D0261505

This book is to be returned on
or before the date stamped below

Making the Peace

Making the Peace

PUBLIC ORDER AND PUBLIC
SECURITY IN MODERN BRITAIN

Charles Townshend

OXFORD UNIVERSITY PRESS

1993

Oxford University Press, Walton Street, Oxford OX2 6DP
Oxford New York Toronto
Delhi Bombay Calcutta Madras Karachi
Kuala Lumpur Singapore Hong Kong Tokyo
Nairobi Dar es Salaam Cape Town
Melbourne Auckland Madrid
and associated companies in
Berlin Ibadan

Oxford is a trade mark of Oxford University Press

Published in the United States
by Oxford University Press Inc., New York

British Library Cataloguing in Publication Data
Data available
ISBN 0–19–822978–X

Library of Congress Cataloguing in Publication Data
Data available
ISBN 0–19–822978 X

1 3 5 7 9 10 8 6 4 2

Typeset by Best-set Typesetter Ltd., Hong Kong
Printed in Great Britain
on acid-free paper by
Bookcraft (Bath) Ltd., Midsomer Norton, Avon

For Leo and Max

The best condition of a commonwealth is easily discovered from the purpose of political order: which is simply peace and security of life. Accordingly, the best commonwealth is one in which men live in harmony, and the laws are kept unbroken. Rebellions, wars, and contemptuous disregard for law must certainly be attributed to the corrupt condition of the commonwealth rather than to the wickedness of its subjects. For citizens are not born, but made.

Spinoza

Political toleration is a by-product of the complacency of the ruling class. When that complacency is disturbed there never was a more bloody-minded set of thugs than the British ruling class.

Aneurin Bevan

Preface

This is a study in British public culture, and like many books about Britain it is mainly about England. The more comprehensive name is used in the title and (sometimes) in the text because it is technically correct, and because it is particularly associated with the polyethnic 'civic culture' of the modern state, notionally pluralist and multicultural. But the vernacular, and even the scholarly slippage between the two is constant. Where this is not due to simple carelessness, it arises from an exploitation of the power of ambiguity which is a characteristic of this culture. English nationality has, at last, begun to be subjected to sustained enquiry—triggered, ironically, by the distinctly careless attempts on the part of Mrs Thatcher's governments to invoke it. For about a century before this, however, after the time of assertive books such as J. R. Seeley's *The Expansion of England* or T. H. S. Escott's *England: Its People, Polity and Pursuits*, it was habitually camouflaged, an operation often carried out with bald-faced deception, as in Enoch Powell and Angus Maude's *Biography of a Nation: A Short History of Britain*. As yet, there is no survey of this process; but a good start is made in 'The English Presumption', in J. H. Grainger's *Patriotisms: Britain, 1900–1939*.

This book would not have been completed without the generosity of many people and institutions, outstanding amongst these the National Humanities Center, North Carolina, in particular its exceptionally capable library staff; the Leverhulme Trust, which honoured me with a fellowship; and the Woodrow Wilson Center, Washington DC. The History Department at Keele University suffered much annoyance from these interruptions to my ordinary career. Ann Seaton gave unstinting assistance in transferring a half-finished book from one wordprocessing programme to another; Nancy Ward performed prodigious feats in the final assembly of text, notes, and bibliography.

C. T.

Woodrow Wilson Center
Washington DC
July 1992

Contents

1

The English Image of Order

What I am striving to keep in our minds is the care, the precaution with which we should go about making things better, so that the public order may not be destroyed, so that no fatal shock may be given to this society of ours, this living body in which our lives are bound up.

George Eliot, *Felix Holt*, 1868

The image of public order in England changed during the nineteenth century. Nobody was, or is, quite sure why. Until the French Revolutionary wars, the English were seen by themselves and by their rulers as an 'ungovernable people'—a fact which flattered while it alarmed those who made themselves responsible for government. The turbulence of the post-war decades became legendary: machine-breaking, arson, and riot were seen as harbingers of open class war. But instead the 1850s brought an unprecedented domestic peace. Historians have found here 'the English miracle', 'the conquest of violence', characterizing the 'age of equipoise'.[1] Quite suddenly, 'public order had ceased to be a national problem. The fabric of society could be taken for granted, and since it was no longer threatened by violence, violence of the old, ruthless kind was no longer needed for its protection.'[2] The decisive moment in this shift was April 1848, which became for Britain as much as for Europe 'the turning point at which history failed to turn'. A decade of Chartist mobilization petered out in London, stifled by middle-class solidarity.[3]

That counter-mobilization of the respectable, the 'triumphant vindication of the English way', as G. M. Young called it, set the state on a new footing.[4] It became a kind of republic in spite of its monarchical trappings. Its magnified legitimacy was accompanied by an enlarged public policy agenda, the most visible part of which was the rapid expansion of the professional police system in the 1850s. While the police could—and can—never have more than a limited impact on 'crime', they quickly found plenty of other concerns.[5] What their daily activities amounted to was the reconstruction of public order in its widest sense. Charles Rowan and Richard Mayne, the founding Commissioners of the London Metropolitan Police, became unusually direct 'primary definers'—to use the term applied, sometimes rather indefinitely, by Stuart Hall—of order.[6]

This unplanned agenda had unanticipated results. The old tolerances within which the people had periodically stepped into the public arena of politics were tightened up. Public space became more constricted. F. M. L. Thompson has reached the glum conclusion that the steady growth of the police presence in the later nineteenth century turned the streets 'more and more into sterile territory on which the public had the right of passage but nothing else', confirming William Morris's more highly coloured remark on 'the impatience of the more luxurious part of society to clear the streets of costermongers, organs, processions, and lecturers of all kinds, and make them a sort of decent prison corridors, with people just trudging to and from their work'.[7] The redefinition of public order, moreover, paradoxically made order-maintenance steadily more difficult, if not indeed impossible. As Allan Silver has suggested, the transformation of the police into what he calls a public bureaucracy 'may raise expectations about the level of public peace it is possible to attain'.[8] It plainly did so.[9] Equipoise would soon tilt back towards anxiety.

The twentieth-century idea of public order is an immensely demanding one. Still, it appears to remain plausible, and not merely to conservatives. This plausibility reflects the special place of order in English public culture, and its deep historical roots. There is copious evidence of a public belief that order once existed, even if it is breaking down at present.[10] The temptation to find out whether it really did is hard to resist. Yet such a line of enquiry does not get very far before it runs into the problem of definition. Public order is an odd, and in a sense un-English, concept. Sir Thomas Elyot's great tract on English gentry character-building of 1531, *The Boke named the Governour*, pointed out that 'the wordes publike and commune . . . be borrowed of the latin tonge for the insufficiencie of our owne language'.[11] While the word 'common' has been fitted to specially English notions—common law, common land, common wealth, common people, and common sense—the other has remained more obviously ambiguous. The accretion of ambiguities was in process while Elyot was writing. The overlapping equivalents, 'common', 'national', and 'popular', were generated by Middle English, according to the Oxford Dictionary; 'community' was added in 1560.

Just what sense of unity did the word rest on? The profusion of boundaries, from estate or parish to nation—and eventually, perhaps, continent—within which the bonds of community have been taken to operate has reflected the conventional wisdom that the process of 'modernization' has involved steady enlargement of vision and communication. The central ambiguity has remained, all the same, between biological individuals and legal or political abstractions. The former make up 'the public', the latter the *res publica*. No writer in the English political tradition should have been more careful of this distinction than Burke, and he assigned to the sphere of the state 'everything that is truly and properly public, the public peace, the public safety, the public order, the public prosperity'.[12] What, we may ask, was not included in these terms? The ultimate answer is hard to find.

'Order' is of course a yet vaster and more multivalent notion. Thomas Elyot simply equated it with the divine scheme of things as a whole, though for him as for most people the bottom line was natural common sense: 'take away ordre from all thynges what shoulde then remayne? Certes nothynge finally, except some man wolde imagine eftsones Chaos'.[13] But order as the antithesis of chaos is an abstraction, not a prognosis. Its manifestations are categorical: Elyot demonstrated the divine order by reference to the heavenly hierarchy, the four elements, the species, and so on. For him, and for the English gentry through to the eighteenth century and beyond, the conservative aspect of order was self-evident. As Peter Laslett has written, 'the ancient order of society was felt to be eternal and unchangeable by those who supported, enjoyed and endured it.'[14] Pope saw that 'Order is Heav'n's first law; and, this confest, / Some are and must be greater than the rest.'

R. N. Berki has recently suggested that order is merely static; 'the peaceful, undisturbed acting out of social relationships'.[15] But this seems more restrictive than the older sense. 'Order thus conceived', a recent historian notes, 'was at once an ideal arrangement of human institutions, a pattern of authority, and an ultimate scheme of values.'[16] The capacity to hold multiple meanings in conjunction may be illustrated by the usage of the House of Commons. The Speaker's call to 'Order!' is an invocation of consensus about the validity of rules for the transaction of business, as is the 'point of order'; the Order Paper simply lists the sequence of items of business; while periodic ministerial Orders form a mode of executing decisions and exerting authority.[17] But the idea of voluntary rule-bound conduct is evidently easier to realize in an institution whose existence is more or less predicated on acceptance of such order, than to deploy as an administrative standard in the less structured public sphere outside the walls of Parliament. It is effectively paralysed by fundamental dissent. Even the timeless machinery of the House of Commons had enormous difficulty in adjusting to departures from the norm such as the filibustering of Irish Home Rulers or the atheism of Charles Bradlaugh. The real world, unfiltered by the mesh of political discipline, is bound to show much more intransigence.

Yet order there must be. Order maintenance is probably seen as the elemental task of government. Admittedly, Confucius held that teaching the people virtue was most important, and that organizing them for defence against internal and external enemies was an admission of failure. Socrates said, more cautiously, that 'it is one of the tasks of government to make its citizens virtuous'.[18] Humanist republicanism of the Machiavellian stamp, seminal to the modern political tradition, took virtue to be the active component of public order. But this produced a puzzle. When nineteenth-century English officials spoke of order they seem to have raised two quite distinct, even contradictory images. One was negative, one positive. The negative image was mere absence of disorder; its purest form would be the empty street. On this view (which is perhaps too popularly attributed to officialdom) people are a problem to be managed. In the positive image, order arises out of the co-operative interaction of self-disciplined individuals. It is a view of social harmony. On this view the people may sometimes be a problem but they also contain the answer: the consensual capacity—ranging from 'sense of community' or 'civic responsibility' through to full-blown 'national consciousness'—which the sage administrator can draw forth.

These two images were habitually put in the same frame by the process of casual elision which the English public tradition brought to a fine art. Combining the roles of subject and citizen, giving obedience and consent, was made possible by a semantic tolerance akin to freedom of conscience. 'Public order' as such was hardly emphasized until this century: not until 1920 did a statute contain the word 'order' in this sense, and the first Public Order Act was not passed until 1936.[19] Though the classical tradition identified the safety or security of the people as the ultimate justification of public power (Cicero's *salus populi suprema est lex*), the English tradition was hesitant in recognizing the state.[20] Ambiguity about the individual and institutional meaning of security was fundamental.[21]

English renaissance political thought blurred 'civil order' into 'cyvyle lyfe and polytyke ordur', or 'cyvyle ordur and polytyke lyfe', equably enough.[22] The characteristic English device of studied indefinition (as Bagehot said, 'we like to have the rigidity taken out of an argument') was integral to the common law tradition. A mountain of individual case law suffocated general principles. The layout of Tudor treason laws, for instance, so close to the heart of the state, seems to have been deliberately unsystematic.[23] The apotheosis of the common law at the hands of Sir Edward Coke had an enduring impact on English national consciousness; indeed, it fixed a large part of its vocabulary. In this sense Coke can be seen as the principal draughtsman of the English self-image. What J. G. A. Pocock has called the 'common-law mind' and the 'common-law interpretation of history' emerged from 'deep-seated and unconscious habits of mind' . . . 'the product, in short, of English history itself'.[24] The common law interpretation both flattered and manacled the English, demonstrating as Sir John Davies said 'the strength of wit and reason and self-sufficiency which hath been always in the People of this Land', and denying the validity of any foreign influences, comparisons, or standards.[25]

By the nineteenth century, the gulf between the common law tradition, with its ingrained aversion to abstract definition, and the continental legal world, was all but unbridgeable. This 'powerful stream of medieval thought flowing into the seventeenth and eighteenth centuries, its strength surviving at least until the coming of philosophical radicalism', gave shape to English public thought. The Roman conception of public power had no place in this legal culture. In fact, the public power itself remained unidentified; English constitutional law had no notion of *Staatsgewalt*.[26] There was thus a void in the representation of the public, and the concepts of public order and public security were generally subsumed in common law language as 'the rule of law' and 'keeping the peace'. Both are suitably complex notions. The rule of law does of course have an abstract significance: it was this that liberals everywhere in Europe deployed against arbitrary government and 'feudal' justice. The essence of liberalism was the insistence that government must be under the law, and that the law must be the same for every citizen. Many treatments of 'liberty' since the nineteenth century have equated it with 'due process'.[27]

In common usage, the rule of law became a rather cruder formula, whereby obedience to law must be signalled by visible law enforcement. Long before the nineteenth century, measurement of the 'degree of law enforcement' became the vital factor in what Keith Wrightson identifies as the endemic confrontation between 'central regulation and local customary practice'.[28] Avoidance of open confrontation in this long, slow contest was the lodestone of order, and the loose texture of the eighteenth-century law enforcement system allowed it to contain this reciprocity. Historians are in fairly sharp disagreement about the precise mechanics of eighteenth-century justice, but the process of argument has thrown out suggestive metaphors characterizing the remarkable capacity of the English law to enlist public endorsement. E. P. Thompson has posited the 'imbrication' of a semi-autonomous legal value-system and a largely customary society. Thompson's view that the law must be taken seriously, and not dismissed as a crude instrument of class domination, is in effect a reassertion of the common law interpretation in Marxian, or rather Gramscian, terms.

Imbrication is not of course fusion so much as interlocking: it enables roof tiles to keep rain out, for instance, or fish scales to flex, but does the law have a similar utility? Obviously it does, or at least—which is more relevant in society than in meteorology—it is perceived to have. Thus the rule of law was hegemonic, sustaining the ruling class by mobilizing the consent of the ruled.[29] Following Thompson, Douglas Hay developed a particularly dramatic account of the hegemonic function of the eighteenth-century legal system, stressing its exploitation of capriciousness. Such erratic enforcement could only be functional in an unsystematic legal culture. Writers who have modified Hay's account have done so by stressing the extent of participation in the legal system by the 'middling sort', and the growing professional coherence of lawyers.[30] The result is a broad confirmation of Thompson's delicately balanced mechanism of hegemony, in which ideology is a reciprocal instrument, forming a genuine constraint on the governing establishment.

Alternative metaphors have characterized the law's grip in more fluid terms than 'imbrication', though with some loss in mechanical clarity. Anthony Fletcher and John Stevenson have divined a 'reservoir' of popular consent, and noted the 'affinity' between state law and local custom.[31] These more organic metaphors express if they do not altogether explain the way in which central power advanced by insinuation rather than confrontation. Eighteenth-century statutes followed the common law path of accretion rather than definition. Several legal historians have explained the striking increase in the number of capital offences during the century by the fact that English legislators 'lacked general definitions ... with the result that they were constantly having to add particularity in order to compensate for generality'.[32]

The self-image of the English as a law-abiding people ('law-keeping and law-seeking') has been salient since the later Middle Ages. Such things as 'that peculiarly British institution, "the law of the queue"' are still capable of arresting anthropologists. Around the turn of the nineteenth century, Maria Edgeworth read a large contrast between English and Irish civic culture from the characteristic English threat 'I'll have the law of you!'

(which she saw as an expectation of justice), as against the Irish 'I'll have you up before His Honour' (in the hope of partiality). The underpinnings of this widely attested attitude remain obscure, but the place of the common law at the core of the English national self-image was plainly crucial in its transmission.[33]

Perhaps the most solid basis for the culture of law and order remained that other grand construct, the peace—honorifically assigned to kings and queens, but essentially common. 'Every man ought to endeavour peace', as Thomas Hobbes enjoined, with the characteristic rider, 'as far as he has hope of obtaining it'.[34] Hobbes offended his countrymen's instinct by calling this a 'general rule of reason', and 'the first, and fundamental law of nature', but he undoubtedly expressed their practical precept. This activist injunction is plainly different from mere quietism, as enshrined for instance in the maxim 'Ruhe ist die erste Burgerpflicht', which E. J. Hobsbawm tells us was the slogan of every German princeling. But the difference points to the heavy duty which the word 'peace' has to perform in English public discourse.

Even in purely legal terms, Glanville Williams pointed to the 'surprising lack of authoritative definition of what one would suppose to be a fundamental concept in criminal law', and Ian Brownlie saw that 'definition may vary according to the functional context'.[35] Setting aside the primary meaning ascribed by the Oxford dictionary, 'freedom from, or cessation of, war', which by the nineteenth century (though not in Hobbes's time) had become largely reserved to international relations, we come to the second: 'freedom from civil commotion and disorder; public order and security'. Already we have both negative and positive formulations, and the first of a flood of synonyms. Only further down the list do we reach 'quiet' and 'tranquillity', which are the nearest equivalents to the German *Ruhe*. These we might dismiss—like Rousseau, who sneered 'On vit tranquille aussi dans les cachots; en est-ce assez pour s'y trouver bien?'— but for the fact that they were once very popular with the definers of public order. When the colours of the newly raised Manchester Volunteer Corps were consecrated in February 1798, at a time of imminent danger of French invasion, the *Manchester Mercury* noted that one of the principal tasks of the force was 'to preserve and secure internal tranquillity and social order'. Not long afterwards, the local authorities observed to the Home Office that the Manchester Weavers' Association might be 'converted at any time into a most dangerous instrument to disturb the public tranquility'.[36] And tranquillity was the keyword of the first job descriptions issued to the Metropolitan Police by Rowan and Mayne.

The two basic senses, positive and negative, or we might say optimistic and pessimistic, fertile and sterile, remain salient. The Oxford dictionary appropriately cites Clarendon's usage: 'Peace is that harmony in the state, that health is in the body' [1727]. But from this blithe organicism the dictionary brings us up rather short by citing Mark Pattison on the 1889 dock strike: 'Peace and order were maintained by police regulations of German minuteness and strictness.' Here indeed is a negative image, and it is interesting that the same faintly obscure comment furnishes the usage for the dictionary's definition of 'public order' (the nineteenth meaning of 'order'): 'the condition in which the laws or usages regulating the public relations of individuals to the community, and the public conduct of members or sections of the community to each other; the rule of law or constituted authority; law-abiding state; absence of insurrection, riot, turbulence, unruliness, or crimes of violence'. It seems that Pattison's picture is specially appropriate, and that the negative image of order is stronger than has usually been thought.

It is difficult to be sure about this because one of the most intractable issues for English historians in recent years has been the measurement of orderliness in English society since the Middle Ages. Any attempt to measure disorder, or even actual violence, short of open insurrection, runs into the well-known problem of criminal statistics: since no set of crime figures can be known to be reliable, we can never be certain how to calculate shifts over time, to compare different periods or areas. We are driven to use more impressionistic evidence, some of which is flatly contradictory. There is plenty of testimony—often, of course, English—to the innate orderliness of the English people. According to Alan Macfarlane, for instance, 'the many who travelled through England in the late sixteenth and seventeenth centuries give a strong impression of an orderly, controlled and non-violent society'. Against this we must count the evidence of the 'ungovernable people', and Lawrence Stone's insistence—itself disputed— that the peace-loving golden age of the village is a political myth.[37]

Whether allegedly innate or culturally constructed, this characteristic has continued to be disputed. To take two ill-sorted examples only: Russell Chamberlin's attempt to discover 'the idea of England' recognized that the self-portrait that the 'modern Englishman' would give of 'his race' would include docility and readiness to obey the law, yet foreign visitors over several centuries had seen in the English 'not simply a violent people but a ferocious one', renowned for sickening cruelty towards animals, relishing public executions, and so on.[38] Geoffrey Gorer's more deliberate exploration of Englishness in the 1950s, using survey data, perceived 'the central problem for the understanding of the English character' as 'the problem of aggression'. English 'gentleness', Gorer thought, 'would seem to be a comparatively new phenomenon. ... English people of the seventeenth and eighteenth centuries were remarkably pugnacious and violent'; they persisted in enjoyment of cruel amusements, from bear-baiting through Shakespearian drama to public executions, as well as riot and affray. He posed, but could not answer, the question whether this pervasive violence had disappeared, or had merely been displaced.[39]

This sort of collective psychoanalysis remains ultimately inconclusive, though several of Gorer's findings were more than mere curiosities.[40] Was there a great pacification in the nineteenth century? The answer must depend on what is meant by 'peace', and this had always been socially negotiable. The establishment of the public peace in the Middle Ages was a many-faceted process, in which the royal effort to control the traditional violence of territorial magnates was both assisted and impeded by a public which applauded the extension of royal justice while resenting the extension of central administration.[41] John Bellamy's study of the later Middle Ages adduces a 'crisis in public order' in the fourteenth and fifteenth centuries, and suggests that there were major differences in perceptions of order. The Parliament of 1388 was not unusual in calling for 'better keeping of the peace'; but Bellamy notes that while 'the giving of livery illegally was a crime with serious consequences for public order, the king failed to deal with it either fairly or firmly'.[42] Cynthia Herrup's study of the seventeenth-century legal system concludes that although 'some common definition of a desirable peace was necessary if the structure was to function ... nothing demanded absolute concord'.[43] Compromise and co-operation were encouraged, if not demanded, by the exiguous administrative capacity of the state. A crisis of order, meeting the criterion proposed by Frantisek Graus—a widespread perception that essential values and symbols are threatened—must necessarily be a subjective matter.

What certainly happened in the nineteenth century was a shift in the general perception of the common peace.[44] This was most clearly visible in changing reaction to rioting. It was always easier to recognize a breakdown of order, or breach of the peace, than to specify the lineaments of order. Disorder, tumult, and disturbance are visceral realities. Riots, in particular, were amenable to legal definition, in a well-known cadence of collective action embracing affray, unlawful assembly, and tumultuous petitioning. (Though modern historians may well doubt whether the legal definition is very useful as a 'functional definition'.[45]) The impact of the 1714 Riot Act, and the persistent confusion it caused, is of course notorious.[46] As well as providing a vernacular expression for stern reaction, it established the curious time allowance of one hour for crowds to disperse, after which their assembly became felonious. It also enshrined the basic test of public alarm, that of putting a person of 'reasonable firmness' in fear. It has struck many as being a specially English law, not just in its 'reasonableness', but still more in its ambiguity: nobody was ever clear—lawyers apart— whether the reading of the Act by a magistrate guaranteed a crowd an hour before lethal force might be used (in law it did not, since that would have abridged both the common law and the prerogative powers of the executive), or merely announced that deadly force might be withheld for up to an hour as long as the crowd showed signs of dispersing. The first, erroneous, interpretation has habitually prevailed over the correct one.

An important reason for this was the special function of popular tumult in English public life before the great pacification. As Eric Hobsbawm contends, the city mob in the eighteenth century 'was not simply a casual collection of people united for some ad hoc purpose, but in a recognized sense, a permanent entity'.[47] The eighteenth-century ruling establishment accepted a surprisingly—to modern eyes—high level of public disorder as part of the political process.[48] This view had deep classical roots: Roman oligarchy strengthened itself by incorporating the protests of the lower orders. Machiavelli thought that the tumults of ancient Rome were 'a manifestation of the highest civic *virtù*'; '"all legislation favourable to liberty is brought about by the clash" between the classes, so that class conflict is not the solvent but the cement of a commonwealth'.[49] Peter Laslett likewise holds that 'on those rare occasions when overt conflict came about, it did not necessarily represent a weakening of the national political consciousness, but rather an assertion and intensification of it'.[50] It would no doubt be an exaggeration to say that the English gentry built their vision of order on conflict, but they accepted protest as inevitable and legitimate. H. O. Arnold-Forster's didactic *Citizen Reader* of 1886 told children that in earlier times when 'riots and disturbances broke out ... the people committed acts of violence, which however unwise they may have been, showed how real and great was the suffering which had been caused'.[51] This comforting late-Victorian wisdom was premissed on the abolition of such suffering and hence such violence.

J. H. Plumb observed that, whereas in Europe riot turned in the end into revolution, 'in England alone it faded into insignificance in the nineteenth century'.[52] (Hector Berlioz cruelly concurred, lamenting that his friends the Chartists had no more idea of how to conduct a riot than the Italians had of how to write a symphony; the French, one infers, were best at both.) Plumb's attempt to distinguish pre-modern, or 'pre-revolutionary' riots from their modern successors was rather unclear, as it characterized the former as 'a deeper convulsion in the very bowels of society'. Where these might be is anyone's guess. Others have charted a shift in the meaning of 'contentious gatherings' from reactive food riots to more controlled protests over working conditions.[53] The authorities had their own view: in 1796 the Home Office circulated a memorandum pointing out that 'a riot occasioned by persons disaffected to the government, long premeditated' was to be taken more seriously than a mere 'sudden collection of idle and mischievous people'.[54] This choice of adjectives effectively determined the conclusion, and the memorandum did not weigh the significance of a spontaneous gathering of formerly law-abiding people. But it is important that the official view linked modernization together with politicization. The tendency to read protest and disturbance as a threat to the state became more firmly established in the following century.

The notion of civil emergency was evolving, somewhat contentiously, at this time (Dr Johnson deplored the first signs of the modern usage of the word emergency as 'a sense not proper'). E. P. Thompson has argued that the wave of repressive legislation epitomized by the Waltham Black Act was passed 'under colour of emergency'. His critics hold that the official sense of crisis was generated by fear of a rival élite rather than fear of broader popular resistance.[55] The issue is important, and its resolution has been hampered by a shortage of synoptic history. In the apparently revolutionary epoch of the early nineteenth century, it remains unclear whether 'revolution' was a real possibility and whether the authorities believed it to be.[56] The evidence has been read both ways. The authorities have frequently been accused of alarmism and brutality—the 'Six Acts' and 'Peterloo' are the ineradicable symbols of this indictment—but recent historians have more often remarked on their equanimity and moderation.[57] F. O. Darvall found it 'astonishing' that the anxiety and terror of the authorities and manufacturers in face of the Luddite outbreaks 'should have been so restrained'.[58] Eric Hobsbawm and George Rudé showed how many local magistrates were ready to parley and 'remonstrate' with the Swing protesters in 1830, impelling Lord Melbourne to insist that 'they will deem it their Duty to maintain and uphold the Rights of Property, of every Description, against Violence and Aggression'.[59]

Melbourne's alarmism is well known. Hobsbawm and Rudé find both him and his predecessor Peel hawkish on disorder. Yet it is interesting to see that on the day after the first machine-breaking in the south, Peel set down a strikingly clear statement of the moderation needed for the maintenance of order in the long-running northern industrial disputes:

There are two evils opposite to each other—but equally dangerous—to be guarded against—the one precipitation on the part of the Masters—and a want of temper and prudence in resisting the demands of the combined workmen—the other—the confirmation of the influence of the combination through the exhibition of fear, and through concessions extorted by fear alone.... I trust that the Master Manufacturers are fully impressed with the importance of being clearly and manifestly in the right—of having the opinion of all reasonable and well judging men in favour of the measures, to which they may think it necessary to resort, from a conviction that they are perfectly just....

It is well therefore to be prepared for the worst—doing every thing in the mean time, to prevent extremities, and employing force, if it must be employed,—only in a case where the necessity is urgent—and the policy and justice of interference by force—unquestionable.[60]

Peel's partiality is hardly in doubt. He thought the workers' demands unreasonable, and their methods intolerable. He was also, his biographer says, 'clearly under the impression that the labourers were being directed from some hidden source'.[61] Such alarmism only throws into sharper relief his insistence on holding to a middle way, as when he urged the Manchester magistrates to organize a local citizen force drawn from all social classes, and repeated that 'if a collision took place, it should be on an issue where not only the law but public opinion would be on the side of the authorities'.[62]

The zenith of moderation was reached during the decade of Chartist agitation before 1848. Major-General Sir Charles Napier, military commander of the Northern District (at Manchester) in 1839–41, colourfully exulted that though 'half the land has been openly in arms' there had been 'not a drop of blood spilt on the scaffold'. The legal historian Leon Radzinowicz set out to explain this remarkable performance, and attributed it to wise policy: avoidance of emergency legislation, the use of more sophisticated intelligence-gathering methods, strict adherence to the rule of law, and leniency in punishment. Framing all this, Radzinowicz identified Lord John Russell's commitment to the traditional right of public assembly. 'The people had a right to free discussion. It was free discussion which elicited truth. They had a right to meet.'[63] This was the core dogma of post-utilitarian liberalism, and its fusion with the common law on this point undoubtedly supplied the crucial element in the official perception of the difference between a meeting or demonstration and a riot. But the line was notoriously hard to draw; the avoidance of definition placed a daunting responsibility on the local magistracy. In 1839 the Nottinghamshire magistrates 'bluntly asked for clearer guidance' on the question. Was a large meeting to be regarded as illegal if some of the people at it were carrying arms? Should a meeting be declared illegal, even though nobody was armed, if the numbers of people assembling were calculated to cause apprehension? To these and other similar questions clear answers were never to be given.[64]

The leniency or severity of the official response to what was perceived to be the challenge of Chartism cannot of course be judged in absolute terms. Sentences of transportation were freely, and some have said promiscuously, handed down. The largest batch of transportations was from the Potteries after the 'Plug Plot' disturbances, sometimes called the General Strike of 1842. Over 250 Potteries Chartists were arraigned before a Special Commission in Stafford in the first fortnight of October 1842. Most of their offences had been committed in Stoke, Fenton, Hanley, and Burslem on 14 and 15 August. On the second day the magistrates had withdrawn the troops to the middle-class stronghold of Newcastle under Lyme and abandoned the other Potteries towns to the rioters. A sympathetic historian has seen these events as 'a desperate saturnalia by men and women who were hungry, penniless and determined to assert their power through looting and destruction of property'.[65] This would set the outbreak within the tradition of urban riot. But Dr Fyson also sees the events of August as a 'memorable' contribution to 'the national crisis of 1842', and a 'phenomenal outbreak of popular discontent' which threatened the existing form of class society. If it was so, the reaction of the authorities may indeed have been moderate. After the single military action in Burslem on 16 August, when troops opened fire, killing one man and putting the rest of the crowd to flight, the magistrates thought that the area remained in 'a most disorganized and revolutionary state'.[66]

The juxtaposition of these adjectives points to the great uncertainty which persisted through the Chartist decade. How could you recognize incipient revolution? One of the most frequent complaints voiced by officials and employers was of 'insubordination', which may express even more acutely than 'disturbance' the disorienting anxiety which fuelled a sense of crisis. (Though usually a negative term, it could also take positive form, as in the need 'to maintain a higher state of subordination'.[67]) Uncertainty was magnified by the law itself, as we have observed. The pressure put on magistrates in the early nineteenth century was immense, and the traditional magistracy gave way under it. When the Home Secretary, Sir James Graham, told Queen Victoria in the midst of the August 1842 disorders that he was 'by no means satisfied with the activity of the magistrates', he was making a common complaint (though his additional charge that 'the mill-owners have shown a want of proper spirit in defending their property' was less common).[68] The weakness of local justices in face of mass protest was repeatedly castigated by senior ministers, and they were gradually stiffened by an infusion of stipendiaries, and ultimately of course by the creation of a professional police.

The succession of early nineteenth-century crises of order has been constructed by historians into a general crisis of the old regime. On this view, the unreliability of the magistracy, and above all their erratic shifts between excessive willingness to placate rioting crowds and excessive eagerness to call on military assistance—divergent but related responses—gradually eroded the long-standing resistance of the gentry and urban middle class to the idea of professional policing. (Classically stated in 'the remark of a personage who had been robbed on the highway: "At least", he cried, "we have no Marshalsea!"') The charm of the old refrain 'We buy exemption from crime too dear, if we purchase it by the loss of happiness and virtue' began to fade. It was as if the uncertainty of the English way became too much even for the English to endure.[69]

There can be no doubt that some strands of the process usually called 'modernization', in particular the uncontrollable and unprecedented course of urbanization, imposed a destructive test on administrative machinery which had evolved to regulate the agricultural villages and commercial towns of the previous century. And only the looming apprehension of moral collapse created by the explosive growth of cities can explain such outbreaks of respectable hysteria as the London 'garotting' scare of the 1860s, which was talked up by even so solid a repository of common sense as Trollope (who was privately sceptical of the whole scare, yet could not resist putting a garotting into *Phineas Finn*).[70] But if the fact of urbanization was definite enough, its impact on attitudes was not straightforward. All modernization theory, even its most sophisticated variants, carries the illusion of a single 'great transformation', from traditional (or yet more tendentiously 'pre-modern') society to modern. The reality is always more fragmentary and incoherent, as has become clear in the rewriting of English police history. Once the history of the police was a distinctly Whiggish story of harmony between the need for order and the preservation of liberty. In this story the English, long hostile to the notion of police because of its association with French state tyranny, at last discovered that it is possible to arrange a police system which is both efficient and democratic.[71]

Modern histories of policing depart from this optimistic, not to say miraculous vision. The most corrosive recent interpretations have utilized the Gramscian idea of social control, in which the people assist in their own subordination. In essence this is a powerful explanatory device. Though the cruder usage of the term 'social control' as simply an intensification of central control has been effectively criticized,[72] more sophisticated use of it has undoubtedly sharpened our awareness of the police as a part of the mechanism of hegemony, a vehicle for the transmission of cultural values. The vivid image of the policeman as 'domestic missionary' fits well with Wrightson's picture of a perennial tussle between central and local concepts of order in early modern England. Thus a clear-headed study such as Wilbur Miller's *Cops and Bobbies* recognizes that 'order may not have been partisan, but whose order it was and the way it was upheld were political issues'.[73]

The besetting weakness of most 'social control' accounts has been their tendency to treat the exercise of power as a one-way transaction. Manipulation may be direct or circuitous but in the social-control perspective it is deliberate and downward. Yet the best case-studies can only be read as showing the reciprocal nature of power—not merely limited by the shortcomings of the state apparatus, but also disputed and shaped by a larger kind of social negotiation.[74] In the context of public order, all this amounts to saying that the cherished English tenet of participation may have been in some respects illusory, but was not in essence a sham. The institution of the special constable demonstrated the tenet's concreteness: as one commentary put it,

it is only in accordance with our national character and the whole system of preserving law and order in this country, by which the people are encouraged themselves to contribute to the maintenance of the peace, that special constables are appointed, if possible, from among the actual parties in conflict.[75]

The police had far-reaching capacity to determine, both in the abstract and in daily practice, the content of order. Indeed, it seems to be generally accepted that this—rather than the prevention or detection of crime—was their principal function. 'Police were solely employed in this manner which commanded respect for the establishment throughout the Country'.[76] The Staffordshire constabulary were typical in being raised 'specifically in response to the fear of disorder', and only subsequently to tackle ordinary crime.[77] For a long time, perhaps as long as a century after the elaboration of the 'policed society' in the 1850s, local élites had a genuine role in the policing process, especially in the definition of police functions. The 1856

Act gave Chief Constables a position of considerable independence, and the military background of the early incumbents, coupled in many cases with long tenure of office, moved this in the direction of the largely uncontrolled power which they would exercise a century later.[78] But the process was gradual, involving the free (rather than, as in recent years, manipulated) consent of police authorities.

The dominance of community leaders in defining the tasks of the police and, in effect, the nature of order, was very marked in the boroughs. One of the most complex studies of police history so far written, by Carolyn Steedman, argues that the development of mid-nineteenth century policing was shaped by the provincial watch committees' 'understanding of social discipline and community'. Community was above all locality. Police 'expertise' was, in rural areas, no more or less than a full understanding of the mesh of local social relations. The most important quality possessed by good policemen in such a context was not professional skill but virtue: hence there could be little or no question of technical 'operational' matters beyond the competence of a watch committee to assess and supervise. Operations were specified precisely by the instincts of the middle class. Thus the metropolitan emphasis on 'preventive' policing was widely rejected in the provinces because it called for excessive numbers of police—at excessive cost—and threatened 'an alien peace, imposed upon communities, rather than arising from an ordered set of social relations'.[79]

The police of the metropolis were ordered differently. The power of the Home Secretary was absolute, in itself a striking constitutional innovation. Most of it was delegated in practice to the Commissioners, and the first two of these, Rowan and Mayne, effectively defined the image of the 'bobby'. They laid down a rigorous code of personal conduct, fusing respectability, impartiality, and iron self-control in face of provocation. Before the notion of 'moral policing' became more than a xenophobic bogy, the moral fibre of the police themselves was pivotal in securing public acceptance. Rowan and Mayne soon came to believe that countrymen made the best police, a belief which the *Quarterly Review* refined in 1856 with the nineteenth century's instinctive social Darwinism (in this case preceding zoological Darwinism).

Intelligence of a certain kind...may be carried too far; your sharp Londoner makes a very bad policeman; he is too volatile and conceited to submit himself to discipline.... The best constables come from the provincial cities and towns. They are both quicker and more 'plucky' than the mere countryman from the village—a singular fact, which proves that manly vigour, both physical and mental, is to be found in populations neither too aggregated nor entirely isolated.[80]

Two more tangible things also defined the public figure of the police: uniform and armament. A mid-century American observer thought that part of the 'great moral power' of the London policeman 'lies in his coat'.[81] The colour of the uniform was carefully chosen, though there has been some uncertainty about its exact signification. It was hardly, as some writers have suggested, an unambiguously civilian get-up; indeed it was distinctly military, in colour, cut, and accoutrement, and became gradually more so. The famous helmet which appeared later in the century, and has stayed in use because its moral value outweighs its impracticality, was directly modelled on the Prussianized headgear adopted by the army after the German victory over France in 1871. (This fashion was soon shelved by the infantry, and now adorns only the ceremonial rig of military bandsmen.)

The unmistakably military style and, in many respects, behaviour of the new police—naturally christened a 'force'—was, however, balanced by their public abjuration of lethal weapons. No record exists of the reasoning behind the decision to create an unarmed police.[82] The issue may scarcely have arisen as such, if the consensus view is right: since English hostility to foreign gendarmes was so strident, and the English could only with great difficulty be brought to accept any professional police, they would certainly have rebelled openly against an armed force. The Peace Preservation Force raised by Peel in Ireland—the first 'Peelers'—and the Royal Irish Constabulary as it emerged in the 1830s would not have been acceptable precedents. While it should perhaps be remembered that in Britain before *The Sweeney* the non-lethal armament of the police was not to be despised (Engels was correct, if sarcastic, in writing of 'the soothing power of the policeman's truncheon'), there can be no doubt that the moral confidence implicit in the unarmed posture of the 'bobby on the beat' supplied a kind of psychic armament. 'The mob quails before the simple baton of the police officer, and flies before it', a *Quarterly Review* article reassuringly intoned in 1870, 'well knowing the moral as well as physical force of the Nation whose will, as embodied in law, it represents'.[83]

It is apparent that a deliberate distancing of the police from the army was dictated precisely by the well-attested unsuitability of regular military forces for the task of internal peacekeeping. The British army had of course no conscript element; thus while its discipline might (in theory) be better, its legitimacy was tainted. It was in fact a provocative force in the domestic context, and its successes in restoring order were dependent on its appearing in sufficient strength to overawe crowds. Unfortunately for the authorities, the volunteer formations like the militia were scarcely less provocative, and were certainly less competent.[84] Yeomanry of the sort whose murderous unsteadiness had caused the Peterloo massacre were the worst offenders, but no military formation was really suited to the volatile atmosphere of riot. The problem was not confined to England, but the imprecision of the English law magnified the instability. The Bristol riots of 1831 impressed this indelibly on the military mind. The commander of the troops called out to aid the civil power subsequently shot himself while awaiting court martial on the charge of having failed to open fire on the rioters soon enough. The mayor of the city, indicted before the high court, was convicted of failing to 'hit the exact line' between inadequate and excessive force in repressing the disorder.[85]

The common law principle of necessary force was a daunting one for the man on the spot to translate from doctrine into action. In 1833, after the violence of the Coldbath Fields demonstration, *The Times* perceived that the dispersal of a mob turned on one moment of crisis 'as fine and sharp as a razor'.[86] General Napier, whose masterly deployment of troops—and unswerving fidelity to liberal principles—during the early Chartist demonstrations won him wide praise, was supremely conscious of that evanescent line. 'As things are,' he wrote, 'the soldier has all the responsibility, while, at the same time, no precise power is confided to him, no line of conduct defined for his guidance.' Napier drily set down the dilemma of the military officer turned involuntary peace officer: 'His thoughts dwell upon the (to him) most interesting question, "Shall I be *shot* for my forbearance by a court martial, or *hanged* for over zeal by a jury?" '[87]

Like other soldiers after him, Napier was disinclined to accept the common lawyers' assurance that he had nothing to fear from an honest jury, which would understand the pressures of 'fear, danger, confusion, hurry'. What he and they wanted was that 'the duties of the one' (the civil authorities) should be 'defined up to a certain point, where the duties of the [military] should begin, so that neither may be placed in a false position'.[88] This was just what English legal tradition militated against. The guidance sought by peace officers had to be found in their own minds. The operability of common law assumptions presupposed a common acculturation, at any rate of the governing class. Only this common sense could obviate the need to define the powers of the executive in an emergency, and hence to define the state itself. What W. L. Burn sees as 'the notable, one could properly call it the astonishing, degree of social cohesion' of mid-Victorian England sheltered the state from public scrutiny.

The decisive test of common sense occurred, by common consent, in the springtide of 1848. A leading part in the paralysing of Chartism was played by the Chartists' own subscription to the 'English way', the declared belief that England was 'a different kind of nation', and that revolution was a foreign phenomenon.[89] Nothing could illustrate the hegemony of this notion more exactly than the open letter of Ernest Jones in the *Northern Star* in July that year: 'A truly brave people are never themselves disorderly, and have sufficient energy to prevent disorder in others.'[90] But more substantial still was the flocking of the middling sort to the standard of order.[91] The overwhelming and unexampled enrolment of special constables bore out the confidence shown by cabinet ministers and officials before the Kennington Common demonstration. Charles Trevelyan urged that 'Chartists should be made to see that there is a power in Society itself sufficient to put them down'.[92] There was, but just what was it? Trevelyan was evidently not speaking in any direct sense of a *pouvoir publique* vested in the state. Rather he drew on the widely diffused belief in a primal English sense of community.

This belief incorporated the conviction that the community was the producer, not the product of the common law. Once again, the Chartist Ernest Jones (whose Welsh ancestry was modulated by his upbringing in north Germany) gave precise voice to it: 'the right of public meeting in the open air' had been, he said 'maintained ever since the witenagemot of the ancient Saxons'. The Teutonic foundation of the English political system was a deep collective faith reconfirmed by Bishop Stubbs's monumental constitutional history, which suggested that 'the polity developed by the German races on British soil is the purest product of their primitive instinct'. In their early 'community of institutions and languages' the English 'possess a basis and a spring of life, from and by which they may rise into a great homogeneous people, symmetrically organized and united, progressive and thoroughly patriotic'.[93] Though Stubbs laid less emphasis than the amateur enthusiast Ernest Jones—or his fellow professional Edward Freeman—on the continuity and significance of the witenagemot itself, he produced a powerful statement of organic popular unity, harmonizing liberty and order. The very 'complexity and inconvenience' of the English system proved it to be 'natural, spontaneous, and a crucial test of substantial freedom'.[94] This paean to native empiricism, 'the principle of adapting present means to present ends', was in marked contrast to the earlier view of Bentham—going back to Hume—that the complexity of English political and judicial institutions constituted a bulwark of aristocratic privilege rather than popular liberty.[95]

It is not necessary to stress that a model of community lifted from the blurred mists of antiquity (the only surviving record of original German social forms was second-hand, via Tacitus and Caesar) was not in any straightforward way adaptable to the nineteenth-century experience. In so far as urbanization and industry had produced new social cleavages, it was paradoxical to resolve them by appeal to assumptions that were not merely pre-modern but prehistoric. Yet it does seem that the English way in domestic progress, as distinct from foreign affairs, was to call up the old world to redress the balance of the new. As England became materially more urban, it became morally more rural. Trollope thought it axiomatic that the English character was formed in the country, and explicitly (if implausibly) contrasted this with urban cultures like those of the USA, Italy, and even France.[96] Martin Wiener has put together telling evidence of what he calls 'the decline of the industrial spirit' after 1850.[97] In so doing he has amplified a perception which flashed before earlier writers, such as G. M. Young, who wondered 'why, in a money-making age, opinion was ... more deferential to birth than to money, and why, in a mobile and progressive society, most regard was had to the element which represented immobility, tradition and the past'. Young's tentative answer was essentially English: 'perhaps the statement will be found to include the solution'.[98]

Wiener's catalogue of paradoxes is longer, and no more easily explained. Why, for instance, did the public schools, without any central direction, become so coherent a system? Why did the domestic vernacular of William Morris and Norman Shaw have such a ready appeal? We are here up against the kind of occult resonances which make the abstract music of Elgar more 'English' than the deliberately local evocations of Delius.[99] The main thing is to register that the rediscovery of rural England took place in the late nineteenth century and was largely southern in its topographical connotations. The hollyhock-swamped thatched cottage as a dominant motif of the countryside—a term itself of twentieth-century coinage— belonged to the area which had originally been known as 'Merrie England', and whose rural nature was thrown into sharper relief by the pattern of urban growth in the nineteenth century.[100] The still centre of public order in the Victorian official mind seems to have been as distinctly rural and southern as the supercharged national identity propounded by Kipling or Belloc, both of whom located it even more precisely in Sussex.

By coincidence the only public order project of the century to be deliberately designed and promulgated, and given the faintly un-English label 'plan', originated in the same place. When Sussex erupted with 'Swing' turbulence in the winter of 1830–1, the Duke of Richmond 'enrolled a [special] constabulary force of shopkeepers, yeomen and "respectable" labourers, organized them in sections and districts under local commanders, and sent them out as mobile units to occupy villages'.[101] The system was developed by his brother, Lord Lennox, at Chichester, and ultimately the 'Sussex plan' was espoused by Lord Melbourne and broadcast to the provinces: copies were found by Hobsbawm and Rudé as far from Chichester as Carlisle. It was probably the skeleton of Trevelyan's ghostly 'power in Society' of 1848. Certainly it was urged on the Irish Constabulary at that time by General Lord de Ros, who explained to the Inspector-General the order-restorative potential of

intensive patrolling of the sort which was pursued during the riots in Kent and Sussex in 1830, when, with comparatively few troops, the face of the country was so perambulated, that all attempt at outrage was entirely paralized & order restored immediately.[102]

The southern counties supplied what Ford Madox Ford, searching for the spirit of England, identified as that 'precise green valley that was ... the heart of the country', and what may be thought of as an ecology of order for the administrative class. The English village and Piltdown man, as a literary critic puts it, 'together offered incontrovertible proof that all humanity, civilization, and beauty can be traced to Sussex'.[103]

The salience of rural relationships in the image of order was grounded on the fundamental role of the magistracy in order maintenance. Even after the establishment of the professional police there remained a strong belief that the best guarantee of public order was the resolute magistrate ready to make face-to-face contact with a disorderly crowd. The Justice of the Peace was the bedrock of the system, and the petty sessional division became 'the essential unit of rural police distribution' after the 1856 Act, so that the new law 'actually strengthened the power of rural justices'.[104] That power derived from the social prestige of the landed gentry, and it remained substantially true of the nineteenth as of the seventeenth century that the legitimacy of the judicial system was underwritten by that prestige.[105] The survival of landed power into the nineteenth century is admittedly a disputed question. J. C. D. Clark's recent insistence that a coherent *ancien régime* persisted well beyond 1832 runs counter to a conventional consensus that modernization was well under way by then. He is right to point out the odd way in which the inconsistency between the fate of the old aristocracy as displayed in Lawrence Stone's classic *The Crisis of the Aristocracy* (1965) and its later power as displayed in another classic study, F. M. L. Thompson's *English Landed Society in the*

Nineteenth Century (1963), has been ignored. And although it may be mischievous of him to suggest that 'the real cultural and financial bankruptcy of the traditional landed elite' did not finally come to pass until the 1930s, when the historians of the 'Old Guard' (as he jocularly calls them) 'were young, and were struck by it', the continuing work of Professor Thompson seems compatible with such a conclusion.[106]

The issue is important for understanding the image of public order. If officials had in the back of their minds an image which was essentially bucolic, with a cautious admixture of professional enforcement machinery, it would not be hard to see how an idealized concept of civil peace was constructed, wreathed in the sanguine glow of the 'conquest of violence'. The countryside was no longer a dangerous place. The severity of the Swing repression had played a major part in neutering it, cowing the landless workers and generating the surly servility of 'Hodge' that was so plain to Victorian observers. The decisive taming, the enclosure process which strangled the old yeomanry, eradicated the clash between peasants and modernizers—whether capitalist or socialist—that marked the European experience.[107] The English 'way of life' could be safely located in a sanitized, peasant-free countryside.

Whether or not one likes the Gramscian terminology, the idea of hegemony in its very imprecision fits comfortably with English assumptions about public order. As E. P. Thompson says, the idea of the rule of law was a bastion of the establishment, but like any fortification it restricted those it defended. The reciprocity of the English way was real enough to keep it going. The adaptability of the system, so vital to the 'Whig interpretation', drew on a kind of cultural negotiation around the dominant symbols of public life. The public itself, public interest, public order and public security were manipulated with a skill so great as perhaps to be unconscious. Whether, as Tom Nairn and others assert, the system is now in crisis, and nineteenth-century stability has become 'paralytic over-stability, the adoptive conservatism ... turned into the feeble, dwindling, incompetent conservatism of the last generation' (before 1977), and whether 'the appealing, romantic social peace is inseparable from the twilight', it seems to be true that English public discourse has lost 'the idea of the virtuous power of popular protest'.[108] The progressive tightening of public order over the last century has tilted the old notion of balance against that idea. This realignment may be the most enduring of all Victorian values.

2

The Indian Negative

Disguise it how you will, it is force in one shape or another which determines the relations between human beings.

James Fitzjames Stephen, *Liberty, Equality, Fraternity*

Coercion and Codification

It is sufficient to hear an English gentleman speak of his Irish and English tenants to perceive that he considers the first as foreigners, in connection with whom all the laws, human and divine, which he is accustomed to obey in dealing with the latter, lose their authority and cease to restrain him.

Émile Boutmy, *The English People*

'Coercion in Ireland was a very different problem from the maintenance of order in England', F. C. Mather remarked. 'Nineteenth-century statesmen did not confuse the two.'[1] It is notorious that even under the Act of Union, Ireland was administered in an exceptional way, more like a grand colony than an integral part of the United Kingdom. The executive housed in Dublin Castle was headed by a Lord Lieutenant who was also, and more appropriately, known as the Viceroy. His Chief Secretary was a Whitehall minister who was sometimes a member of the Cabinet, sometimes with greater political weight than his nominal chief, but always a constitutional oddity.[2] In a formal sense, Ireland was integrated with Britain: Irish MPs sat at Westminster, and Irish law was English law—more so, indeed, than Scottish law was. But here the most telling differences repeatedly emerged. The law was often unenforceable because of passive or active resistance. When the latter became intense, emergency legislation—'coercion'—was liberally applied, not least by Liberals. Law and order was a fragile linkage: the attempt to enforce the law regularly precipitated outbreaks of disorder. Ireland was a congenial place for miracles, but the 'English miracle' did not manifest itself there.

The British government came closer to recognizing the category of political crime in Ireland than was altogether comfortable. This was a function not so much of direct political resistance as of the special kind of intimidatory violence associated with the land struggle. The ordinary crime rate in Ireland was rather low, but what engrossed attention was 'outrage', the label attached by the authorities to violence with no evident personal motive. This kind of amorphous terrorism, usually carried out at night by oath-bound local secret societies or 'associations', was understood as communal enforcement of a popular 'unwritten law'.[3] This peasant resistance was extremely tough; it rendered parts of Ireland ungovernable some of the time and ensured that the central police force remained armed and semi-military in nature. Because it was not expressed in terms of direct challenge to the state, outrage could be more or less contained by the adjective 'agrarian' applied to it by the police. But agrarian crime was unmistakably political in a looser sense: it articulated a broad refusal to internalize the English legal order.[4]

By mid-century the English notion of the innate lawlessness of the Irish had been reconfirmed. Even where there was no visible sign of disorder, the English could see that there was no genuine public peace. Commenting on the situation in Westmeath in 1871, for instance, *The Times* observed that the county was tranquil, but it was 'the tranquillity of a society paralysed by terror': 'the appearance of order is deceptive. Its real meaning is not that law is supreme, but that law is dethroned.'[5] The Prime Minister, W. E. Gladstone, deprecated the kind of alarmism which screamed for repression, but he saw the same basic gulf between English and Irish society. 'Why is government easy in this country? Not, God knows, from want of criminal elements amongst the population, but from the vigorous and healthy tone of social life, which makes men of whatever class an ally of the law.'[6]

His answer, of course, was not repression but reform. Yet the nature of the reform he embarked upon was itself symptomatic of the gulf. His 1870 Land Act signalled the start of a dramatic volte-face in the Liberal assumption that progress was inevitable and that England provided its model. Steps had been taken in the 1830s to integrate English and Irish land law in the belief that Ireland must follow the English path, the path—as Sir Henry Maine was to put it—'from status to contract'. Gladstone's Irish Land Acts, above all the second in 1881, displayed the radically different notion that what was appropriate for England might not be universally valid.

Thus the distinct, demi-colonial status of Ireland became more rather than less marked over the first century of Union. The awkward tension between the English image of social order and its Irish reversal represented the sort of problem which was perhaps easier to face up to in more remote or exotic parts of the empire. The contradiction was certainly very visible in the grandest imperial possession, India, and it was confronted by much the same means: it was ignored. Imperialist writers such as the historian Sir John Seeley lamented the lack of public interest in the amazing fact that England was responsible for the destiny of this vast subcontinent. Macaulay before him marvelled that 'this subject is to most readers not only insipid but positively distasteful'.[7]

This aversion served to avoid confronting the uncomfortable issues thrown up by the pretty unambiguous dependence of British rule on military force. The rebellion of 1857 was always called a 'mutiny', a form of mental quarantining which minimized its political significance and authorized the torrent of bloodshed with which it was suppressed. Official violence did not become a major subject of public debate, however loudly liberals such as Frederic Harrison might lament that the Indian rebellion had 'called out all the tiger in our race', and insist that 'that wild beast must be caged again'.[8] The issue came into sharper focus in 1865, when a much smaller rising was suppressed in Jamaica. Governor Eyre was accused of abusing martial law powers, and his case became a battleground between those who, like Harrison, feared that the 'Indian way' was fast feeding back through the other colonies towards England itself, and those—headed by Thomas Carlyle—who relished the chance of asserting that force was the ultimate arbiter of government.[9] The intensity of the intellectual civil war over the Jamaica case displayed the depth of the clash between the two images of order.

For all the later Victorian efforts of imperialists such as Seeley and Sir Charles Dilke who urged the creation of a 'Greater Britain', in which England, Britain, and the Anglo-Saxon colonies would be fused into a somewhat mystical entity, in practice political culture developed separately.[10] An important symptom of this impermeability was the saga of legal 'codification' which ran over a half-century from the 1830s to the 1880s. The Indian Penal Code written by Macaulay in 1835 and finally enacted in 1860 was a remarkable achievement, a mental eqivalent at least of the great military conquests by which the growth of British India was conventionally marked. Sir James Fitzjames Stephen, who followed Macaulay and Maine as legal adviser to the government of India and who revised the Indian legal system in the early 1870s called the Penal Code 'a work of true genius'.

The rigorous administration of justice of which it forms an essential part has beaten down crime throughout the whole of India to such an extent that the greater part of that vast country would compare favourably, as far as the absence of crime goes, with any part of the United Kingdom except perhaps Ireland in quiet times and apart from political and agrarian offences.[11]

The key to this 'triumphant success' was Macaulay's systematic presentation of the English criminal law 'freed from all technicalities and superfluities'. Stephen wrote later in his great *A History of the Criminal Law of England* that until he had been in India he 'could not have believed it possible that so extensive a body of law could be made so generally known to all whom it concerned in its minutest details'. He even made the startling assertion that the average Indian citizen had a better knowledge ('accurate and comprehensive and distinct') of the Penal Code than English lawyers and judges had of the criminal law. What was more, 'all the ingenuity of commentators' had failed to introduce any serious difficulties: 'after twenty years' use it is still true that anyone who wants to know what the criminal law of India is has only to read the Penal Code with a common use of memory and attention'.[12]

These discoveries, revolutionary in the context of the common law culture, led Stephen on his return from India in 1872 to take up once again Bentham's idea of a 'complete code' of law for England. This classical utilitarian project had already stalled several times in face of traditional attitudes. In 1833 commissioners were appointed 'to digest into One Statute all the Statutes and Enactments touching Crimes', and then 'to digest into One other Statute all the Provisions of the common or unwritten law', and finally to report 'how far it may be expedient to combine both these Statutes into One Body of the Criminal Law'. As Radzinowicz bluntly notes, 'they were at it for fifteen years'.[13]

Two further commissions, in 1837 and 1845, carried the process on, producing thirteen hefty reports and many bills; but 'the only outcome of these stupendous efforts, costing the nation a fortune, were the Criminal Consolidation Acts of 1861', through which the common law survived intact. The reform movement 'had spent itself'.[14] A brief revival in the 1860s was mourned by *The Times* in 1871 as having expired prematurely. Fitzjames Stephen's entry into the fray once more resuscitated the project, and his draft Homicide Law Amendment Bill of 1874 got as far as referral to a Commons select committee, which, however, decided that homicide was the wrong place to start. Stephen then went ahead independently, writing a *Digest of the Laws of Evidence* on Macaulayan principles, and quickly following it with his famous *Digest of the Criminal Law* in 1877.

This prodigious single-handed achievement confirmed Stephen's status as the virtual 'Codifying Commissioner' for England (the title thought up for him by *The Economist*). With the support of the Lord Chancellor and the Attorney-General, his apparently irresistible momentum carried him into the drafting of new Parliamentary bills. In June 1878 the Criminal Code Bill was introduced into the House of Commons, and referred to a Royal Commission. A favourable outcome was seen as a foregone conclusion until the Lord Chief Justice, Sir Alexander Cockburn, stood up at the last moment against the tide of codification. 'Stephen's supreme effort had come to nothing', Radzinowicz writes, adding an epitaph on it which makes the outcome seem inevitable: 'As codes go, this one was good . . . but its chances had been wrecked by the deeply rooted hostility against codification per se and its threat to the common law.'

The common law of this country, like the forces of growth which determined it, is sui generis; it constitutes an integral part of the national heritage, and discharges a political, social and moral function which is more precious than the shapely codes which seekers after legal paradise aspired to create.[15]

This implication of continental utopianism would have been intolerable to Stephen, who saw himself as an apostle of realism and clearheadedness. He inveighed against the squeamish and woolly-minded liberalism which, in his view, had suffocated the original (and, to use one of his favourite adjectives, manly) vigour of utilitarianism.

Stephen gave stentorian voice to the Indian negative of the English experience, insisting on an elemental perception of social relations which English public discourse had—whether deliberately or unconsciously— suppressed. *Liberty, Equality, Fraternity*, his most extended critique of J. S. Mill's *On Liberty*, gained its sometimes disconcerting force not from elaborate argumentation but from the simplicity of its governing idea. This idea had been most brutally expressed by Carlyle in his sulphurous denunciation of Chief Justice Cockburn's summing-up in the Jamaica case:

anterior to all written laws and first making written laws possible, there must have been, and is, and will be, coeval with Human Society, from its first beginnings to its ultimate end, an actual Martial Law, of more validity than any other law whatsoever.[16]

Stephen was hardly less muscular in his insistence on the primacy of force in the creation of peace and the maintenance of order. Even his agnostic liberal contemporaries were dismayed by his assertion that 'both religion and morality are always and must be coercive systems'.[17]

Stephen had no patience with the veil of pseudo-democratic consensus which had been draped over the English state. 'It is impossible to lay down any principles of legislation at all', he insisted, 'unless you are prepared to say, I am right, and you are wrong, and your view shall give way to mine.'[18] This was, of course, the statement which the British had, after protracted hesitation, finally made about the relationship between their culture (or 'civilization') and that of India.[19] As Stephen pugnaciously put it, 'Our law is in fact the sum and substance of what we have to teach them. It is, so to speak, the gospel of the English, and it is a compulsory gospel which admits of no dissent and no disobedience.'[20]

Liberals could stomach this under colour of progress—hence the importance of the campaigns against *suttee* and *thuggee*—but they could not stomach Stephen's readiness, indeed eagerness, to recognize that the same logic underpinned the process of politics in England. To them, Stephen appeared as an apostle of coercion. Perhaps the most shocking moment in *Liberty, Equality, Fraternity* comes when Stephen squares up unflinchingly to the responsibilities of Pontius Pilate for the maintenance of public security in Palestine. Explicitly linking the *Pax Romana* with the *Pax Indiana*, and rolling forth the sonorous Virgilian injunction, 'tu regere imperio populos, Romane, memento . . . pacique imponere morem', he holds that 'An Englishman must have a cold heart and a dull imagination who cannot understand how the consciousness of this must have affected a Roman governor.' Pilate's position was 'not very unlike that of an English Lieutenant Governor of the Punjab'. His 'duty was to maintain peace and order in Judea', not to recognize the teacher of a higher form of morals, or a more enduring form of social order. If he had followed Mill's precept of religious liberty 'he would have run the risk of setting the whole province in a blaze'.[21]

By this dramatic exercise in *einfühlungsvermögen* Stephen was in effect counterposing a religion of public order to the Christian religion. His more explicit assault on the 'religion of humanity' was more than an attack on the English adherents of Comte. Frederic Harrison put himself in this somewhat exotic category, but his positivism was closer to the English mainstream than was Stephen's muscular realism. 'Even common sense may be overdone', Harrison remarked at the start of his counterblast against 'the religion of inhumanity'. Harrison refused to admit the validity of Stephen's monolithic image of force, and held to the traditional distinction between physical and moral force, or power and authority. 'The ultimate appeal to muscular power is found to be most valuable as a negative and repressive force, but to have very little value as a positive and incentive force.' Stephen's belief in the positive capacity of coercive force could only lead to an overmighty and oppressive state, if not to outright state-worship. 'The only true solution', Harrison optimistically asserted, 'is the growing one—the principle that the authority which commands physical force should confine itself strictly to the vast field contained in the material existence of society . . . without pretending to teach or preach.'

Harrison's deepest visceral revulsion was towards the unmistakable influence of Indian government on Stephen's outlook. His book 'teems with Oriental impressions', Harrison noted; he 'forgets how dangerous are the analogies of the East'. The growing custom of administrators to say 'we manage these things better in the Punjab' was ominous because it derived from the experience of ruling 'one of the least developed of human societies, where the germs of moral civilisation and intellectual freedom are hardly visible', and over which 'an empire founded on conquest' had all too recently been 'cemented amid a deluge of blood and passion'.[22]

The clash between Harrison and Stephen was at root a conflict over the nature of the present danger. Stephen saw it in liberal sentimentality: his evident fear that liberalism risked setting the country 'in a blaze' reflected, as Harrison remarked, the Indian government's awareness of sitting on a volcano. He put this vividly in an article written ten years later:

No country in the world is more orderly, more quiet, or more peaceful than British India as it is, but if the vigour of the government should ever be relaxed, if it should lose its essential unity of purpose, and fall into hands either weak or unfaithful, chaos would come again like a flood.[23]

This strenuous and exhilarating vision of government was potentially corrosive of the whole English public tradition. Harrison saw the great danger as lying in the application of Indian attitudes to an advanced society where public order was the product of 'moral civilisation', and where the coercive action of an overmighty state could destroy the legitimacy which its predecessors had built up.

Ship of State or Body Politic?

> It would be difficult in the whole compass of language to find a
> metaphor so commensurate, so pregnant, or suggesting so many points
> of elucidation, as that of *Body Politic*, as the exponent of a State or
> Realm.
>
>   S. T. Coleridge, *Church and State*

Sir Ernest Barker described *Liberty, Equality and Fraternity* as 'the finest
exposition of conservative thought in the latter half of the nineteenth
century', but it was not much closer to the mainstream of English conservatism than it was to liberalism. Its true ancestor was *Leviathan*, and
its challengingly simple public philosophy suffered the same repudiation.
Yet one may wonder whether it was not Stephen's deliberately un-mealy-
mouthed delivery, rather than his message, that was objectionable. For
alongside the hopeful individualist truisms of liberalism went a curiously
robust tradition of respect for the state as the symbol of public life.

Frederic Harrison's injunction that the state should not pretend to 'teach
or preach' was of course a relic of a more uncomplicated age. Burke may
have been able to make a satisfactory distinction between the legitimate
material functions of the state and its encroachments on the private sphere,
but by Harrison's time the boundary was irretrievably blurred. 'Collectivism'
was inexorably encroaching upon individualism.[24] But the power of the
modern state did not spring forth fully armed from the heads of the Whig
legislators. Writing of Macaulay's account of the trial of Warren Hastings,
'one of the great moments of a free constitution', John Burrow focuses on
the symbolic role of Westminster Hall in Macaulay's narrative. 'There is
here, expressed not philosophically but rhetorically, a high idea of the state
and the law as the enduring public thing in the lives of men, and of the
dignity, at its highest even the glory, of the men who minister its rituals
and shape and transmit its precedents.' Burrow adds that 'if this seems
obvious enough, it is not, after all, one of the ideas one tends most readily
to see as dominant in mid-Victorian England'.[25] It is perhaps fair to
say that the English state tradition has been supplied with an extensive
wardrobe of sheep's clothing. Insiders and outsiders alike have been struck
more by the self-deprecatory tone of Bagehot's version of the constitution
than by the iron sense of authority which underpinned it.

Admittedly, Bagehot declared that 'the natural impulse of the English
people is to resist authority', and that 'We look on State action, not as our
own action, but as alien action; as an imposed tyranny from without, not
as the consummated result of our own organized wishes.'[26] But this rather
complacent salute to the traditional self-image—summed up in his remark

that the English were not 'un vrai peuple moderne' like the Americans—came at the end of a disquisition which impressed most of its readers with a very different point. This was his potent image of the constitutional monarchy as 'a *disguise* [which] enables our real rulers to change without heedless people knowing it'. Republics had only difficult ideas in government—that is, they involved political thought—whereas constitutional monarchy 'has an easy idea too'. It was literally the visual imagery of power, 'the *theatrical show* of society', to which the masses deferred. Bagehot set deference at the core of the constitution, and his confident analysis of the machinery of hegemony remained persuasive for a century or more.[27]

The idea of a 'deference culture' loomed large in academic political scientists' work on Britain, seeming to explain the general public indifference to the enlargement of state power, as well as the authoritarian structure of the legislature and the political parties. In the last twenty years it has been subjected to sharper criticism, though much of this serves mainly to show how perilously subjective is the notion of 'political culture', and how problematic is the assessment of 'strong government' or 'effective government'. A leading critic of deference theory observes that 'in an historical and comparative perspective it is probable ... that the English have a peculiar lack of any concept of "the state"'.[28] He instances the comparatively slight role played, especially in economic development, by a centralized 'authoritarian government', and the traditional hostility of working people to the 'state apparatus'. The nub of his argument, that a crucial part in the maintenance of authority has been played by the consistent readiness of élites to adjust to public opinion, the reciprocal nature of power, and the ample evidence that 'a large section of the public not only feels that it has the right to try to influence government policy but also that its efforts stand a good chance of being successful', will by now be familiar enough.[29] This is how hegemony works.

The two great public metaphors, the body politic and the ship of state, are both profoundly authoritarian. The first is perhaps less obviously so than the second, indeed it might even be perceived as democratic in spirit. But the ethos of organic democracy is very different from liberalism. From Shakespeare's Menenius to Bagehot himself, the biological argument was agin the citizen, submerged in

this wonderful spectacle of society, which is ever new, and yet ever the same; in which accidents pass and essence remains; in which one generation dies and another succeeds, as if they were birds in a cage, or animals in a menagerie; of which it seems almost more than a metaphor to treat the parts as limbs of a perpetual living thing, so silently do they seem to change ...[30]

The 'essence' of a society could only be divined by a seer such as Bagehot, able to grasp 'that which is mystic in its claims; that which is occult in its mode of action'. The mass of the people remained as he said, spectators in the theatre of power. Props and effects veiled the reality of the state, and few tried to penetrate the 'intellectual haze' which, as Bagehot said, was preferred by 'men of business'.[31] The English were imagined as a pre-eminently practical people. Rarely, in English public discourse, does one hear assertions like Coleridge's of the necessity 'to form and train up the people of the country to obedient, free, useful, organizable subjects, citizens, and patriots, living to the benefit of the state, and prepared to die for its defence', or Haldane's 'Belief in the state as real equally with the individuals in whom it is realised and whom it controls, this is the foundation of orderly government.'[32] Such Hegelianism would be repudiated by native empiricism. It is quite possible to write the history of English conservatism, for instance, without reference to Coleridge; indeed it is quite normal. Haldane's doom is equally instructive. Yet these two thinkers at both ends of the nineteenth century were not so marginal as they can be made to appear.

In practice the English version of public power was a compromise, eschewing the rhetoric of the organic state (the 'teaching and preaching' which Coleridge wanted and Harrison dreaded) but conserving a core of almost arbitrary power under the colour of public security. The 'secret state' which has aroused some public—or at least journalistic—appre-hension in the last decade may be unprecedented in its present scope but it is not new in principle. It does not merely date back to the first enactment of contemporary official secrecy legislation in 1911, which has conventionally caused some puzzlement because it was carried so easily by a Liberal government. The puzzle has to be carried back at least as far as the 1840s, when the government faced down a small constitutional crisis over the security of the public mail.

When the Home Office practice of opening letters was revealed in 1844, soon after the introduction of the penny post, a minor storm of public indignation was raised. The first line of defence for the Home Secretary, Sir James Graham, was simply to refuse to discuss the issue at all, on national security grounds. The second, when this proved inadequate, was a secret select committee of the Commons. This revealed that the practice of letter-opening had been carried on by every British government since the Commonwealth. The only reason it had now come to light was that the Home Office had gone on from domestic targets to a formidable foreigner, none other than Mazzini, who was of course aware of such practices but had plainly not expected to encounter them in Britain. Some English people shared his surprise: such a system might suit Russia or France, 'but it did not suit the free air of a free country'.[33] *The Times* wielded the ethnic club menacingly:

The proceeding cannot be English, any more than masks, poisons, sword-sticks, secret signs and associations, and other such dark ventures. Public opinion is mighty and jealous, and does not brook to hear of public ends pursued by other than public means. It considers that treason against its public self.[34]

This confidence was in process of being betrayed; another jealous god was dying.

The Parliamentary debate sharply revealed the ultimate incompatibility between the two senses of public security. Macaulay came out on the side of individual security, insisting that all letters were private, and that long experience 'shows us that the benefits arising from the strict observation of the security of private life, without the exercise of arbitrary power, much more than counterbalance all the advantages to be derived from the contrary system'.[35] The official view focused on the security of the state, though without quite naming it, and emphasized the alarming possibility that with a secure mail 'every criminal and conspirator against the public peace would be publicly assured that he should enjoy possession of the easiest, cheapest and most unobserved channel of communication'.[36] And the Home Office had the last word—or, rather, silence. When new claims of letter-opening were raised in early 1845, Graham simply stonewalled, refusing either to confirm or deny the allegation. Thus matters rested.

The Habit of Authority

> The 'typical' English gentleman exercised authority, indeed he *was* authority. No wonder, therefore, he worshipped it.
>
> Colin Richmond

The subject of 'paternalism in British history', the subtitle of A. P. Thornton's remarkable essay *The Habit of Authority*, has not been widely studied. Indeed it is hard to think of rivals to Thornton's barbed work. This started from the observation that 'the "genius of English liberty" has been nurtured under the protection of governments more in sympathy with individual right than with any view of "social justice", or of the rights of men in general'. The parallel fact that government in England had been supported to a degree uncommon in other countries called for examination, but Thornton could think of only three books which had undertaken this: Butterfield's *Whig Interpretation of History* and *The Englishman and his*

History, and Sellar and Yeatman's *1066 and All That*. If his tongue was sidling into his cheek at this point, he was very serious in his central contention that 'There would never have been an Empire at all had there not been, in the English character, a habit of authority—and this habit would not have survived without its obverse, a habit of respect for its exercise.'[37]

He followed this with a pungent account of English submission, which he saw as becoming habitual after the Norman conquest. The tenacity of the Normans was what distinguished them from other depredators, but it was facilitated by English pragmatism: 'the strength of the "Norman Yoke", as the Plantagenets, Jack Cade, Levellers, Diggers, and Tom Paine understood, lay not in its oppressive force, but in the acquiescence of the English people that it was a useful yoke, under which useful work was done'.[38] The reasons for this acquiescence, and for the success of 'the governors of England' in elevating 'law and order' from a necessity to a principle, are less clearly adduced. Why did the moderation so characteristic of English Toryism become the social contract under which the gentry were accorded such immense deference? Thornton held that even in the nineteenth century 'what the people required of this governing class was a particular kind of perception, an ability as it were to read the runes of the general will', so that English paternalism, 'far from suffering marked defeat as a sturdy and independent democracy came pouring through the gaps in the pale of the constitution, took on a new lease of life'.[39]

The nearest he could get to explaining the ascendency of this class was to invoke Pascal's notion of the head start given by the upbringing of a 'man of quality': 'the "clear gain of thirty years" was the most powerful weapon in the aristocrat's armoury', and its use was 'a potent agency in keeping England, socially speaking, a colonial society, with habits and conventions imposed from above'. This was done by 'the magnetic attraction of English aristocratic attitudes themselves'; 'The wish of the people, as everyone agreed, was to be governed by gentlemen';[40] 'the idea of aristocracy did represent an ideal in the English community. Men acknowledged that standards had been set, and respected the authority that had set them.'[41]

However difficult it might be for an English person to gainsay Thornton's assertion, its lack of specificity is a problem for the historian. The argument is largely negative: 'if the doctrines of utilitarianism had been thoroughly comprehended and accepted by the people, then surely the peerage and the monarchy with it, would have vanished in some great explosive revolution of the 1840s'.

English society, despite the dislocations that the processes of industrialism had caused, was still close-knit. There was such a thing, though never so publicized as its fellow in the United States, as a national outlook, a generally accepted method of dealing with life, even if it was most often defined in terms whose negative aspects had an easily-exploited comicality: 'not playing the game', 'not cricket', 'not done', all of them implying the existence of some aristocratic code of action.[42]

The insertion of 'aristocratic' here is tendentious, and the American comparisons which Thornton deployed rather capriciously remain as treacherous as they are enlightening. We are left with the puzzle of why, if the American 'national outlook' was so highly publicized, Americans lacked (according to H. G. Wells in 1906) that 'living sense of the state' which, Thornton suggests, Wells had singled out as an integral part of the English national outlook. In fact, Wells hardly did this. Though he did imply that England possessed that mysterious capacity to frame long-term collective aims which he found missing in America, he stressed that the great mass of prosperous middle-class people in England also lacked that 'sense of the state'.[43] So where could one find that 'general will' whose runes the gentry were prized for reading? And how, since the 'original motivation' of authority in England was always brutally simple in Thornton's view— 'self-preservation'—did the establishment discover its subtle secret, self-restraint? Thornton merely comments that 'since flexibility had always been found to be an asset to this policy, its rigid doctrines were accordingly few'.[44] Here we see the 'English way' with sharp clarity, but are told no more than that it 'had always been found'.

Thornton's historical exploration of what he labelled paternalism was against the grain of collective assumptions, as much so, it may be thought, as Fitzjames Stephen's had been. But it did not raise a comparable stir. What he characterized, in speaking of Burke's evaluation of the laws of commerce, as 'complacency at this astronomical level' (which, he added, 'can seem a more thwarting foe than tyranny itself'), was no less pervasive in the decades following the Second World War. Harry Eckstein's outstanding essay on the British political system, written in the late 1950s, noted that the habit of deference was 'generally glossed over' in modern commentaries. Yet Eckstein thought it the only possible explanation of the striking discrepancy between the British system and other modern democracies. He remained agnostic on the issue 'whether Britain is a democracy or not': 'British government is at least supremely constitutional in character'.[45] And that is a supremely English adjective. We all know what it means, but that meaning is not to be found in the Oxford dictionary.[46]

3

Flawed Equipoise 1880–1914

The traditional love of liberty, the traditional sense of duty to the community, be it great or small, the traditional respect for law and the wish to secure reforms by constitutional rather than violent means— these were the habits ingrained in the mind and will of Englishmen.

James Bryce, *Modern Democracies* (1921)

Against the Regime of Casual Crowds

The contrast between the image of orderliness assiduously cultivated by the establishment, and the persistence of substantial disorder through to the Edwardian age, was not much noticed until recently. The title of Donald Richter's *Riotous Victorians* (1981) was deliberately disconcerting. Richter argued that 'the widely-held belief in the public orderliness of Victorian society' was a 'gross misconception'; Britain remained, until the 1890s at least, a 'very disorderly society'.[1] He may have overstated his case somewhat, but the evidence goes far to sustain his point. The decade of the 1880s, in particular, witnessed a turmoil dramatically at odds with the broad meliorism of the modernization process.

The decade began with the intensification of rural conflict in Ireland into what was soon called the 'land war'. This was the most extensive breakdown of law and order since the 1798 rebellion, and though less sanguinary than that had been, it was in some ways more formidable.[2] The Liberal Home Secretary, Sir William Harcourt, warned Gladstone in July 1882 that the spirit of the people was 'every day more and more hostile to law'. In Ireland 'we are in a condition of things which is only not actual rebellion because there is neither the courage nor the force for an open attack—In all other respects the state is one of civil war.'[3] The challenge was not simply that of public violence, but a more corrosive unpicking of public security, through the practice of ostracism or 'boycotting'. Gladstone's government tried to legislate against this through the Prevention of Crime Act in July 1882, which Gladstone endorsed reluctantly with the argument that while 'the evil, which there is in boycotting, dwells more or less in the breasts of most men', its elevation into a system created 'a monstrous public evil, threatening liberty ... and seriously endangering the peace and order of the country'.[4]

The defective peace of Ireland was an endemic problem throughout the years of the Union, though English indifference taught Irish activists that only when ungovernability became epidemic would it engross real political attention. Gladstone's declaration of his mission to 'pacify Ireland', after the apparently ineffectual spate of Fenian action in the mid-1860s, initiated a series of attempts to balance coercion with 'conciliation'—the latter within the tight limits of liberal economic principles. Gladstone's two land reform laws tried to moderate the power of landlordism in Ireland, ending the reign of strict English property law but refusing to use public funds to assist the creation of a peasant proprietary. When they failed to disperse the burgeoning Irish national movement, Gladstone moved on to 'Home Rule' as the only way of saving the Union. Unionists refused to accept it as such, and followed Gladstone's defeat by trying to kill Home Rule by helping the tenantry to buy out the landlords. These vast, divergent, and indeed revolutionary trajectories shared a common aim: to make Ireland secure. They were in spirit both public order policies, whose positive aspect was unfortunately more visible from the English than from the Irish side; the negative inspiration of Home Rule was to become more stultifying as Gladstone's successors manœuvred to deal with Unionist threats of violent resistance.

Gladstone, like Balfour after him, felt himself to be organizing the 'resources of civilization' against anarchy. At the height of the land war crisis, the 'manliness and prudence' (Gladstone's words) of the proconsular Earl Spencer, the Viceroy of Ireland, proved sufficient to face down the challenge. But the threat spilled out from Ireland itself. The American branch of the Fenian organization launched a campaign of dynamite bombings in England. Irish anarchy fused with Russian anarchism to spawn a terrorist alarm of the sort that was to become more familiar in the following century.[5] Here and later, in the 'Plan of Campaign' agitation, the notion of political crime obtruded awkwardly into English public discourse. (It would remain alien a century later, even after the temporary concession of 'political status' to IRA prisoners.) In the English view, a political crime was not a crime committed for political reasons; or, as A. J. Balfour put it, a crime did not become political because it was committed by a politician. A political offence was one which had been framed for political reasons—as where membership of certain political organizations, or publication of certain political ideas, were made criminal offences—and which lay outside the 'normal' criminal code. This robust distinction does not seem to have been widely grasped, however, and has led to complications in international law, especially extradition law.[6] To hang on to this strong sense, we need another category—public crime, perhaps—to denote the commission of 'ordinary' crimes with political motive. (The term 'order defiance' has also been proposed for this kind of action.[7])

Either way, however, there is no escaping the fact that the modern state security system began with the creation of the Irish Special Branch in the 1880s. The indefinite threat of terrorism, whose actual destructive capacity was always hard to get in proportion, was enhanced by a growing sense of the fragility of civilization. The state might be becoming more powerful but the social order seemed less robust. Bernard Porter has suggested that changes in political climate—'the bundle of liberal assumptions and prejudices' in this case—may 'happen suddenly, with a crisis, or slowly, with the gradual erosion of an ethos'.[8] Both tempi could be found in the generation of what George Dangerfield indelibly labelled 'the strange death of liberal England'. In Porter's account the 'vigilant state' grew out of a widening discrepancy between political and economic liberalism, subverting the old optimism that sound political systems were 'best defended by having no defences'.

A real test of liberal assumptions was set up in the arena of Trafalgar Square in late 1887, when persistent demonstrations were mounted, initially against unemployment, and later against the first permanent Irish 'coercion act', Balfour's 1887 Criminal Law and Procedure Act. The scale of the crowds stretched the Metropolitan Police to the limits of their capacity. Sympathy for the Irish was probably less important in this mobilization than a sense of the need to assert the public right to use the square, which was being squeezed by the growing activity of the police. Richter labels the events 'the struggle for Trafalgar Square', rather than riots or disturbances, and plainly some such issue was felt to be at stake. The police saw the control of public spaces, especially such symbolically freighted spaces as Trafalgar Square, as a central task. The Commissioner of the Metropolitan Police, Sir Charles Warren, justified his early ban on meetings in the square as being 'absolutely necessary in the interests of public peace'; it was 'not safe to wait till a breach of the peace has actually taken place before taking police measures'.[9] This absolutist version of public safety was vehemently endorsed by the *Spectator* on the apocalyptic ground that 'if a mob can do these things with impunity, the People loses all rights, and its sovereignty is superseded by a regime of casual crowds'.[10]

But the police view was still contested within the government. Even in 1883, amidst the shock and alarm of the first terrorist attacks, Harcourt maintained the old liberal attitude, or prejudice. When the Metropolitan Board of Works decided to ban public meetings on Peckham Rye, on the basis of powers it had assumed in 1877, the Home Secretary lectured them that

There is not a village or town in England, which has not some open space where gatherings of this kind can take place, and it would be intolerable if the population of London amounting to four millions of people, were destitute of such opportunities which are naturally and legitimately desired. . . . Unnecessary repression of this character creates discontent and disturbance, and so far from tending to public order is calculated to provoke irritation and tumult.[11]

Harcourt's Conservative successor, Henry Matthews, preserved the same attitude towards police eagerness to stifle public protest. Admittedly, during the Trafalgar Square conflict he deferred to the argument of extreme necessity made by Warren, and approved his indefinite ban on public meetings, which in the event ran on from November 1887 to October 1892. It was this ban which triggered the final explosive confrontation on 13 November, when a crowd of some five thousand was broken up by resolute police action—with a battalion of Grenadier Guards prominently on display—in what George Bernard Shaw called 'the most abjectly disgraceful defeat ever suffered by a band of heroes outnumbering their foes a thousand to one'.

The police relished this triumph, but Matthews never wholly accepted the action. Though he continued publicly to support Warren's successor, Monro, he remained privately critical of his assumptions. Finally, when Monro banned a parade of Friendly Societies in 1890, Matthews was driven to protest that 'these men are the pick of the working classes, perfectly orderly, with an excellent object in view. It would be disastrous to get the police into collision with them.' Of course, Monro's idea was to avoid collision by prohibiting the parade, but Matthews rejected this negative view. 'Processions are *not* necessarily illegal', he insisted. However 'troublesome to the police' demonstrations were, 'it will not do to go beyond the law in dealing with them. In the case of Trafalgar Square', he reminded Monro, 'the law was strained to the utmost; but public safety and public opinion supported the action of the police. That would not be so in this instance.'[12] Here was a particularly clear statement of the discretion assumed to be at the core of order maintenance. The creation of order was a reciprocal process in which the contribution of public opinion was vital. Since there was no way of measuring public opinion exactly, it had to be gauged by 'touch', rooted in a common sense of order.

That common sense was disintegrating at the turn of the century—partly as a result of the very success of the police in minimizing breaches of the peace. As order was stretched more extensively, fears of its fragility burgeoned. One recent historian has noted a growing apprehension that traditional modes of public assembly were at least as dangerous as they were beneficial to society, and a growing confidence on the part of the police of their ability and their right to clear the streets.[13] The successors of Harcourt and Matthews were to give way imperceptibly to this confidence. Whether, on their own reading of the public interest, they were right to do so is not an easy question to answer. Public opinion is a shifting and elusive element in political calculation and history-writing alike. Examining the early 1890s, Bernard Porter has taken the reception of Sherlock Holmes as a straw in the wind. Conan Doyle's bizarre creation, perilously combining conventional signs of gentility with images of subterranean decadence, was initially a flop. His popularity in the mid-1890s would, Porter suggests, have been hard to imagine ten years earlier, his ultimate status as an English icon presumably still more so. The incorporation of disguise into the Holmes detective method can be read as a plain indication of shifting public tolerances, and Holmes is indeed a world away from the simple repositories of manliness and gentlemanliness whose standards dominated earlier popular fiction.[14]

A modern comparative study of political crime in Europe has noticed the extent to which the English legal system, up until the 1890s, involved the public, in the form of the jury, in the definition of political offences. On this view, the trial of John Burns and others for sedition and incitement to riot in 1886 was 'the high water mark of English judicial liberalism'. In this period, judges were apt to call upon juries to look at political cases 'in a free, bold, manly and generous spirit towards the defendant'. In 1886 Lord Cave instructed the jury in the Burns case to consider motive as well as result:

if you think that these defendants . . . had a seditious intention to incite the people to violence, to create public disturbances and disorder, then undoubtedly you ought to find them guilty. . . . On the other hand if you come to the conclusion that they were animated by an honest desire to alleviate the misery of the unemployed . . . you should not be too swift to mark any hasty or ill-considered expression which they might utter in the excitement of the moment.[15]

Barton Ingraham remarks that after this tidal point 'one can detect a gradual, but steady, decline' in the liberalism of the judiciary. The old situation depended, as he notes, on an extraordinary public consensus of opinion.[16]

The difficulty of maintaining consensus in face of major public stress became acute during the Boer War, which generated an unfamiliar crisis of national confidence. The violent assaults of patriots on 'pro-Boer' meetings brought on a Parliamentary debate on the underlying asumptions of orderliness. Though stout defenders of the absolute right to free speech remained on the Liberal side, the Conservative view was more subtly balanced: the Home Secretary urged that 'there are times when men's feelings are strongly excited, and when allowance ought to be made for it'. Since this was such a time, he held that 'those who are calling these public meetings ... ought to be very careful not to endanger the public peace'. Arthur Balfour trawled deeper into constitutional thought, maintaining that

the right of free speech in this country is of a kind which ought not to make the persons who wish to give their views to the world absolutely oblivious of the conditions under which they speak and of the disorder to which their speeches may give rise, and of the public difficulties and dangers which may ensue.[17]

More important than the supercilious tone here, perhaps, was the negative syntax and the veiled indication of the essential identity of public order and public safety.

Industrial Treason

The two pre-war decades produced a new sense of crisis. The threat of organized labour to modern society was identified in the early 1880s by the leading economic philosopher W. S. Jevons. 'Our elaborate system of trade and industry' was more vulnerable than simpler societies to 'serious emergencies' caused by reckless strike action. Faced with what he labelled 'social treason', Jevons saw no answer but compulsion, or what might now be called industrial conscription, necessitated by the collapse of traditional communal responsibilities. If the community would not operate naturally, it must be reconstituted by force: 'there should be some legal authority capable, in the last resort, of obliging citizens to perform essential duties'.[18] This uniquely modern sense of threat to the life of the nation soon became more acute. The Yorkshire miners' strike of 1893 overstretched the local police and brought the intervention of troops. The resulting lethal affray at Featherstone, where two miners were killed and at least fourteen wounded, was treated more seriously than more sanguine events earlier in the century had been. The ultimate sanction of the state in preserving order was subjected to extended reappraisal, though the debate was kept out of the public realm. The Liberal Home Secretary, H. H. Asquith, silenced Parliamentary questions by the same method used by Sir James Graham in 1845. Featherstone remains etched on the collective memory of the labour movement as a classic instance of state repression, but the establishment saw it very differently.[19] The official conclusion was that the traditional way must continue to be followed.

Much the same was true of the official response to the South Wales miners' strike of 1910, though 'Tonypandy' was to become an image of repression even more vivid and durable than Featherstone. Indeed, what is remarkable about the South Wales crisis is that the Home Secretary, Winston Churchill, so far from giving rein to what Dangerfield called his 'native militarism', kept the extent and form of military intervention under exceptionally strict political control. No previous Home Secretary had set out such precise conditions for the use of troops. What Churchill did was to send to Pontypridd a military commander, General Nevil Macready, with large but indeterminate powers to co-ordinate the local and national forces of order. Macready gave the impression of carrying in his pocket a dormant commission to act as military governor, and brilliantly exploited this vague threat to achieve an almost bloodless pacification.[20]

The originality of Churchill's policy has not always been fully grasped. Recent writers have noticed that his decision to take order-maintenance out of the hands of the local authorities—which seems to have occasioned no Cabinet discussion—stood traditional public order doctrine on its head.[21] This was, indeed, sufficiently obvious at the time: as the Chief Constable of Staffordshire noted,

The curious precedent has been provided . . . of a General Officer being placed in command of troops but acting under the orders of the Home Secretary: and of the Police sent from London, ostensibly in aid of the Glamorgan police, being practically under the orders of the officer commanding the troops and not the Chief Constable.[22]

Somewhat less obvious, perhaps, is that through this instinctual creation of a civil–military supremo (a word even more foreign than 'commissioner', and equally useful) Churchill turned the weak spot of the English way—its reliance on individual judgement—into a strength by giving enhanced power to a carefully chosen man. This was the colonial technique coming home to roost.

Macready, assisted by a few similarly inspired junior officers, gave a *tour de force* demonstration of how to walk that fine line whose perils Napier and Haldane had so vividly depicted. He showed that, with the right man in the right place, the English method of peacekeeping was still effective. But by the same token he showed how dependent it was on the choice of that individual. He was able to exploit the indefiniteness of the structure of authority, and the substantial residue of sensitivity to the rhetoric of orderliness amongst 'respectable' working people. When he arrived in South Wales, he found that the local police were in the pockets of the mine owners, who believed that the revolution was at hand. In their view, the miners' marches and pickets were more than mere protest or disorder. They wanted to 'flood the valleys with troops', and to surround each mine with 'a ring of steel'.[23] Macready astonished both masters and men by taking—and showing that he took—the view that the main cause of the conflict was the action of the employers in enforcing a wage cut by a lock-out. He acted as if he believed that the state had a duty to stand above the dispute, and to refuse to allow its forces to be manipulated by one side under the colour of protecting property.

In the circumstances, this was a revolutionary stance. The local police certainly had no such idea of detachment, any more than those who assumed the role of their paymasters. Macready's disconcerting impact on the local establishment heightened his influence over the 'responsible' miners' committees. These he lectured with traditional paternalism, telling them that:

although I could not believe that any of the strikers would be so foolish and un-British as to embark on [violent]action, . . . if anything in the shape of revolver shooting or bomb throwing [occurred] the military would be obliged to intervene at once, the result of which could only be disastrous to the strikers.[24]

The effect of such homilies was equally traditional: one miners' representative, 'a very sensible man—quite alive to the folly of riotous behaviour' . . . 'was quite sensible over the matter and promised that he would do his best to influence the men. I pointed out that we were determined to maintain the strictest discipline among the protective forces, as well as to maintain order among the strikers.'[25] 'That it is illegal to congregate on highways or on railway stations or to follow or molest persons is quite a surprise to a striker. When the limitations of the law became known by means of notices it was much easier to induce the men to listen to reason.'[26] In the end, Macready got the Joint Committee to agree that 'in order to preserve the good name of the valley it was essential that those who desired the continuance of law and order should themselves exercise their influence in preventing anything in the shape of disorder and not necessarily wait for the intervention of the police.'[27]

The apparition of Macready in South Wales showed that the old deference relationship could still work, if the authorities demonstrated their acceptance of its reciprocity. Macready was able to secure, by and large, public acceptance of his own definition of order because he was able to cast it in a sufficiently traditional guise, and to show his conviction of the need for consensus. He 'condescended' in the old style, with tact and grace. Yet even he perhaps deluded himself about the extent to which he was functioning as the medium for the spirit of community. His general's uniform, and the carefully-staged visibility of his troops, gave him an exceptional position. The Metropolitan Police, whose efficiency obviated the need for direct military confrontation of the strikers, were themselves acting in a quasi-military role in relation to the locality. Macready's commission of the peace by no means turned him into an ordinary magistrate.

His success, extravagantly lauded by a relieved government, served to disguise the unresolved inconsistencies of the English system. For ten years afterwards, through successive moments of crisis—the strikes of 1911–12, the Ulster crisis of 1912–14, the resort to conscription in the Great War, the Metropolitan Police strike of 1918, and the Irish guerrilla war of 1920–1—Macready straddled the gap between doctrine and practice. But during this time the underlying problem was becoming more acute. The *Daily Mail*, the voice of lower-middle-class patriotism, branded the transport dispute of 1911 'a strike against society', which 'could only succeed by the destruction of society itself'.[28] This hysterical tone was to become the mark of the twentieth century.

Jingoism shaped all life, after the social Darwinian fashion, as war, and the primary focus of its anxiety was of course international. But visions of national struggles for survival inevitably brought anxiety about internal strength. The Anglo–German antagonism, as it mounted in the decade before 1914, fed back into fears of domestic disloyalty, and a loss of faith in the resilience of the national community. 'Spy scares' were only one, if the most lurid, manifestation of this anxiety. What G. R. Searle has called 'the quest for national efficiency' articulated a novel prepossession with military power.[29] Its exponents felt their way uneasily amidst the still-robust liberal orthodoxies. Once national security was thought to depend on measurable quantities like public discipline and state power, rather than the 'spirit of liberty', the deficiencies of the English way must begin to be cause for alarm.

Emergency Powers

Until the outbreak of the European war, however, the traditional orthodoxy prevailed. No formal doctrine of civil emergency was worked out. The pressure for some such definition was growing, and was certainly not confined to the margins of the national efficiency movement. Featherstone had compelled Whitehall to give unwonted attention to the perennial problem of determining the proper use of force to restore order. Inter-departmental committees cogitated for some years afterwards. A judicial commission chaired by Lord Bowen interviewed civil and military officers with responsibilities for peacekeeping, and heard plenty of evidence of their dilemmas when faced with decisions of life and death. In spite of all this it reasserted the dogma that individual commissioners must do their best in the spirit of the common law.[30] A similar line, recognizing the 'peculiarly onerous' responsibility cast on military officers in civil disturb-ances, but deciding that it was 'not possible or even desirable to attempt to regulate that responsibility more clearly', was taken by the Commons select committee convened in 1908 after troops had been deployed to restore order in Belfast.

The committee went so far as to admit that it 'would have been glad to find a mode of defining [the power to use force] with more precision'—a significant admission—but it was guided by its weightiest witness, the future Liberal Lord Chancellor R. B. Haldane. Haldane, who had sat on the Bowen Commission, produced some memorably terse statements of the English way. 'A man is on the verge of two precipices, and he has to get along, and he does get along.' If the committee were to frame regulations to 'save the officer from falling over these precipices', as some of its members wished, 'you will make the law go over the precipices'. Here was plainly said what military officers had often thought. Haldane dismissed the notion of a joint civil–military authority to take responsibility: it was 'much better to have one man whom you can hang, if necessary'. This brutality of expression—whether or not consciously echoing Napier—was as revealing as it was uncharacteristic of Haldane himself.[31]

By this time, the army, encouraged no doubt by the mounting popular alarm about the threat of German invasion, was beginning to push harder for formal definition of powers to prepare defensive operations. It affected to take the view that such powers should be quite simple to define, though it was well aware that lawyers would take a different view. The undercurrent of barely suppressed hostility fed by this conflict came close to the surface in 1909, when the War Office revived an earlier call—made in 1888—for an Emergency Powers Act. The scope of the original demand had been extensive, including powers to arrest spies and expel aliens, as well as to use any lands, roads, and water supplies, to construct communications, to requisition local authorities to 'do anything necessary for the public safety', to place any fortress on a war footing, to put civilians under the Army Act, and to raise volunteer forces.[32] (The stated justification for such a state of emergency would be 'imminent national danger', perhaps derived from the German legal *Zustand drohende Kriegsgefahr*.)

This demand was met by the government with the finely honed skills of sponge-wall technique. Sir Courtenay Ilbert, the parliamentary draughts-man, drily observed that 'the elaboration of a statutory emergency code would appear to be an academic exercise on which a Government official would not be justified in spending his time unless he happened to be in the enjoyment of superabundant leisure' (even more, presumably, than was required to construct that luxuriant sentence).[33] 'Like most lawyers', a senior military staff officer tartly commented, Ilbert 'objected to a clear straightforward measure that everyone could understand'.[34] He set the official lawyers to search out and list all the legal powers already available. They came up with a stupendous 576-page volume of statutes affecting the military forces of the Crown, 'a monument of legal stupidity' which, so far from satisfying the army's demand, reinforced its belief that simplification was imperative. The Crown lawyers reiterated the common law orthodoxy that in event of invasion or imminent risk of it, 'military officers should exercise such complete powers that any attempt to specify [them] in detail or to express them in statutory language might involve the danger of restricting or limiting them'. Time was to show that this argument was far from nugatory, but it naturally cut no ice with the army. Nor did the pious advice that officers must 'trust to the patriotism, good sense, and consider-ation of their countrymen for indemnity', or the opinion that sensible juries would not convict soldiers for exceeding their powers in such circumstances. All in all, the lawyers held, there was 'no probability of English statesmen being willing to place permanently on the statute book provisions corresponding to those under which a state of siege may be declared in France'. Government would 'no doubt continue to rely on the discretion and courage of officials', and 'a civil or military officer who hesitated to take such risks would be unfit for his post'.[35]

Lord Wolseley, the Adjutant-General, fumed that it was 'difficult to speak with any patience of such academic platitudes'.[36] His junior, Sir John Ardagh, made the point more diplomatically by spelling out the military dilemma in interpreting the rule of necessity.

by the law of necessity an officer may do anything that he considers necessary, but he must be prepared to explain the reasons for his acts and be judged for them on their reasonableness; thus an officer would be justifed in ordering the inhabitants of a town to remain indoors unless provided with a night pass between 6 p.m. and 6 a.m., but he would not be justified in ordering them to go to the enemy's cantonments to get information, and in shooting them if they refused.[37]

This much was clear enough, but most action was likely to fall somewhere in between. In practice, officers were certain to be intimidated, if not paralysed, by 'dwelling upon', as Napier had put it, a putative jury's attitude.

The renewed military demand for clarification took some account of these earlier confrontations, but still insisted on the need for definition of a possible state of emergency or 'extreme national danger'. In such a state there should be powers to requisition local authorities to organize labour, to evacuate civilians, to alter the telegraph system, to raise military forces, proclaim martial law, and billet troops in private houses. It also called for the strengthening of the 1889 Official Secrets Act to make it more effective (or less ineffective) against spies.[38] The mere mention of martial law and the billeting of troops, such salient public taboos since the Petition of Right, probably doomed the proposal. Martial law was a vexed question which had been practically excluded from English legal thought since the seventeenth century. As a result it became—fundamental though it was—the most uncertain element of all in the structure of public power.

Doubts about the definition of martial law, and its source—whether the royal prerogative or the common law power of the executive to meet force with force—and doubts indeed about its legality, persisted through the nineteenth century.[39] The furore over Governor Eyre's use of martial law in Jamaica threw them into sharp relief, and appeared to vindicate the common law version. Chief Justice Cockburn denounced martial law doctrine as repugnant to the law of England. The ascendancy of the common law was confirmed in the 1880s with the publication of A. V. Dicey's *Introduction to the Study of the Law of the Constitution*, whose pithy eloquence and self-assurance made it the nearest thing to a written constitution that England has ever recognized. Dicey defined martial law as 'the power of the government or of loyal citizens to maintain public order, at whatever cost of blood or property may be necessary'.[40] In his polemical writing, he added a moral gloss, denouncing what he took to be a popular belief in the capacity of 'five ignorant young officers ... by the inspiration of heaven or the Devil' to administer 'some unknown system of ready-made equity', as an absurd delusion.

The noticeable fact, however, is not the imbecility of mind, but the utter lawlessness of spirit, displayed by men who often assert that martial law is—to use a horrible expression I have seen in a Conservative print—'the one thing needful' for Ireland . . . The men who desire it really wish for a proclamation that unrestrained force of the sword has taken the place of the restrained and just force of the law.[41]

Dicey's central assertion was that continental definitions of 'state of siege' or emergency powers would be supererogatory (and indeed harmful) in England, because the common law provided all conceivable powers with a reach and flexibility beyond the wit of any legislator. All it required was that the necessity of the actions taken to restore order could be demonstrated subsequently in a court of law.

It was precisely this requirement, which lawyers found so elegant, that soldiers found so unnervingly impractical. Just what was necessary? Even the complacent official summary prepared in 1881, noting that 'the law would fall far short of what is needed for the preservation of society if it did not allow all necessary measures to be taken for putting an end to unlawful assemblies, riots, and insurrections', admitted that 'the difficulty is to ascertain what is this necessary degree of force'.[42] A modern writer on crisis government in western democracies has noted that 'there is a healthy difference of opinion concerning what this criterion permits'.[43] Here 'healthy' is distinctly ambiguous: the dispute has been vigorous, but whether it has been beneficial is much more doubtful. At least it is not easy to say who benefited from the uncertainty. In classical common law perspective it is the public which is protected from military tyranny; and no doubt some memory of seventeenth-century events underpinned the long-standing aversion to martial law. The problem for the twentieth century was that the immobility of English legal thought on this issue left the law in a shape designed around the kind of warfare which had gone out with Monmouth's rebellion. The twentieth century was to see the appearance of many complex, politically sophisticated kinds of 'low intensity conflict' to which the old legal tests could be applied with the utmost difficulty, if at all.[44]

The use of martial law to crush the Boer guerrilla campaign in South Africa revealed the beginnings of this process. Some lawyers, notably Sir Frederick Pollock, argued that the expanding scope and nature of modern war enlarged the principle of necessity far beyond its traditional limits.[45] The traditional test of a state of war, whether or not the ordinary courts were sitting, was no longer valid. The case of D. F. Marais seemed to demonstrate that a marked shift of interpretation was taking place. Marais's appeal from the sentence of a military tribunal, on the ground that martial law was illegal because the civil courts were still sitting, was quashed in a dramatic decision by Governor Eyre's old defence counsel, Lord Halsbury.[46] The case became a zone of combat for jurists who saw it as opening the way to a new style of arbitrary state, and the issue remained—as will be seen—locked in a legal contention that was never finally resolved. Unsurprisingly, the Crown law officers gave it as their opinion on 17 July 1913 that

There seems to us to be great danger in endeavouring to make an exhaustive list of the powers which the Executive may exercise in time of emergency. The great merit of the common law is that it will justify even an unprecedented course of action if it is fairly covered by the maxim *salus reipublicae suprema lex*. We are convinced that it is far better to rely upon the good sense of the community and the necessities of the case backed up if need be by a Bill of Indemnity when the crisis is passed.[47]

What was unmistakable in this protracted legal–military dialogue was the contrast between the heady official rhetoric of public spirit, and the army's sceptical sense of reality. Thus the lawyers believed that if an officer loopholed a house for defence, the owner would accept the necessity of the damage. The army had no experience of such ideal citizens. Indeed, its general view of the public spirit was decidedly gloomy. In an Army Council memorandum in late 1908 addressing the issue of public order in a general emergency, the writer noted that though he was not

an expert on the subject of the control of a large civil population in time of possible panic, I can readily understand that with vast numbers of ignorant, underfed, and discontented unemployed, together with the alien and criminal population, the Government might have a weighty question on its hands at a time when all the energies of our naval, military and civil authorities should be devoted to repelling the enemy.[48]

Such pessimism was not confined to the seclusion of the Horse Guards. Doubts about public morale ran through police and Home Office correspondence, summoning up the stern resolution of earlier authorities in earlier grand emergencies, like Sir David Dundas in 1796—'in this state of things no man ought to remain neuter, and the lukewarm should be more than suspected. On the tranquillity of the Capital everything depends.'[49]

In 1909 the Chief Constable of Lanarkshire, for instance, offered the view that 'in the event of invasion civil tumult would certainly occur, in any case the dregs of the population would seize their opportunity to cause disturbance and to loot'. In such circumstances not only the police, but the special constabulary too, would have to be armed. But in preparing for this, the authorities would tread a fine line.

It is quite recognized that there would be the strongest opposition to any training of the civil police that would suggest its being given a military character, but I think the fact that the rifles and necessary equipment would be stored at the nearest Military Depot and only issued when the Territorial forces were mobilized, and that the Constables would never be exercised with arms, after recruit training, and never shoot the annual musketry course as a body, would soften any feeling of antagonism.[50]

The Metropolitan Commissioner told the military commander of the London district in 1910 that the Home Office was

of opinion that the time has not yet come, though it is near at hand, when I could without giving rise to general and understandable apprehension on the part of the public make the enquiries necessary for compiling a Special Constabulary register for each Police Station in the Metropolis.[51]

The object of the planned mobilization was clear: 'by the maintenance of Order I understand that we should have to maintain it against the turbulent amongst our own residents only, and could not be responsible for repelling attack in any form'.

Imminent Civil War

The sense of general crisis in the body politic of pre-war England may have been exaggerated. It is still a moot point when, or whether, Liberal England 'died'. The title of Dangerfield's book will resonate whatever scholars may make of its content. It is a conventional truth that 'the Irish question not only involved England in bloody civil war outside the country but almost led to internal war in England itself'.[52] In England itself, none the less, public order did not become a salient public issue. The most overtly critical events were contained without much drama. The parliamentary struggle of 1909–10, which finally broke the political authority of the House of Lords, could be seen as a constitutional crisis, but it was resolved by characteristic English means. The irruption of suffragette violence into the public policy process turned out to be less destabilizing than might have been expected.[53] The sharpest pressure on the old conventions came, certainly, in Ireland. The easygoing approach of Asquith's government to the threat of civil conflict was in itself powerful testimony to the persistence of liberal assumptions. Jevons, hardly complacent about the drift of events, had thought that old-style insurrection was a thing of the past. Though it was 'still a serious crime to purchase arms and to organize and drill a body of men in order to oppose the State, or any of its authorities', there was 'little harm to be feared' from such actions.[54]

This was indeed the view of Asquith and his Irish minister, Augustine Birrell, for months after the Ulster Volunteer Force began to do these old-fashioned things.[55] Both relied (whether consciously or not) on the absorptive capacity of English consensualism to digest the jagged fundamentalism of Ulster Protestants. In this way they sauntered to the brink of a catastrophe which they could never quite bring themselves to believe in. They nearly went over it in March 1914. The Curragh crisis tore a far uglier scar in the tissue of consensus than Asquith's practised skills managed to make it appear. The determination of 58 cavalry officers to resign rather than take part in operations to 'coerce Ulster' was not in strict terms a mutiny. No direct order was ever disobeyed. But its impact was none the less dire: the government was faced with a political conflict in the army, and the consequent paralysis of its Irish policy.[56] The implications of this could be disguised, but not wholly escaped. The crisis had been precipitated not by the government's desire to try conclusions with the UVF, but quite simply by the absence of any formal emergency routine under which the army could be deployed. The rhetoric of order was still—as Hubert Gough acknowledged—adequate to secure the compliance of the officers with any instruction to uphold law or protect property. But neither the Cabinet nor the War Office could, or seemed at first to see any need to, determine the practical difference between 'preserving order' and 'coercing Ulster', in circumstances where Ulster's method of asserting itself was to prepare to resist the British government by military means. It was General Paget's resultant wild hypotheses about 'leading his army to the Boyne' and setting the province 'in a blaze' which gave the Goughs their opportunity to take a stand.

The virulence of their partisanship, and the potentially fatal rift it opened in the officer corps, have recently been illustrated with a starkness missing from previous attempts to contain the crisis within the discourse of consensus.[57] Though there was a substantial weight of military opinion behind the attitude of the 5th Division artillery chief—

We ask our own men to fight against strikers who are in many cases of their own class and with whom their sympathies must often lie. Arguments of strike leaders no doubt appear just as convincing to them as those of Unionist leaders to us. ... How can we ask men to obey us next time if we fail when put to the test—our defection will certainly be made the most of by the leaders of all the parties of disorder from seditionists in India to syndicalists in England. We shall be introducing syndicalism into the army.[58]

(of the artillery, Gough characteristically sneered 'A large number of their senior officers would do *anything*!')—the mutineers' victory was a political nightmare.

Its first and perhaps gravest consequence came in Dublin barely a week before the outbreak of the war in Europe. The affray on Bachelors Walk was a pre-echo of Amritsar, documenting the loss of establishment consensus on how to respond to the threat of revolution. On the face of it, the landing of guns by the Irish Volunteers was a very serious threat to public security, as had been the Ulster Volunteers' gun-running in April. The different police reaction has always been attributed by Irish nationalists to governmental bias, but it seems clear that the government itself was anxious to avoid any provocation in either case, even in face of what would once have been seen as open sedition. After the Curragh, the lexicon had to be adjusted. The difference set in at a lower level: the Dublin Metropolitan Police proved unexpectedly less inert than the RIC, and called out troops to oppose the Volunteers. When disaster ensued, the government blamed the police. While nationalist opinion was inflamed, the blow to administrative morale in Ireland was crippling. The outlook was bleak indeed on the day that Serbia rejected the last clause of the Austrian ultimatum.

The Great War saved the army and the political system from a confrontation beyond their experience, and the lesson of this was not lost. Suppressed memories of the Curragh would condition the reflexes triggered by later emergencies. Things would never be quite the same again.

The Secret State

Amidst the elaborate and apparently endless debate about the possibility of harmonizing emergency powers with the conventions of the English way, two specific innovations stand out with heightened prominence as time passes. In the critical decade of the 1880s, a political police was finally established, and the law of official secrecy was framed. The Special Branch of the Metropolitan Police, of course, began life as the Special Irish Branch, and could be applauded as a relatively moderate response to the provocation of Fenian terrorism. Plainly the government had to do something, and since a state of emergency was out of the question, some less open mode of anti-terrorist action was inevitable. Covert action was, moreover, validated by the belief that it was not only more prudent but also more effective. Small secret gangs could only be countered by surveillance and undercover penetration. Such departures from traditional conventions of official behaviour were amply justified by the public danger. (In fact, as *The Times* had remarked forty years before, the conventions had always been illusory.) Because they were so amply justified, no formal justification was called for. Bernard Porter says of the Special Branch in this period, 'the public generally did not seem to want to know about it, and governments were happy not to enlighten them'.[59] Senior police officers, like public lawyers, preferred informal to formal powers. Their reasons, of course, were quite different. The result was that only one statute, the 1883 Explosive Substances Act, was required to bolster the available emergency powers.

The sense of crisis in 1883 was muffled by the overhang of conventional constraints on state power. Yet the conventions were perceptibly changing. Gladstone might protest against the provision of police guards for the homes of senior ministers, but he endorsed the view that the plea of public safety should override normal political processes. When Harcourt proposed new legislation to control explosives, Gladstone wondered 'whether it may not, as a case of public safety, be one in which we ought by communication beforehand to try to secure a cooperation of parties in the House of Commons'.[60] Whatever the motive in this case, this sort of instinctual bipartisanship was to be a principal means of eliminating the public discussion of public security.

The reasonableness of the state's response served to disguise the perhaps accidental way in which the power to define the public interest was passing out of the sphere of public accountability. The protection of the Special Branch from external scrutiny enabled it, as Porter concludes, 'to carve out quite a considerable little empire of its own in one of the more shrouded corners of the British state'.[61] Its contribution to public security can never be measured. How often it saved the public, or part of it, or the government, from whatever threat, could only be understood on the basis of its own definition of public safety. Occasional glimpses can be got of the contours of this definition, with sometimes a sense of the direction in which it is shifting. More often, however, the moments at which the veil of secrecy has been torn away have revealed nothing but the individual assumptions of agencies and agents, from Henri le Caron to 'Spycatcher'. (There seems no reason to believe that, however odd his later offences, Peter Wright's early sense of purpose in entering government service was anything but typical.) The entrenchment of official secrecy has served to facilitate the avoidance of definition.

The first Official Secrets Act, in 1889, was innocuous enough in appearance, but it established the coupling of external and internal security which was to be steadily tightened over the next century. The first bill was described as 'an exceedingly simple one' by the Attorney-General: its purpose was 'to punish the offence of obtaining information and communicating it against the interests of the State'.[62] In so far as there was any public concern about the measure—and Parliamentary debate was exiguous—it was obviously subordinated to the growing alarm about foreign spies. But the civil service was at least equally concerned to discipline its own members. As we have seen, the army's main complaint against the 1889 Act was that it did not permit effective action against spies, but the civil service found an equally serious deficiency in its failure to impose penalties for receipt of official information. The receivers were, of course, almost always journalists working for English newspapers rather than foreign governments. This target was decisively hit by the 1911 Act, whose somewhat deceptive official title is 'An Act to re-enact the Official Secrets Act 1889 with Amendments'. In fact it was a revolutionary law, whose sudden forcing-through must be accounted one of the most extraordinary episodes in modern legislative history. The motives for the government's indecent haste have never been satisfactorily established.[63] Recently opinion has tended rather strongly to the view that the government took advantage of the 'spy scare' to secure a law which enlarged the powers of the state far beyond what was needed for their ostensible purpose. The weightiest expression of this view was the 1972 Franks Committee Report, which noted that the legislation had been prepared over a long period, and that it was consistently operated not merely in 'matters connected with the safety of the State', but as 'a general check against civil service leaks of all kinds'.[64]

A somewhat different perspective has been drawn in K. G. Robertson's comparative analysis of governmental secrecy in three 'liberal-democratic' states. British governments may have seen 'democracy as implying that the traditional civil service view of itself as part of government must be ended and that it must be brought under the control of those who had been elected'; part of that control process was the Official Secrets Act.[65] This explanation is clearly plausible in theory, though it would be strengthened if there were any direct evidence of two such divergent views. The absence of evidence about the attitudes, assumptions, and—perhaps—theories of ministers and officials leaves the issue in a quintessentially English state of ambiguity. Thus the Franks Committee found that in the absence of any definition, either in the 1911 Act or any of its successors, or in any formal regulation, of the terms 'authorisation' and 'duty to communicate'—or indeed of the term 'official information'—the practice of civil servants was to exercise their own judgement. Officials became self-authorizing though responsible to their minister for errors of judgement; 'in other words they are self-authorising provided they are cautious and do not embarrass the Minister', as Robertson notes.[66] The uncertainty of the Act makes for caution; ultimate reliance is placed on the socialization of civil servants into the governing ethos of adminstration. This simple extension of the 'English way' was bound to cause new problems as the scale of 'official information'—practically defined as any information in an official file— expanded during the twentieth century beyond any earlier imagining.

4

In Defence of the Realm

What had been done for the defence of the realm was done for the defence of capitalism and no one was startled or shocked. The English alone possess the art of making the boldest constitutional changes without raising their voices by a fraction of a tone.

H. N. Brailsford[1]

Constitutional Dictatorship

Until August 1914, Parliament had never conferred upon executive or military authorities of England such power over the rights of the people.

Harold Bowman, 1915

The deluge of the First World War transformed the public power in England. Set beside the spectacular mutations of other belligerents—Russia, Germany, Austria-Hungary—the English constitutional revolution has attracted little attention. Interest in it started at a low level and has gone on declining. A few legal writers at the time saw in the Defence of the Realm legislation a 'violent disregard of traditional and hitherto respected civil rights', 'a sensational measure, the first time in England for at least 250 years when the power to sentence a civilian to death without trial by jury had been given a legal sanction', a 'bloodless revolution', 'to all intents and purposes military dictatorship', or held that as a result of it 'at the present moment, the Common Law lies under the iron heel of militarism'.[2] A modern American legal historian has remarked that 'what is surprising—if not shocking—to the foreign observer in the light of English history in the preceding century is the alacrity with which the English surrendered practically the totality of their cherished liberties to the discretion of Government officials during an emergency.'[3]

English historians, however, have not seen things this way. The Defence of the Realm Acts 1914 and 1915 (DORA)—the acronym coming to sound more cute than sinister as time passed—make only fleeting appearances in standard histories of the war. A. J. P. Taylor's *English History 1914–1945*, hardly an establishment view, contains a bare handful of passing references. Arthur Marwick's pioneering social study of the war, first published in the same year, went so far as to print the first DORA verbatim in its main text (something even legal textbooks do not do), on the ground that it would be 'so often referred to in the course of this book'.[4] In fact there follow a scant dozen references to it. His more general studies of the impact of war on society hardly touch on it. Sir Llewellyn Woodward's massive *Great Britain and the War of 1914–1918* does not mention DORA until page 464, and consigns its substance to a brief footnote. J. M. Bourne's otherwise luminous *Britain and the Great War* merely glances at it, as does Stuart Wallace's study of academic postures (though all his subjects were affected, and one—Bertrand Russell—was imprisoned by the Act). Trevor Wilson's gargantuan work has one sentence on it.[5] Other histories of modern Britain have noticed the impact of DORA in the industrial sector, but not the constitutional.[6] It is an American literary historian, Samuel Hynes, who has gone furthest in tracing its cultural significance.[7]

One might conclude from this that the small fuss about DORA was indeed a fuss about nothing. Another way of explaining 'the docility with which the people of this country submitted to the abrogation of many of their most cherished rights'—as Sidney Clarke put it in 1919—is to recognize that whatever DORA may have done, it had popular sanction.[8] Whether 'they stopped the constitution as a miller would stop a wind or water-mill' (as was said in 1801 of the bill to reimpose martial law on Ireland), this time it was not a *coup d'état* but a democratic revolution. The evidence for seeing DORA as revolutionary is weighty rather than bulky. There was singularly little public discussion of any of the Acts, and that little was coloured by war temperature if not war fever. Harold Bowman, writing at the safe distance of the *Michigan Law Review*, showed surprise at the sketchy argument advanced by the Home Secretary, Reginald McKenna, when he introduced the first bill in the Commons on 7 August 1914, and the exiguous debate that followed. (Indeed, he was able to print the debate in full as a footnote.) McKenna's observation that there would be no capital punishments under the new law 'apparently in his view disposed of all objections as to the possible arbitrariness of the measure'.[9] In the Lords there was no debate at all.

When the first amending bill was brought in two weeks later, McKenna justified the extension of military authority with the simple statement that 'the House will see that it is very necessary and desirable that such an extension should be made'. Again, the second reading debate consisted of a single interpellation concerned with the vagueness of the phrase 'reports likely to cause disaffection or alarm'. This terminological inexactitude came in for more forceful criticism from Lord Robert Cecil when the Defence of the Realm Consolidation Act had its second reading on 23 November. Cecil tried to get McKenna to specify what the government would view as 'reports likely to cause disaffection': disaffection from what, for instance? The bill did not mention the king; did it mean the government? McKenna more or less admitted that public safety could not be defined. It did not seem to have occurred to him that the bona fides of the government might be questioned. 'It is obviously necessary to have something of this sort', he offered almost diffidently, though he saw that it would be difficult to prove that such offences actually assisted the enemy. Rather, 'all disaffection and all untrue alarm is weakening'. He ventured that if, in committee, 'suitable words are suggested for insertion in the Order in Council I do not think the Government would have the slightest objection'.[10] But (need one add?) no such words were suggested. The English tradition could not easily produce any.

The essence of DORA was very economically expressed in the brief text of the first Act; on this foundation were later built amendments, consolidations, and an awesome mass of regulations. The government ('His Majesty in Council') announced that it had 'power during the continuance of the present war to issue regulations . . . for securing the public safety and the defence of the realm', and to 'authorize the trial by courts martial and punishment of persons contravening any of the provisions of such regulations . . . as if such persons were subject to military law'. The regulations were designed to prevent information being obtained for communication to the enemy or for 'any purpose calculated to jeopardize the success of the operations of any of His Majesty's forces or to assist the enemy'.[11]

Later changes did not touch the core of this bold assertion of public power, couched in archaic prerogative terms but not in any strict sense deriving from the prerogative.[12] The only substantial amendment arose in the House of Lords, where the DOR Consolidation Act ran into lively censure in November 1914. Lord Loreburn, while stressing that 'power ought to be given to prevent acts which are dangerous to public safety', insisted that 'the point is, who is to try those who are guilty of these offences?' He could see no reason why, if the civil courts were still sitting, they should be superseded by courts martial, and proposed an amendment which guaranteed British subjects a civil trial where possible. In debate he pointed out that the question 'was never even ventilated in the House of Commons', the August Acts having been passed 'when nobody was here, and it was all done in a hurry'.[13]

This protest was turned on its head by the government: the absence of opposition in the Commons—which as Lord Crewe slyly insinuated had a better title to be the guardian of liberty—was adduced as evidence of the Act's innocuousness. The Lord Chancellor regarded it as self-evident that 'we are in a state of war and are fighting for our lives, and have to take exceptional powers'. The Earl of Halsbury, however, whose judgement in the Marais case had been seen by some critics as undermining the safeguards of civil trial, now came out strongly for the old standard. 'I do not think', he suggested witheringly, 'that the liberty of the subject is so trifling a matter that it can be swept away in a moment because some of us are in a panic'.[14] The amendment was supported by Lord Bryce, who was 'not aware that there has ever been any precedent for such a proposal as is now made': 'The only question is whether the British subject is not entitled, as he has always been in time past, to have the constitutional protection of being tried by a civil court while there is a civil court there to try him'.[15] In the heat of debate—albeit brief—Halsbury condemned the new law roundly as 'about the most unconstitutional thing that has ever happened in this country'.[16]

The weight of this criticism eventually had some effect. Though the government maintained in November 1914 that to admit Loreburn's amendment would be to destroy the whole bill—and by this insistence brought Bryce and Halsbury to heel—Lord Parmoor's persistence eventually led to the Amendment Act of March 1915, which guaranteed civil trial to British subjects under something like the old rule. Aliens were, it is hardly necessary to add, excluded. Conservative peers still issued dire warnings of the danger to national security, accusing Parmoor of having negated the whole impact of DORA, and robustly asserting that they would rather be tried by court martial than the high court in any case, since it would be quicker and cheaper. In fact, the amendment made no dent on the basic law, whose punitive scope had indeed been increased by the Consolidation Act to include the death penalty.

Bowman raised the question why this 'precedent that might conceivably lead to the undermining of all the "monuments" of English liberty' met with virtually no resistance. He pointed out that, although several Parliamentarians recognized that the new law broke with old 'customs' and 'traditions', 'no one ventured to assert that such acts were beyond the power of parliament, or that they were unconstitutional'.[17] (The fact that Halsbury did so seems to have escaped his notice.) In other words, values which had once been exalted to primacy in English history, especially 'custom', were now subtly downgraded. Here the effect of an unwritten constitution can be quite plainly seen. There was no standard against which to measure the powers now taken, nor any way to determine whether 'immediate necessity' (or in American terms, 'clear and present danger') or 'reasonable necessity' should be the criterion for their exercise, or any way of defining danger to the state. A desultory if ill-tempered discussion of the term 'other special military emergency' during the Lords debate on the first 1915 Amendment Act was the only public recognition that modern warfare had broken the old rules. Such nit-picking about abstractions was as uncongenial as ever to English peers.[18] Bowman concluded that the government had invented the novel rule that 'although the general security of the inhabitants of the British Isles did not appear to be seriously threatened, it could make rules intended to operate generally and for the period of the war, drastically curtailing or totally extinguishing the ordinary rights of all the people'.[19] English history contained unshakable grounds for rejecting this contention, but it did not provide any way of measuring a threat to 'general security'.

The point, of course, was that in the circumstances of 1914 such matters were academic. Nobody wanted, or dared, to risk understating the gravity of the situation. Extremity naturally generates extremism; 'la patrie en danger' is a cry which seems to paralyse the intellectual faculty as it stimulates the visceral. Those who had earlier denounced the modern worship of action now embraced it. A Liberal such as McKenna might speak apologetically of the need to do 'something of this sort', but the fundamental logic was simply the need to 'do something'. 'Fighting for our lives as a nation', the ultimate sanction was to be judged not by a jury but by history. The Attorney-General, Sir John Simon, wielded a barely veiled threat when he said that MPs should 'be sure they took adequate steps; they would be forgiven by posterity if their steps were more than adequate'.[20] Since error was no doubt inevitable, it was best to err on the side of assertion. Yet Simon knew as well as anyone that the whole English tradition of emergency action had been premised on the belief that error must be avoided or punished. Whatever might be their fate at the hands of posterity, Members of Parliament believed that they would certainly be punished by living voters for any failure to meet the emergency 'with decision, without wavering, with a might that would overwhelm every disloyal spirit and an authority that would strike the note of discipline and obedience throughout the nation'.[21] Halsbury's sneer that 'some of us are in a panic' was a truly radical dissent from the national religion.

Rather than wondering at 'the docility with which the people submitted to the abrogation of their rights', it makes more sense to see the people as participants, if not prime movers, in this abrogation. The mass psychic mobilization that signalled the creation of the first total war could not find many direct targets: persecution of ethnic Germans, or more extravagant assaults on German culture or German dogs, represented a relatively minor engagement. Sacrifice, on the other hand, offered the only universally available means by which individuals could assert their identity with the threatened nation. National sentiment, not government, was the architect of this revolution. J. M. Bourne is no doubt right to say that the extension of state power through DORA was a 'series of ad hoc responses', driven by perceived necessity but with 'no overall plan, no philosophy of action'.[22]

This very fact increased, if anything, the impact and penetration of the wartime change. A pervasive sense that traditional conventions and restraints were inappropriate to a 'struggle for survival' such as this—a reversal, in effect, of classical liberal conviction—issued in something more than a mere temporary suspension of the constitution. Bonar Law's declaration in February 1915 that 'at a time like this powers of dictatorship must be given to the government' was probably made, and received, in the belief that England was resurrecting the ancient Roman republican institution known to every schoolboy through the virtuous, self-effacing figure of Cincinnatus. Indeed, the major study of crisis government written shortly after the Second World War by the American political scientist Clinton Rossiter specifically identified the English conduct of the Great War as a vindication of his concept of 'constitutional dictatorship'.[23] Rossiter labelled DORA 'perhaps the most radical Parliamentary enactment in the history of England, indeed in all the history of constitutional government'. This was, at any rate, no attempt to play down its significance. It established 'a virtual state of siege'. Rossiter did not openly dissent from the early denunciation of DORA by Professor J. H. Morgan of University College London (who was, in fact, one of the more vehement patriots among the academic community), as 'martial law and something more', 'a blot on the statute book . . . which recalls nothing so much as the kind of legislation hitherto reserved for uncivilized Protectorates', or from Lord Parmoor's denunciation of the pusillanimity of the wartime House of Commons: 'at the present time [1917] the idea of Parliamentary government in this country is nothing more than a farce'.[24]

Rossiter accepted that the 'delegated dictatorship' built on the simple foundation of DORA was unforeseen and presumably unintended by the Commons, and hence in spirit illegal. He was bleakly realistic in his view of subsequent Parliamentary scrutiny:

Parliamentary approval of the regulations was not provided in the statute, the members apparently clinging to the mistaken belief that it was not legislative power which they had delegated but simply the authority to issue supplementary rules and orders. Although some decrees were attacked in Parliament, none was ever withdrawn as a direct result, nor was there ever in all the years of the war a general debate on the Defence of the Realm Act.[25]

Never once in the course of the war did Parliament show that it retained any of its ancient independence and initiative in legislative matters. Its only value was to give a democratic form to the dictatorial edicts of an autocratic Cabinet.[26] But he was wholly optimistic about the outcome of this, citing Lloyd George's successful exercise of 'a vigorous cabinet dictatorship' through the agency of the War Cabinet as evidence of the superior adaptability of the Cabinet system of government in a major crisis. Its great advantage over the presidential system lay, Rossiter said, in its 'ability to forge the close union of executive and legislative so often indispensable in an extended period of national emergency'.[27] He minimized the longer-term dangers of such fusion. 'Such', he intoned, 'are the ways of the greatest of Parliamentary governments'.[28]

It is true that, as Rossiter observed, the possible far outstripped the actual threat to individual liberty. Even the massive, unprecedented, and— on paper—alarming spate of DOR regulations did not jar too much on the daily lives of most people. What Morgan called the 'net of restrictions so finely woven, so ingeniously designed, that it enmeshes every act of the citizen', remained for the most part invisible. The authorities used 'restraint and circumspection' in exercising DOR powers, though it is likely that even if they had not done so there would have been little public complaint, let alone resistance. DORA was an irritant, undoubtedly, and many officials abused it somewhat: too often, in Sidney Clarke's opinion, they 'sought the easy method of departmental ukase to procure powers which they were not inclined to or could not obtain from Parliament'.[29] But the traditional moderation of the English establishment remained its surest instrument. Bowman accurately noted that 'if the government in any degree yielded to the always present temptation of such occasions, its matter-of-fact, almost droning doing of the business was a perfect disguise. It showed nothing of that love for the display of power, the passion "to stand revealed . . . in the storm and thunderbolt" of which Hallam writes.'[30] But to conclude from all this that nothing essentially changed would be to exaggerate the role of the government as the mere agent of 'the primal instincts of the people'. In so far as it acted in this role, it necessarily did so by setting up institutions and procedures, and these would leave a permanent imprint on English political culture.

Exigency of War

> I may say now that as long as the provisions of the Defence of the Realm Act as it now stands on the Statute Book give nothing more than is needed in this national emergency, the argument that they are novel and do violence to our constitutional traditions is an argument of very little weight.
>
> Sir John Simon, February 1915

One of the most remarkable changes which the war brought with it was a novel addiction to rapidity of action. 'Dispatch seemed in the mood of everyone.' The brevity of the debate on the first DORA, and the almost equally dramatic curtailment of normal Parliamentary procedure—which had never worshipped expedition—have already been noticed. The conclusion of the long-drawn-out pre-war civil–military altercation over emergency powers was equally rapid as soon as war began. After the law officers' opinion was written in July 1913, the War Office continued to press for a substantive measure. The Prime Minister agreed in November to refer the issue to a subcommittee of the Committee of Imperial Defence (CID), and in March and April 1914 further papers were prepared. The pace remained leisurely. The *ad hoc* subcommittee did not meet until 30 June, two days after the assassination of Archduke Franz Ferdinand at Sarajevo, and Ireland still seemed more threatening to internal peace than did anything that was happening in Europe. (The lethal affray in Dublin after the Howth gun-running, which happened in spite of the government's best efforts to avoid taking any action, engrossed attention at the time of the Austrian ultimatum.) A tone of detachment prevailed.

The subcommittee discussed three degrees of emergency: first, a precautionary period', corresponding to the earlier concept of 'imminent national danger or great emergency'; second, a war not involving invasion; and third, an actual invasion, which the War Office representative thought was the 'only condition under which a proposal to establish martial law would be entertained'. As we have seen, the soldiers were looking for definite powers in the first two situations. Sir John Simon reiterated his familiar view that it was not 'expedient to pass legislation of the nature proposed'. A statute 'would seem to be an indication that the powers under the common law were regarded as inadequate, and would of itself weaken those powers'. Instead he now suggested a proclamation to 'enlighten the public on the powers which it is lawful to exercise in time of emergency'.[31]

In the event, however, no such proclamation ever appeared. Instead, the 'precautionary period' passed without any action, but the declaration of war brought a statute, which may well have been regarded as a proclamatory statute, but which was in effect an enabling law. The most careful examination so far made of this odd process finds no explanation for the 'rapid about-turn in policy'. The War Office's 'shopping-list of powers', it seems, 'managed to be slipped through the [sub]committee undebated and without challenge'.[32] Haste was the hallmark of the social-Darwinian species of war. It gave at least the appearance of speed. Liberals may paradoxically have been more vulnerable to this diffuse military blackmail than a Conservative administration would have been. Michael Bentley's sympathetic suggestion that 'the war's demands and pace gave Liberal politicians no space, no time, no air', vivid as it is, may exaggerate the actual pressures of war-management, but certainly conveys the moral pressure under which ministers such as McKenna were impelled to act.[33] The naming of Lord Kitchener as Secretary of State for War was a self-denying ordinance which surely sprang from a sense of inadequacy, heightened in the spring of 1914 by the government's mishandling of the Curragh affair. A man less like a textbook Liberal would have been hard to imagine. The only Liberal war minister of stature, Haldane, who had in any case proved a feeble support during the Curragh crisis, was eliminated from public service by the supposed unpopularity of his respect for German culture.

DORA itself should probably not be described as a panic measure, but it was a clear example of the haste-process. It sat oddly aslant to the rhetoric of consensus. Lord Robert Cecil's most eloquent criticism of the Act was that it might seem to indicate that the government did not trust the people. The government did not directly refute this construction, and went on to use DORA systematically to censor news and stifle public criticism. There was something in Cecil's point, though of course ministers could not see themselves through the eyes of an opposition which had recently branded them as 'a revolutionary committee which had seized upon despotic power by fraud' (through the abolition of the Lords' veto). The coiner of this memorable description, Bonar Law, sharpened Cecil's criticism of DORA by tackling head-on the elusive issue of the distinction between the national interest and the interest of the party in power. He attacked the notion offered (outside Parliament) by the Solicitor-General that DORA would apply to 'criticism of such a character that it might destroy public confidence on the Government which at the moment is charged with the conduct of the War'. Under this rule, Bonar Law protested, the famous—and famously patriotic—criticisms of the Aberdeen government's conduct of the Crimean War would have been illegal, indeed quite possibly punishable by death.[34] This penetrating point was left hanging in the air by the Treasury bench, no doubt in the interests of rapid closure of the debate. Of course, nobody on that bench had the least intention of executing the Leader of His Majesty's Opposition for doing his patriotic duty. But the legal implications of the new offence for lesser folk were as perilous as he contended. It would be too much to say that DORA created a form of state terror; but the malleability of its powers was unnerving. They were soon being wielded as a dark threat by the less principled members of the executive.[35]

The paralysis of traditional standards in the shock of war was plainly marked in the judicial interpretation of cases which arose under DORA and its Regulations. Whether or not one accepts the view, strongly expressed by a modern legal historian, that the case law of this period 'reveals ... judicial abnegation regarding the protection of civil liberty' (in contrast with a more protective attitude towards private property rights),[36] there can be no mistaking the readiness of judges to display the kind of brutal realism championed by Fitzjames Stephen. It was particularly noticeable in cases arising under Regulation 14, authorizing the internment of persons considered by the Home Secretary to pose a threat to national security. Attempts, such as that in *R. v. Halliday* [1917], to have this regulation declared *ultra vires* the enabling Act, produced rulings such as the Lord Chancellor's that 'it may be necessary in time of great public danger to entrust great power to His Majesty in Council, and that Parliament may do so feeling that such powers will be reasonably exercised'. Although this case was noteworthy for the vigorous dissenting judgment by Lord Shaw, insisting that the liberty of the subject must be upheld even in a national emergency, the significant outcome was, as Lowry writes, that 'the real or actual necessity for the measures chosen was not justiciable, as the majority would not inquire into the executive definition of the threat to "public safety"'.[37]

The remarks of Lord Justice Scrutton in another Regulation 14 case, *Ronnfeldt* v. *Phillips* [1918], remain none the less striking for having been cited several times (though in legal, not general histories):

It has been said that a war could not be conducted on the principles of the Sermon on the Mount. It might also be said that a war could not be carried on according to the principles of Magna Carta. Very wide powers have been given to the Executive to act on suspicion on matters affecting the interests of the State.[38]

Sometimes quoted also—again in lawyers' footnotes—and surely no less significant, was Sir Frederick Pollock's curt reaction to Shaw's dissenting judgment. 'It is my private opinion that in time of war there is no such thing as the liberty of the subject.'[39] It is true that this opinion was delivered in a private letter to the American jurist Oliver Wendell Holmes, and Sir Carleton Allen tolerantly observed that 'such dicta are permissible in correspondence *en pantoufles*, but it is difficult to believe that in more deliberate discussion Pollock would have maintained this as a serious proposition of law'.[40] Still, the dictum did not stay private, and it seems most likely that it expressed rather accurately the informing attitude of most judges. The parallel but opposite plaint of Lindsay Rogers that 'there can no longer be the proud boast that in time of war England leaves untouched the safeguards of the citizen against the Executive' may have cast a romantic haze over the reality of the past.[41] But there could be no doubt that things were not what they used to be.

In general, a recent legal historian holds, DORA led to 'a threefold diminution of the judicial role' in British legal culture. The first was the self-imposed restriction on review of the delegated legislative powers of the executive. This had particular impact in the sphere of individual rights, and began a process of attenuating, if not extinguishing, the doctrine of *ultra vires*. The second lay in the manner in which the DOR powers were constructed, to render them 'judge proof', so that even if the judges had been disposed to critical examination of these powers, there would have been no opportunity for such examination. The third was the granting under Defence Regulations of judicial and quasi-judicial powers to the executive, in particular powers to intern and to try by court martial. To resist this multiple diminution of its role, the judiciary would have had to show 'a degree of activism which would have been unusual even by normal standards'.[42]

An equivalent shift can be seen in the application of the state secrecy law. David Williams notes that since the 1911 Act 'the judiciary has shown no readiness to interpret narrowly the terms of the official secrets legislation'.[43] The new standard created by the Official Secrets Act (OSA) was displayed in the first important case brought in 1913, the prosecution of a former senior gunner on HMS *Agamemnon*, G. C. Parrott. Despite the absence of any direct evidence of the information alleged to have been communicated, and the antiquity of the pre-Dreadnought on which Parrott had served at the time, a guilty verdict was brought in at the Old Bailey. The underlying assumption was spelt out by Justice Darling: 'It is common knowledge that there is no country in Europe which does not want to know a great deal about other nations which those nations do not want to communicate.'[44] Why they should not want to, or whether communication would in any definite way damage their security, were not matters for anyone but the executive itself to judge. When Parrott appealed, the Court of Criminal Appeal laid down that under OSA a jury could infer an actual communication of information from the general circumstances of the case, and the onus was on the defendant to show that such communication was not prejudicial to the state (a virtually impossible task if the state was not to show the way in which it believed that it had been prejudiced).

Besides confirming the presumption of guilt, the Parrott appeal also determined that the term 'enemy' in the OSA was to be taken to mean any country 'with whom we might some day be at war', as Justice Phillimore put it. Following Darling's version of common sense, this included every country in Europe, at least. Plainly what was important, as later use of the law was to show, was the protection of official information *per se*, not the prevention of demonstrable damage or benefit to any party. Ultimately, in 1919, it was made clear that all official information—i.e. all information in official hands—not only 'official secrets' which might be presumed useful to a potential enemy, was protected by the law.[45] Under colour of an indefinable national security, a much more concrete system of state security was rapidly put in place.

Did the state trust the people? It is clear from even the short argument over DORA that the earlier orthodoxy—that freedom was the surest defence of a free country—had been overthrown by the supposed demands of war. It is also clear that the mass of the people participated eagerly in the war effort, at least for the first year. Neither censorship nor propaganda were alien impositions so much as popular demands. Public order was less of an issue than for a hundred years past. It did not altogether disappear from the official agenda, however. In the spring of 1915 the War Office prepared a military scheme for the suppression of civil disturbance in London, which took as its premiss the assertion that 'the existence of a state of war not only increases the probability of civil disturbances occurring and the probable extent of their area, but also renders the suppression of such disturbances a matter of vital importance to the safety of the nation'.[46] The reasoning behind this view of the probability and extent of distur- bances has not been preserved for us, but it is clear that the Home Office did not dissent from it. The ministry's main concern was to stress that the military scheme 'should be treated primarily as a precautionary measure which might be put in force before disturbances have taken place on a large scale'. It would not imply any surrender of the responsibility of the civil authority.[47]

The extensive recasting of the War Office draft by the Home Office did, however, show that there were some lingering disharmonies between civil and military understanding. The Home Office expunged enthusiastic military expressions such as that 'there should be no reluctance on the part of the civil authorities to demand military aid', or that 'the time for peaceful persuasion, warnings, and the ordinary methods of dealing with disorderly crowds will have passed, and that for prompt and decisive military action will have come'. The ministry also removed a reference to the DORR on the familiar ground that 'the matter is not much affected' by the Regulations; 'the powers given by the Common Law and embodied in the King's Regulations are ample for dealing with all disturbances'. It noted that Paragraph 965 of the King's Regulations 'has been somewhat misunderstood'. It was not the case that military officers could exercise their own judgement about whether to respond to a call for assistance from the civil authorities, only that they should not give orders to charge or fire on a crowd unless satisfied 'that this course is necessary'.[48]

Behind this misunderstanding lay the experience of Macready in South Wales, where promiscuous requisitioning of troops by magistrates had, in the military view, compromised the operational flexibility of the army. Macready's answer had been to establish his own intelligence service to determine the need for military action, and this received wisdom was incorporated directly in the War Office scheme for London. The Home Office 'suggested', however, that it was 'not necessary in London to establish a special military intelligence system': the Metropolitan Police would be able to provide accurate information, and 'no information supplied by such an intelligence system would justify the Military Authorities in refusing to send troops when requisitioned by the Civil Authority'.[49] Thus if there was general agreement about the danger of public disorder, there was little sign that the civilians were changing their long-standing view of how it should be dealt with. Necessity was still the rule. Even in wartime, the crowd remained a touchstone of normality.

Insurrection

> No course is open to the Government but to take every possible
> measure to break the murder gang and to enforce the authority of the
> law.

Winston Churchill, 1920

While it is not altogether strange that public order in Britain ceased to be a
salient issue for the duration of the war, it is more surprising that a similar
quiescence descended on Ireland. Irish public commitment to the war
effort was greater than nationalists more extreme than Redmond's party
liked to suggest, but it was by any measure smaller than the British, and
was in visible decline from 1915 onwards. In these circumstances, the
general tranquillity of Ireland during the first half of the war was an
unlooked-for bonus for a hard-pressed government. Agrarian violence fell
away under the steady effect of the pre-war land transfer programme;
elections were suspended for the duration; DORA provided extensive
controls on traditional foci of tumult like fairs and meetings; and even the
suspension of emigration did not at first seem to produce the battalions of
discontented young men which might have been anticipated. Unfortunately,
the midpoint of the war produced the most spectacular outbreak of
domestic political violence since the eighteenth century: it appeared localized
and transient, but it should have shattered any complacency about the
state's capacity to impose its conception of order.

The place of the 1916 rebellion in the development of Irish nationalism
lies some way outside the scope of this account, but the British reaction
throws intense light on the configuration of order in the official mind. The
coup de main of Easter 1916 was, of course, an exceptional emergency
beyond the control of the civil power from the instant that an unarmed
Dublin Metropolitan policeman was shot dead in Upper Castle Yard
on the Monday morning. On the following day the Viceroy proclaimed
martial law in Dublin. This was done in the heat of the moment, in—one
might say—the proper spirit of martial law, the spirit of desperation. The
sequel two days later, when the Cabinet announced the extension of
martial law throughout the island for one month, was more unorthodox.
Martial law was widely regarded as unacceptable in the domestic sphere,
even in extremely critical circumstances. It had not been resorted to during
the Fenian insurrection of 1867 when the suspension of habeas corpus had
been found adequate, even though quite large military forces had been
deployed against the rebels.

The same powers of internment were readily available in 1916 through the immediate suspension of Section 1 of the Defence of the Realm Amendment Act 1915. And in fact all the arrests, trials, internments, and executions carried out in 1916 were carried out under DORA, not martial law. So martial law was not imposed because it was necessary; it had suddenly ceased to be politically odious and had become symbolically desirable. The arguments against it had scarcely diminished in force. On 28 April, the day after the Cabinet decision was announced, Birrell rehearsed the traditional view in urging Asquith to rescind it: both the law officers and the under-secretary, he telegraphed, were 'strongly of opinion that for the moment Proclamation of Martial Law for the whole of Ireland most inadvisable'. 'All useful powers already exist', he insisted, while 'we anticipate grave possibility of very bad effects produced if Martial Law is extended to the very large areas which at present show no sign of disturbance'.[50] Fifty years earlier this would hardly have needed saying to a Liberal Prime Minister.

Now, however, the arguments in favour of martial law had received novel reinforcement. On top of the unadorned reasoning of the Inspector-General of the RIC, that martial law should be proclaimed wherever rebels were likely to gather in 'formidable' bodies[51]—the argument that had not prevailed in 1867—came the view advanced by the Irish Attorney-General that the army must force the 'unconditional surrender' of the rebels and punish them by 'military law' (a quite illegal proposal, since the rebels were not under the Army Act). The core of this idea was the reassurance of the public, who had an 'extraordinary belief in the magic term "martial law"'.[52]

How the Attorney-General managed to convince Birrell that he was an adherent of the traditional negative view of martial law is one of the minor mysteries of this confused time; more interesting for the development of emergency powers was the unstable interplay between symbol and reality over the next few years. Martial law did not exist: as Asquith soon recognized, 'there is no single case in which it has been or is likely to be necessary to resort to what is called "martial law", and there is no adequate ground for its continuance'.[53] General Maxwell too, dispatched to Ireland with trumpeting of 'plenary powers under Martial Law over the whole country', realized that 'it seems to be thought that I have been vested with powers that I do not possess'.[54] The traditional public aversion to military rule, whatever the Attorney-General might think, re-emerged: 'A grievance has been manufactured because martial law has been declared. All public bodies spend their time in passing resolutions against it.'[55] Since English lawyers had always held that martial law could only be tolerated in circumstances of overwhelming necessity, the situation was puzzling. In the past the authorities had always gone to great lengths to avoid or disguise the use of martial law. Now they had to hand a modern legal instrument perfectly adapted to the war emergency, but actually preferred to pretend that they were using one which had previously been regarded as barbaric.

That this was no mere temporary aberration was attested by the range and volume of criticism which dinned upon the government over the next months. Irish Parliamentary leaders denounced the 'military dictatorship' and warned that the 'madness of your soldiers' would destroy Lloyd George's attempt to negotiate a settlement of the Irish question. Lloyd George himself, though he had long since ditched his pro-Boer past, found it congenial to describe Maxwell's administration as 'stupid and fatuous'.[56] Yet the government went on implying that martial law was in force, even as late as March 1917. The Chief Secretary for Ireland, Henry Duke, took the line that formally revoking the proclamation of martial law would be read as a political statement. 'Martial Law is important to Ireland chiefly as a declaration of policy', he wrote in September 1916, and was so closely associated with Maxwell himself that 'to rescind the Proclamation during Sir John Maxwell's command would be idle'. In March 1917 he still held that 'a proclamation that there is no martial law' might lead people 'into acts of violence or insurrection on the supposition that there is not power in the hands of the government under the existing law to deal with matters of that kind'.[57] How this could be, when Asquith had made clear that the rebellion had been dealt with precisely under that law, was not easy to see.

In fact the government was playing a dangerous, and finally fatal game with labels. It was permitted to do so by the uncertainty of the English law compounded by the disorganization of rebellion and war, and was drawn into this course by a persistent misreading of Irish public opinion. Nearly a year after General Maxwell recognized the shift of organized political opinion, Duke was resting the case for maintaining nominal martial law on the need to reassure the loyal public. By that time it was clear that what reassured the loyal public antagonized the rest; the problem was to work out whether this was a risk worth taking. An administration steeped in the rhetoric of consensus had no disposition or aptitude to tackle such a problem. The tendency to assume that the great majority of the public was fundamentally law-abiding and therefore ready, if sufficiently reassured by displays of governmental strength, to hold or return to 'constitutionalism' remained dominant for five years after the 1916 rising.

This five-year period witnessed the most drastic decline in public security since the height of the land war a generation earlier. Now, however, the shape and incidence of violence was vitally different. Urban disorder spread beyond the traditional framework of Belfast sectarian conflict. In Cork city, for instance, the tally of riots grew from 2 in 1915, and 7 in 1916, to 24 in 1917, 16 in 1918, and 23 in 1919. But the main foci of crowd formation were vigils outside prisons, and the funerals of republican hunger-strikers. Such demonstrations were hardly disorderly—if anything the reverse. That is not to say that they might not have been treated as a public order problem. If they had been aggressively or even sternly policed, there can be little doubt that extensive violence would have followed. But the authorities carried over the hands-off approach which had prevailed during the pre-war confrontations. (The one great pre-war exception, the Howth gun-running, of course confirmed the police in their caution.)

The official interpretation of Irish opinion was subject to some internal contention, especially in the last year of the war, when Viscount French was appointed Lord Lieutenant of Ireland. French's arrival coincided with a big shift in the expressive mode of Irish dissent. Until then, the government's anxieties had been focused on the issue of military recruitment. Since recruitment in Ireland remained voluntary even after the intro-duction of compulsory service in Britain in 1916, the interpretation of Irish support was made in basically negative terms—inadequate enlistment. Explanations of this were constructed in a balanced form which tended to disguise the element of active opposition; for instance, the Inspector-General of the RIC noted in October 1916 that while strong feelings of disloyalty were 'kept in check' by the belief that martial law was in force, that belief also formed a major barrier to recruitment.[58] The casual reader of such an analysis might conclude that if martial law were rescinded, recruitment—rather than resistance—would rise.

The great crisis of the war in 1918, however, brought the issue to a head—almost. The announcement that conscription would be imposed in Ireland generated a huge movement of protest, so that resistance could now be measured in positive rather than negative terms. At the core of the movement was the reconstructed Sinn Féin organization, which now engrossed not only the old republican fringe but also most of the broad mass of Irish constitutional nationalism. Sinn Féin had always preached passive resistance, and had seen conscription as the most likely mobilizing agent of such resistance; now it was joined by the Catholic Church, while carrying along—and in time being carried along by—the old Fenian organization, which launched an aggressive boycott of the police and began seizing weapons.

Lord French took the view that if this powerful coalition was not stopped in its tracks it would soon be in effective control of Ireland. He wanted to impose martial law area by area, concentrating the available coercive force to eliminate the whole Sinn Féin group. He had powerful Conservative supporters, especially Walter Long, but the Cabinet as a whole choked on his prescription of direct confrontation. It was able to exploit divisions within the ramshackle Dublin Castle executive, offering French the power to impose martial law if the officials of the administration were unanimously in favour of it, a condition French knew he could not meet.[59] French thus became what martial law itself had earlier been, a provocative symbol of military rule—it was natural for nationalists to describe the veteran field-marshal as 'military governor' rather than Viceroy of Ireland—without the coercive power to push matters to a resolution.

In these circumstances drift was inevitable, and an optimistic view of Irish opinion survived even the escalation of republican insurgency in the year after the end of the war. In that period the first assassinations and fatal ambushes were mounted by the renamed Irish Republican Army, culminating during the winter of 1919 in widespread attacks on smaller police stations and an attempt to kill French himself at the gates of Phoenix Park. Lloyd George's sardonic reaction to the narrow failure of this *attentat*, 'they are bad shots', deeply shocked his Irish minister, but is possibly more interesting as evidence of a still-visceral belief in Irish inferiority. Certainly the idea that majority opinion was being duped or intimidated by fanatics underpinned nearly all British assessments of the situation: absence of open disturbance was read as evidence of actual terrorism and, at the same time, potential law-abidingness.

The failure of British ministers to grasp what they were faced with in Ireland was not surprising: in part it was due to the novelty of the Sinn Féin–IRA campaign itself, which was put together as much by instinct as by calculation. The Chief Secretary was frankly at a loss to decide how to deal with MPs who decided to constitute themselves as a separate assembly rather than go to Westminster, and Dáil Éireann was not proclaimed illegal for over six months. It was by no means easy to see, in the spring of 1920, just how far the republican counter-state had undercut the authority of the incumbent regime. Walter Long had tried to impress on his colleagues as early as December 1918: 'I have watched the rise and fall of every political party in Ireland for the last forty years, and I think the present movement is much the most difficult and dangerous of any the Government have had to deal with.' He had urged, 'It is a fair and square fight between the Irish Government and Sinn Féin as to who is going to govern the country.' Lord Wimborne had suggested nearly two years earlier that 'recent events and the present temper of the country preclude the wisdom or safety of half measures'. Nevertheless, hopeful signs remained for those who preferred to see them.[60]

When the head of the civil service, Sir Warren Fisher, was sent to investigate the Irish administration in April 1920, he blamed the blanket ban on Sinn Féin for polarizing Irish opinion, and implied that reform could revitalize the system and help to restore normality. This was no doubt the only reasonable suggestion to make at the time, but it followed immediately after a truly alarming set of popular gatherings which, perhaps more than anything else, demonstrated the headlong movement of Irish opinion away from the official norms. After the attempted assassination of French, the army had been authorized to carry out a series of arrests of republican leaders, who went on hunger-strike in Mountjoy Gaol demanding 'political' treatment. Steadily larger crowds gathered outside to keep a vigil that was orderly but not silent. On 12 April the numbers reached 10,000, according to police estimates, and the atmosphere was intensely charged. Spontaneous popular action had set up a tremendous psychological duel in which the authorities quite suddenly backed down. On 13 April the Dublin trade unions mounted a kind of city-wide general strike; next day the prisoners were released on French's order.

The sense of powerlessness evinced by Lord French and the newly appointed military commander in Ireland, Nevil Macready, derived mainly from the conviction that as soon as one of the hunger-strikers died the government would immediately release the rest, and create an even larger impression of weakness. Thus the releases ordered on 14 April were in their view the lesser of two evils, but by a rather narrow margin, since they were all but disastrous for the credibility of the Irish government and the morale of the police. They heralded a period of enthusiastic conciliation headed by a new Chief Secretary, Hamar Greenwood, in the hope of winning broad support for the new Home Rule Bill. Within a couple of months this period ended, when the conciliator was humiliated by the failure of the summer assizes to secure any convictions for murder against republican *guerrilleros*.

Thus Britain was brought back to war measures. Underlying the confusion of policy since 1916 was the odd collection of legal powers round which executive action had been framed. DORA, standing in for martial law, was only part of this: for all the stern rhetoric of martial law, not even DORA had been systematically or comprehensively used. In 1918 the executive preferred to turn to the 1887 Criminal Law and Procedure Act, which had been specifically engineered by Arthur Balfour as a way of avoiding the habitual reversion to temporary emergency laws earlier in the century. The Crimes Act was used to establish Special Military Areas in 1918 and to ban Dáil Éireann and Sinn Féin as dangerous associations in 1919. Yet by that time it had a decidedly antique air about it, and the attempt to put the assembly of Irish MPs on the same footing as Captain Moonlight was especially dubious, as Fisher mockingly showed. The erratic mixture of DORA and Crimes Act powers ran through to 1920, by which time DORA's days were numbered by the inexorable approach of the official end of the war.

The paralysis of the Irish summer assize in 1920 put the state in a peculiar situation, unprecedented at that time, though it would become more familiar over the next three decades. Whilst there was no question of outright military defeat—realization that the IRA was never going to drive the British into the sea was a defining characteristic of the new generation of Fenian leaders—the legal and administrative system had been steadily paralysed by a combination of civil resistance and violence. Of the two, the first, the withdrawal of consent, was ultimately the more subversive. The distinctive quality of the republican campaign was the systematic use of small-scale violence to underpin the construction of an alternative governmental system. This revealed very clearly the functional limits of the consensus-based British order: beyond repeated public calls for a 'return to constitutionalism', or Churchill's protest that 'No nation has ever established its title-deeds by a campaign of assassination', the powers-that-be (or that had been) had no plausible recourse short of counter-terrorism. The reason for this was the familiar one, that no formal emergency framework was available to contain and direct the use of military force.

Martial law had relapsed from the brief political favour it had enjoyed in 1916 into its more familiar role as constitutional bogy. The erratic nature of British security policy in 1919–20 stemmed from the problem of finding an appropriate status for the army on which the civil power now grudgingly depended. The military profile was successively raised and lowered according to the perceived extremity of the crisis, but the notion of military government was resisted with a conviction absent from most other aspects of Irish policy. The nature of the republican campaign meant that nowhere for more than a short time, never more than a few hours and often merely a few minutes, was there a tangible manifestation of the absolute necessity which, according to common law, would justify the supercession of the ordinary legal process. The law of rebellion had been framed in a time when rebels took the field in serried ranks with pike and sword (as some old Fenians indeed still wistfully longed to), and had already been pronounced inappropriate to the complexities of modern warfare during the guerrilla phase of the Boer War.[61] Something new had to be created, but what?

The answer found for the Irish troubles bore the encouraging, if not rhetorical, title of the Restoration of Order in Ireland Act. The studied neutrality of this terminology was important from the British point of view, though it did not prevent ROIA from being seen in Ireland as yet another 'coercion act'. It was calculated to have the same significance as 'defence of the realm' in war: Greenwood presented the draft to the Cabinet as a 'modification' of DORA to permit courts martial to try capital charges other than those involving 'assistance to the enemy'.[62] Despite the capacious definition of this category now being developed by the judiciary, it was seen as unnecessarily provocative in Ireland after the boomerang effect of the 'German plot' arrests in 1918.

The ROIA was not accepted without demur by the Cabinet; the view was forcefully put that 'it was a decision of the gravest moment to utilize machinery intended for time of war in time of peace', and 'considerable anxiety was expressed at thus handing over the whole administration of the law to soldiers'.[63] But it was a long way from heralding military government. Lloyd George distrusted the army, for reasons rather different from the constitutional scruples of his Liberal colleagues. On the same day that the draft bill was shown to the Cabinet, his influential private secretary Tom Jones recorded darkly that he had been told 'the present Army in Ireland under a policy of "thorough" will "bend" and probably "break"'.[64] Though he did not identify his source, or offer any direct evidence, the history of the next twelve months makes it plain that Lloyd George believed this.

The Restoration of Order Act was thus somewhat illusory, as was the formal declaration of martial law that eventually followed it in December 1920, in face of the enlarged insurgent forces which had evolved in response to ROIA. There was some irony in the fact that the most substantial effect of this Act was to impel IRA suspects to take to the hills and form flying columns, thus magnifying the level of disorder. The underlying policy idea, Jones's suggestion in July that the best course would be to threaten martial law while making a peace offer, was reconfirmed within the civil administration in December. (Meanwhile, as a senior Dublin Castle official noted, the army, thinking that martial law meant 'No more damn civilians', foolishly expected 'to have full control of everything in two twos'.[65])

The idea of threatening more than the state was capable of or willing to perform was not without its critics within the civil establishment. Sir John Anderson, the undoubted chief of the Castle administration, had unsuccessfully opposed a new coercion law in July, and later (successfully) resisted the military demand for the further extension of the area under martial law in January 1921 with the interesting comment that he did not think that such a threat 'would have any particular terrors for the other side': they were more likely to regard it merely as a challenge.[66] This can only be read as a negative evaluation of the impact of martial law at the military-psychological level. The army also found martial law disappointing, but held that its ineffectiveness was mainly due to the restrictions on its exercise. These were both geographical—martial law was proclaimed only in eight south-western counties—and legal. The army consistently failed to establish its minimum demands for real authority: actual control over the police, and suspension of the ordinary law. The spirit in which the first demand was by this time being pressed may be judged from the Commander-in-Chief's venomous remark that the commander of the Martial Law Area (MLA), Major-General Strickland, would 'have to watch the Police very carefully' because the RIC Divisional Commissioner 'will think that martial law means that he can kill anybody he sees walking along the road whose appearance may be distasteful to him'.[67] The autonomy of the police was, however, stubbornly defended by their chief, Major-General Tudor, whose political support proved more enduring than Macready's.

The shifting balance of operational control between army and police was to be a leitmotiv of future counter-insurgency campaigns. The political value of the doctrine of police primacy was too great for it ever to be wholly abandoned, even when the police were demonstrably incapable of responding to disorder except by the virtual adoption of military methods. The negative resonance of outright military control and the constitutional difficulties raised by the concept of a 'third force' rendered the open or covert militarization of the police more or less inevitable. The result was likely to be counter-terrorism because the police disciplinary culture was not designed to control armed forces in situations of extreme provocation and violence.

At the root of this issue lay, as always, the problem of definition. What kind of disorder was the state setting itself to subdue in Ireland? Was this war or peace? Lloyd George told Lord French with rather absurd self-assurance that 'You do not declare war on rebels'; yet there could be no doubt that in a legal sense rebellion was war. But was this rebellion? There were powerful inhibitions on perceiving the IRA challenge as such. The habit of consensus made it natural to view the republicans as extremists who were battening on to the moderate majority by the exercise of ruthless terror: they might be neutralized by an equivalent ruthlessness ('firmness') on the part of the state. On the other hand, the implications of admitting that there might be widespread support for the rebels were serious: if the firm measures required were applied 'there might come a point when public opinion would desert the Government'.[68] The legal tussle over the powers of courts in the martial law area sprang from this mixture of theoretical uncertainty and psychological hesitancy.

If there was one fixed point in the long juridical confusion surrounding the concept of martial law, it was that martial law—however derived or justified—meant the supersession of the ordinary legal system. The tribunals established by the military commander to enforce his regulations had no legal standing, even though it was conventional—if misleading— to call them courts martial. Indeed, there was strictly no need for any formal tribunals; they were merely regarded as a reasonably 'decorous' manner of proceeding. In the light of this, the military authorities in Ireland were flabbergasted when they found that appeals from the verdicts of courts martial in the MLA were regularly heard by the High Court in Dublin, and even the House of Lords. Prosecutions were brought against military personnel who had carried out 'official reprisals' under regulations promulgated in the MLA. On the contention that all this made nonsense of the whole notion of martial law, Macready eventually (after a lapse of nearly four months) issued a proclamation ordering that 'the jurisdiction of all Courts of Justice in all matters whatsoever relating to any claims in respect of damage or injury alleged to have been done by Forces of the Crown' be suspended. He was immediately forced to withdraw it—a humiliation from which he never quite recovered. Before and after this, his protests against the hearing of habeas corpus writs in the high courts were deflected by the government on the ground that the failure of these appeals strengthened the moral position of the authorities.

And all the appeals did fail—except the last. The catastrophe happened in July 1921 when the Irish Master of the Rolls ruled in *Egan* v. *Macready* that the proclamation of martial law had been illegal. Given that this had always been the view of some British judges, such an outcome might have appeared predictable; perhaps the confidence of the authorities that it could not happen rested too much on the wartime complaisance of the judiciary. (Though the judgement has not been admired by later jurists.) In any case, this was a political disaster whose vast proportions were only fortuitously disguised by the fact that the Truce ending the 'Anglo-Irish war' (as it could finally be called) was engineered within a week. Austen Chamberlain's implausible declaration in Parliament that Egan and Higgins had been released 'solely on the basis of the existing circumstances' and that 'civil courts have no power to overrule the decisions of military courts in the martial law area' passed unchallenged in the general atmosphere of relief. In July 1914 the constitution had been saved by war; in July 1921 it was saved by peace.

5

Preparing for Revolution 1919 – 1939

You was feeling revolutionary. I know I nearly did go off the deep end. That's when we nearly had a revolution in Bristol, smashed the tram cars up. But I didn't bother with it, didn't bother with politics. I joined no party, not many did. All politicians is poison, in my eyes.

Bristol wheelwright[1]

The Recasting of Emergency

Very few people appear to realize that they [the unemployed marchers] are a body of men organised by leaders whose avowed object is to subvert the present constitution.

Chief General Inspector of Police, 1923

DORA was formally laid to rest in 1921 at the official end of the war, but its half-life—which looks to be perpetual—had already begun. Its soul went marching on. Transmigration into ROIA marked one path along which emergency powers would move in future. 'Statutory martial law' would eventually appear in various parts of the empire, most pregnantly in Palestine, to confront major civil violence and direct threats to public security.[2] For Britain, its most pervasive presence was to be embodied in a new configuration of civil emergency and an inexorable growth of public secrecy.

The war had been a national crisis which had temporarily transcended old fears and old limitations.[3] But the lifting of the external threat revealed that the internal threat had not been wholly leached out by the international bloodletting. Alarms about the danger of industrial warfare were sounded once again as the shock of demobilization battered the economy. Dormant neuroses were awakened by the police strikes of 1918 and 1919, so close to the heart of the state. The campaign for recognition of the police union (NUPPO) overstretched the tolerance built into English labour law. Once again the government turned to its trustiest trouble-shooter, Nevil Macready, to stifle the threat with his personal brand of reasonable force. Things did not quite fall apart; but 'the night the police went on strike' conjured up a potent vision of social breakdown, even if the reality was experienced by only one city.

In Liverpool, during the August 1919 bank holiday weekend, a crowd outbreak of a primal kind—not triggered by any specific political or social issue—started with the looting of some shops in London Road. The troops called in to assist the weakened city police were indecisively deployed, at one point on Sunday afternoon even firing a volley over the heads of a crowd, in defiance of all previous military orthodoxy. One man was killed by this irregular repression, and rioting intensified that night. The disorders ✗ seemed to belong to an exotic public culture in which street manifestations and violent collective action were a normal mode of social negotiation. But since, as one recent conservative writer has complained, 'the British in the post-war period were essentially a law-abiding people [who] prided themselves that they had reached a stage of social maturity in which disorders prompted by lust for violence or a criminal impulse were relics of a past age', the Liverpool outbreak could only be explained by an un-British eruption of original sin.✗ The 'malevolence of the people' of Liverpool seemed aberrant, as did the military reaction. This was the last time in Britain that the Riot Act was 'read', that troops opened fire on civilians or charged a crowd with bayonets fixed.

But the uncertainties which lay behind the indecisiveness of the authorities were wholly traditional. The Home Office observed that

There is no doubt that in law it is the duty of all persons assembled to disperse when the proclamation is read; and that it is also the duty of all citizens to assist the authorities if called upon, but the juxtaposition of the two exhortations—to disperse and to assist—may cause confusion and hesitation in the minds of orderly citizens, at a time when this is most undesirable.[5]

The prevention of confusion was, the ministry ominously noted,

more than ever necessary, now that in times of industrial disturbance there may be present, not only a mob of strikers and sightseers on the one hand, and magistrates, military, police and perhaps special constables on the other, but also certain citizens who have volunteered to assist the authorities to carry on during an emergency.[6]

This putative category of active citizens was a portent of the times. Yet in face of these new challenges the English tradition remained squarely resistant to clarification. The unstable boundary between lawful assembly and riot was even more brittle in an industrial confrontation, and the Home Office had remarked during the pre-war strikes 'how impossible it is to state the law as to unlawful meetings in any clear and definite shape which would assist the police'.[7]

Everyone who tackled such problems ended up by falling back upon the discretion of the officials present at the scene, especially—and increasingly—the Chief Constable. The dilemma of the magistrate was plainly displayed in an article in *The Justice of the Peace* in May 1920, for all its optimistic tone:

the constant advice and assistance of specialists such as experienced police officers used to handling crowds, and military officers conversant with the effect of modern weapons, greatly modifies and simplifies his position, though he is no more than they exempted from exercising his own judgement and discretion.[8]

Not so long ago, 'handling crowds' had not been an arcane mystery for specialists, but the province of magisterial instinct. Some change was now inevitable, and the special constraints of the common law tradition meant that it was more likely to be administrative than statutory.

The sense of crisis in post-war Britain was potential rather than actual (though degrees of imminence are hard to measure). Responsible people more or less vigorously discounted the possibility of revolution.[9] In particular, the army—which had been brought by the war closer than ever before to the machinery of administration—saw no serious threat to the state. Its reasons were mixed, however. Sir Henry Wilson, Chief of the Imperial General Staff, has been accused in a recent study of strike-breaking of being 'to say the least, a trifle unfastidious' in his contradictory determination that full-scale preparations should be made to stifle industrial 'disorder' and that the army should have nothing to do with them.[10]

Yet the army's strongly expressed desire to be kept out of internal security organization ('nothing could be worse both for the Army & for the State than that it should be supposed that the former is being maintained for the purpose of coercing the latter')[11] reflected the persistence of its ingrained detachment from politics, even the alluring business of laying down the conditions of national security. It seems unfair to suggest, as the same critics have, that 'the military mind' took 'an unusual view of the British constitution as a static and inflexible creation'. When the Adjutant-

General said that military actions to restore public order in 1919 had 'not merely strained the military machine but the British Constitution as well', he was more likely invoking a general public belief in a fundamental (and surely immutable) constitutional principle. Not many people then or later would have been likely to dispute Macdonogh's belief that 'it will be a bad day for the Empire if the Government of this country had to look to the bayonets of its troops for support'. The complaint of Field-Marshal Haig, Commander-in-Chief Home Forces, that both naval and military personnel had been used that year 'to carry out duties which do not correctly appertain to those services'—that is, the maintenance of the King's Peace by police measures ('it is not their duty to act as policemen as they recently did in Liverpool')—was only a pedantic rephrasing of an old military fear that the uncontrolled demands of panicky magistrates would paralyse all regular military training and break the army's units up into 'penny packets'.[12] Haig was nothing if not hostile to socialism, but he plainly thought that the civil authorities had not found the right way to combat it.

In fact, the government's search for a suitable mechanism had already gone through some interesting evolutions. The War Cabinet responded to the early post-war strikes in February 1919 by setting up an Industrial Unrest Committee.[13] The word 'unrest', still used evenhandedly with 'disorders' and 'disturbances', does not seem to have been chosen for any particular reason: six months later the title was changed to the plainer Strike Committee. On 7 October this committee proposed that it should be replaced by a still stronger 'National Emergency Committee', but in the event this imposing title was abandoned and the committee became known as the Supply and Transport Committee (STC). The significance of this humdrum tag is unmistakable. Though Churchill could profess himself unable to 'see the distinction between the war and a civil emergency', the government preferred to make clear that its emergency planning had nothing to do with strike-breaking, but only with ensuring that strikes did not damage essential public services. The fact that such insurance was most likely to prevent strikes from succeeding was perhaps a political bonus to a policy which could be simply justified in the public interest.

The general apprehension of unrest also, inevitably, persisted, and in 1922 a Preservation of Law and Order Committee was created with the tellingly vague remit 'to assist the Home Secretary in any special emergency which might arise in connection with the maintenance of Law and Order ... in view of the potential risks of a situation in which there are two million unemployed'.[14] The contrary pressures of alarm and caution were evidenced in the measures adopted by the emergency committees. The most dramatic, potentially at least, was the Strike Committee's proposal in October 1919 to raise a new body, to be called the Citizen Guard.

With its faintly fishy French-revolutionary echoes, it is not immediately obvious why the Home Secretary believed that 'this name would prove a stimulus to recruiting'. The Guard was not intended to live up to its military title—it was certainly not intended to be armed—but rather to be a variant on the traditional special constabulary. The idea may have originated with the military representatives on the Strike Committee, since Haig expressed the belief that a Citizen Guard would be the best means of relieving the pressure on the army. He no doubt envisaged a force possessing some slightly greater operational capacity than the Specials, for instance the capacity to operate in units. But it soon became clear that the proposal did not command the straightforward public consent on which the government's plans depended. It transgressed the indefinite but powerful public aversion to militarism: in industrial areas especially, as the Home Secretary despondently observed, it was 'supposed that the Guard will be of a semi-military description and will be armed, and it is useless to attempt to explain that it is merely another form of Special Constabulary'.[15] In fact the government made little or no effort to explain why a different form of special constabulary was needed, largely because it had no explanation. If it was minded to argue that a new kind of public order problem required a new kind of force, it quickly abandoned any such idea at the first sign that it would be controversial. It fell back once again on tradition, sticking to the old Specials in name at least, if not to the old notion that they represented the whole community. Reliance on the middle class was more frankly avowed in 1919 than ever before.[16]

The salient point identified by the Industrial Unrest Committee when it first began to put together the machinery which eventually became the Supply and Transport Organization (STO) was the need to maintain the wide-ranging wartime powers taken under DORA. In March 1919 a Strikes (Exceptional Measures) Bill was drafted to prohibit a Triple Alliance strike and permit the confiscation of union funds. It was shelved as the situation eased, to re-emerge in May 1926. Later the Strike Committee focused on the need to preserve the power to commandeer transport and enrol volunteer drivers. The central issue, as Keith Jeffery and Peter Hennessy have convincingly shown, was a political and rhetorical one. Could industrial blackmail be equated in the public mind with the external threat which had legitimized the DORA regime?

Draft handbills prepared in 1919 took the line laid by Jevons, with some purple colouring added: the threat of 'national starvation and the ruin of industry' required every 'citizen' to do his part to help run the railways, drive lorries, save petrol, enrol in the special constabulary, and so on.[17] Lloyd George told the Cabinet that the railway strike in September 1919 'really amounted to civil war'.[18] Yet the invocation of national disaster was potentially double-edged, and sat ill with the confident moderation that had traditionally been the hallmark of the official style. As with the renaming of committees, and the retraction of the Citizen Guard project, there was a visible steadying of the helm in late 1919. Jeffery and Hennessy, following the pioneering work of Desmarais, have painstakingly uncovered the way in which the STO as it developed thereafter formed an epitome of the British governmental mode, 'the smooth administrative machine periodically interrupted by political alarums'. Though the formal responsibility for general policy remained with the Cabinet committee, the departmental subcommittee (which met five times as frequently) 'very largely defined the nature and style of the government's emergency organization'.[19]

The government's traditional faith in public order was obviously strained in 1919. Although the senior ministers, who spent most of their time in Paris conducting the peace negotiations, took a sanguine view—Henry Wilson noted sceptically 'Bonar said he did not believe in a Revolution'— members of the STC were less sure. At an important meeting in January 1920 'fears were expressed that the country would have to face in the near future an organized attempt at seizing the reins of Government in some of the larger cities, such as Glasgow, London and Liverpool'. This half-baked analysis, inspired by the conventional fear of Bolshevism, was accompanied by a rather more plausible prediction that 'it was not unlikely' that the next major coal strike 'would commence with sabotage on an extensive scale'.[20] In face of these dramatic apprehensions, the sense of powerlessness which emerged in the discussions is revealing. Henry Wilson, albeit an unbalanced witness, was no doubt right to conclude that only Churchill and Long were mentally prepared for open confrontation with a big strike. His own fury at the 'incompetence and cowardice revealed' in the STC talks was enough to reverse the army's previous disengagement from the internal security imbroglio, one noticeable step in which was the winding-up of GHQ Great Britain scheduled for February 1920.

When Wilson assembled the War Office directors on 22 January to discuss what was to be done 'in case of industrial unrest & revolution', he found, as he laconically recorded, that 'No one knew'.[21] He did not relish this evidence that most soldiers were less politically-minded than he. Haig's emergency plans were reworked, and forces were assembled in the safe south-east. The planned abolition of the industrial intelligence section of the Directorate of Military Operations (MO4) was abandoned, and troops were clawed back from international commitments such as policing the League of Nations plebiscite in Upper Silesia. The deterioration of government control in Ireland exacerbated Wilson's sense of imminent crisis, and when in October the railway unions threatened to strike in support of the miners he was in full spate, dispatching guards battalions (the least likely to fraternize with the people) right, left, and centre, and 'sending tanks north'. Ministers tried to muffle such provocation, but did not ask him to explain what he intended the tanks to do. The fear of civil war lived on.

In this atmosphere the STC faced up in January 1920 to the need to replace DORA with a permanent special powers act. The first Home Office draft bore an uncanny resemblance to DORA in the breadth with which its powers were sketched, and the committee preferred to work towards a three-stage accession of powers. It spent several weeks trying to establish the bases for such stages. Stage II was envisaged as following the first four days or so of a big or general strike, 'when the struggle was becoming intense'. Stage III would begin when there were 'serious civil disturbances amounting to attempts at revolution'. This interesting and unusual exercise proved to be too complicated, since it transpired that departments wanted all their emergency powers immediately—only thus, they argued, could they ensure that Stage III was never reached. But the resulting all-or-nothing bill was politically more unattractive than the step-by-step model, and the committee took refuge once again in procrastination. Only in the midst of the industrial crisis of October was the eventual Emergency Powers Bill suddenly, indeed precipitately, launched, 'at precisely the time', Jeffery and Hennessy suggest, 'when Parliamentary and public opinion was least able dispassionately to weigh up either its short-term merits or long-term consequences'.[22] Thus caution and fear of controversy can produce the same results as vulpine manipulation.

Like DORA, and the Restoration of Order in Ireland Act which was passed in August, the 1920 Emergency Powers Act (EPA) was rather cursorily scrutinized in Parliament. Initially, on Friday 22 October, the government tried to get both houses to suspend standing orders and pass the bill in a single sitting, but this railroading provoked a range of opposition that seems to have been unexpectedly wide. So the second reading in the Commons was delayed until the Monday, and Royal Assent was not reached until 29 October. This timetable was hardly leisurely, though it was stretched by the inkling of an unwelcome public debate. Even *The Times* deplored the 'untimely' measure, attempting to ignore it until its second reading, and then explaining, 'So strongly have we felt that no more unfortunate subject could come up for debate at the moment that we have not even referred to the principles of the Bill'. The newspaper's objections were a compound of tactical fears—that the government might damage the public belief that it was neutral in the industrial conflict—and a wider commitment to the traditional common law view: the government were 'set on having by force prematurely what they might have by common consent should the time be ripe for it'.[23]

Some Labour members denounced the bill as 'conferring a dictatorship on the Executive', and as a direct attack on the workers. J. R. Clynes, however, sounded the official voice of Labour in accepting the necessity of provisions 'to meet the life needs of the nation'. This acceptance has been broadly shared by later historians, with isolated exceptions such as A. J. P. Taylor, who endorsed the contemporary opposition view that the EPA 'made permanent the dictatorial powers which the government had possessed in wartime', curtly adding that it was 'as big a blow against the traditional constitution as was ever levelled'.[24] Arthur Marwick went even further, characterizing the EPA powers as 'totalitarian authority', though this verbal flourish was not followed up in his subsequent account of the law's long-term impact. Kenneth Morgan, more pacifically, was content to see the law as 'the safest way of preserving civil order without confrontation'.[25]

Once again, it has been constitutional analysts such as Rossiter and Williams who have fleshed out the 'dictatorial' concept of emergency. Rossiter saw the EPA as effecting a 'clean break with the tradition of common law and martial law, indeed with the whole of British constitutional development'. It marked a decisive shift to the continental pattern of emergency powers, and 'set up an extremely controversial instrument of constitutional dictatorship . . . uniquely available as an instrument of reaction'.[26] But of course the controversy was notable for its lack of extremity. Rossiter's explanation of this quietism was one of the recurrent tropes of his analysis, that everything depended on the spirit in which statesmen wielded emergency authority. Lloyd George, in insisting on the continuity of EPA with DORA, voiced a belief in both the analogy between the war and the industrial conflict, and the commonly accepted reasonableness of the DORA regime. The continuity argument, couched in pragmatic rather than theoretical terms, was specially British. As Rossiter observed, 'it is interesting to note the lack of speculation in the debates concerning the constitutional and comparative nature of this law'. Most of the Parliamentary argument was about whether the bill was an outright attempt to coerce the miners, and though the opposition instinctively appealed to 'the Constitution' and 'ancient liberties' against the new law, 'the revolutionary nature of this grant of extraordinary power was at no time clearly expressed'—or recognized.[27]

Even so, 'sensible' amendments were achieved, and the restrictions on the EPA conceded by the government during the week of debate made it 'a much less dictatorial weapon than was DORA'. Each proclamation of a state of emergency was limited to one month, and the declaration was applicable only to industrial actions

of such a nature and on so extensive a scale as to be calculated, by interfering with the supply and distribution of food, water, fuel or light, or with the means of locomotion, to deprive the community or any substantial portion of the community, of the essentials of life (Section 1(1)).

Most important, in Rossiter's view, emergency regulations would only be valid for seven days unless they were confirmed by Parliament, and the maximum penalties which could be imposed under them were specified in the Act. All these limitations 'go a long way towards guaranteeing a circumspect employment of the extraordinary freedom of action which the Act affords', in marked contrast to the dangerously loose terms of the Weimar Constitution's Article 48.

Indeed, it could be argued—especially in the light of this comparison—the EPA represented a restriction of the old common law emergency power (which was much more like Article 48). The restriction was tolerable to government just because it made the declaration of a state of emergency politically feasible, whereas a declaration of martial law had generally been out of the question. The powers theoretically available under common law had never been convenient or handy. To invoke martial law against a strike, even a general strike, would have been unthinkable unless the situation had become one of actual civil war—and even that, as the Irish conflict was demonstrating all this time, was riven with uncertainties. Under EPA, effective measures could be initiated from the first day of a major strike, and certainly before the onset of serious disorder.

The 1920 Emergency Powers Act was a substantial and irreversible redefinition of the British state. The authority of the executive to identify a state of emergency was directly founded on a general notion of public order—regulations were to be 'necessary for the preservation of the peace . . . and for any other purposes essential to the public safety'—but the statute itself made no specific provision for dealing with disorder as such. It was a public order law only in so far as it aimed to prevent disorder. Within a few months, however, the need for more specific public order powers reappeared. In March 1921 a draft bill 'for the more effective Preservation of Public Order' was brought to the STC by the Home Secretary. Its purpose was 'to arm the Government with a convenient weapon against incitement to revolutionary violence' once DORA finally lapsed, and its target was

any person who directly or indirectly solicits, advocates, incites, or encourages the unlawful use of violence, or the commission of any unlawful injury to person or property, either

i) by any persons acting together for the said unlawful purpose or any of them; or

ii) by any person or persons whatsoever, or generally, for the purpose of bringing about thereby a change in the form of government or constitution of the United Kingdom.[28]

This identified a more specifically political threat than had the Emergency Powers Act, but it did not yet get beyond the STC under the chairmanship of H. A. L. Fisher. As with the first Emergency Powers Bill in August 1920, it was thought 'inexpedient' to bring such a measure in during the strike then in progress.

A more significant general argument was adduced by some of the committee, who were

doubtful of . . . the wisdom of placing such a Measure upon the Statute Book at all, preferring to trust to the common sense of the people to treat with contempt the inflammatory speeches and writings against which the Bill is aimed.[29]

The resilience of this traditional expectation of social order served to accommodate the novel framework of emergency powers. Neither ministers nor people seem to have been aware of any significant tension between the two. Officials were above all dedicated to preserving continuity, of rhetoric if not of organization.

There was certainly no bid for dictatorial central power. The reluctance of departments to house and operate the STO was almost farcical. Localism remained a fetish. In 1926 the Home Office drew up notes of guidance which insisted that, though 'there is no simple and compact way of expressing the position correctly',

the *primary* responsibility for the maintenance of order and the protection of life and property is *local* and rests mainly upon the police and the police authorities, though the Justices of the Peace, who formerly had the main responsibility, still share in it in diminished degree, and . . . the central government also have important responsibility, partly supervisory, partly supplemental and partly different from and independent of the local authorities' responsibilities.[30]

Apparently finding this clear, the ministry added that the Home Secretary, 'as police authority for the Metropolitan Police District, has a special responsibility which is partly local and partly national in character; in addition he has responsibility of a supervisory character extending to all police districts'; finally, 'under the Emergency Regulations he now has specific power to require a detachment of police in one district to go in aid of any other force'.[31]

Glossing this, the long-serving Home Office Under-Secretary, Sir Edward Troup—who figures as a kind of reactionary ogre in radical accounts of the period, though he was predictably denounced by Sir Henry Wilson as 'hopeless'—published an article a few years after his retirement in 1922, weighing up the balance of local and central authorities in policing. Taking as undesirable extremes the American model on the one hand ('local autonomy and democratic control gone mad') and the Prussian-German approach ('everywhere the police are impervious to public opinion to an extent which would be intolerable in England') on the other, he modestly concluded that 'the best practicable system . . . must be in some way a compromise between imperial and local control', such as he had helped to elaborate. What was needed was as much local independence as was compatible with effective co-operation and mutual assistance in times of emergency. Anything else 'would be contrary to the genius of the English people'.[32] Troup thus presented the police as an organic system, which had 'grown up naturally' and was 'well suited to the conditions of this country and to the national character', but also theoretically correct.

This persuasive mixture of intense traditionalism—indeed mysticism—and progressive rationality retained its hold in the 1920s. Though states of national emergency were declared under the EPA three times, in 1921, 1924, and during the 1926 general strike, reasonableness was preserved. The handling of the 1921 emergency was characteristic. The crisis was brought on by Lloyd George's decision to 'prick the bubble' of the transport unions' strike threats, and initially triggered some overreactions. The Triple Alliance strike was the most plausible approximation to a syndicalist action to date, and was not surprisingly seen on the right as revolutionary. The committee on military resources chaired by Lord Birkenhead advised the Cabinet not only to call up the reserves but also to raise a new emergency force, this time called the 'Defence Force'. Clearly trumpeting its military parentage, this force, recruited on 8 April 1921 largely from ex-servicemen and territorials on a 90-day enlistment, measured out the military dimension of the new emergency system. Despite being placed under military law, and armed, its reliability remained in doubt, and only a few of its 70,000 men were deployed on protection duties.[33] However transient its utility, this experiment cast a long shadow. When it was stood down, its members were encouraged to transfer to the Territorial Army— though not by the TA itself, which observed with some understatement that 'it was not always the best type of man who joined the DF'. In 1925 a senior territorial officer lamented that 'it is difficult to overestimate the harm done to the TA by the Defence Force'.[34]

The state of emergency was redeclared twice, and eventually lasted from 31 March to 26 July. All this is evidence for Jeffery and Hennessy's suggestion that the government's reaction was only 'superficially resolute', and 'stemmed more from panic than confidence'. But the army was trying to apply the lesson in objectivity taught by Nevil Macready. The War Office cautioned that

The Army must not make the mistake of approaching the officials of a Union or Federation as though their existence was illegal or even antagonistic to the national welfare. When they are directly or indirectly involved in the apparent cause of violence and disorder, it will nearly always be found that their own authority has been usurped by irresponsible Communists, anarchists or local hotheads.[35]

Jeffery and Hennessy note how early the regular military forces were stood down, and they quote testimony that miners recalled to service in a Yorkshire reserve battalion 'saw the funny side of striking and then being called back to the Army to keep order if necessary'.

This stage-Englishness, proof against fears of industrial conscription, was echoed and amplified when Sir Eric Geddes, former organizer of the STO, became the government's financial axe-man and proposed to scrap his creation. His argument in September 1921 was nothing if not confident.

It was essential that for the maintenance of order and decent living the Government should take upon itself during the period of unrest which followed the war, the duty of protecting the community from the irresponsible attacks of extremists. The war had created in the people a habit of looking to the Government for direction and initiative in almost every department of life, and the Government was the only body which possessed sufficient strength to oppose the great industrial organizations. This state of things has now passed. Private initiative has once more reasserted itself.[36]

Some local authorities, especially police chiefs, still took a less sanguine view. Jane Morgan has explored the attitudes of Lionel Lindsay, the long-serving Chief Constable of Glamorgan, in 1921. Lindsay clearly wielded the EPA in an activist spirit, on the ground that the Triple Alliance strike broke 'the most precious law of the land, viz. that the liberty of the subject shall not be interfered with', and amounted to 'wholesale terrorism of peaceful citizens'. He saw one of the big demonstrations held in May 1921 as 'the acme of defiance of the law of the land', and believed that while large police and military forces could temporarily deter strikers from committing acts of terrorism, 'it is only the certainty of exemplary punishment that will cause these terrorists to desist from their criminal conduct'.[37] Thus the restraint of local magistrates in face of the strike was deplored by Lindsay and Troup alike. Even so, it is not likely that Troup approved of the Chief Constable's highly charged language of civil strife. Lindsay's views were not unique among police chiefs, but they were inevitably coloured by his long exposure to some of the most intense industrial conflict of his time.[38]

Equally large apprehensions were evident in the report drawn up by the Chief General Inspector in 1923 on the police response to unemployed marchers. The attempt to 'have them dealt with strictly on the lines appropriate to vagrants' had been an almost complete failure. Lowry apologetically pointed out that

The well recognized necessity for the police to rely on tact rather than force in dealing with any difficult situation must be expected sometimes to lead to what looks like excessive tenderness to potential agents of disorder.[39]

He pinned the responsibility for this on public opinion, which was regrettably 'far from being generally against' the marchers: indeed he thought that 'Very few people appear to realize that they are a body of men organized by leaders whose avowed object is to subvert the present constitution.'

Other authorities preferred to cleave less reluctantly to the path of moderation, confident that the mobilization promised under the EPA would always be on their side. When the first Labour government unexpectedly materialized in 1924, there was some confusion amongst the STO functionaries, habituated to seeing labour as a threat. One of them tried to persuade the outgoing Conservative minister responsible for the organization to ensure that it should 'be wrapped in temporary obscurity and silence' so that the incoming ministry might not discover it. But the ethos of responsible governance sloughed off such openly partisan advice.[40] And, indeed, the new government had already been drenched with that ethos and soon made use of the STO in fulfilment of its duty to reassure the nation of Labour's invincible patriotism. The case of Circular 636 bore this out. Issued on 20 November 1925, this centrally prescribed set of local emergency instructions was a constitutional innovation which might, in the past, have attracted some criticism from the radical side. One scholar has found Labour's preference for silence at this point 'incomprehensible'.[41] Ideologically, no doubt, it is; but, as Kingsley Martin was shortly to observe 'English people prefer to face a problem rather in terms of power than in terms of philosophy'.[42]

The final test of the system was the general strike. Morgan sees 'the widespread use made by the police of the powers conferred on them under the Emergency Regulations' as a special feature of the strike, and notes that the Solicitor General suggested to parliament that public opinion believed that the term 'peaceful picketing' had been interpreted 'with undue latitude and moderation'.[43] He saw no necessity to produce any evidence or definition of this opinion, since it naturally accorded with his own. (The mechanics of opinion-construction by 'primary definers' is not often so clearly visible.) This should alert us to the point that any assessment of the strike is inherently political. Official 'reasonableness' looks from the other side of the mental barricades like ruthless coercion and manipulation of opinion. Yet even from this angle it is clear that the established strategy still worked. The system of order functioned pretty much as it had done in 1848, and Churchill's notorious wish-fulfilment games with the government news-sheet hardly seem to justify the place of honour they hold in radical demonology.[44] Evidence of ministerial panic is inconclusive. The orderliness of the strike, the apogee in a sense of the struggle for respectability, is legendary. The authorities were of course intensely suspicious of the strike's syndicalist resonances, but if the Sorelian myth played any significant part in British workers' attitudes it might have produced as much order as violence, since it projected the optimistic image of a majestic, almost stately transfer of power.

In fact, as distinct from legend, the strike produced plenty of violence and disorder. But the most interesting proof of the underlying impulse to order can be found in the failure of the Civil Constabulary Reserve (CCR), yet another variant in the experimental emergency forces. Born out of the ditching of the Defence Force, this ostentatiously non-military body was none the less obviously different from the old Special Constabulary. Its members were actually sworn in as Special Constables, but issued with truncheons and steel helmets. In the event this odd confection proved far more provocative than either the police or the regular troops, who were preferred as agents of a neutral 'law and order'. Strikers reacted to the CCR by contrast as agents of class war ('a species of strike breaker and "black and tan"', as the GOC London District remarked), and attacked them without restraint.[45] This unexpected 'vindication of the more traditional arms of the state', as Morgan puts it, underlines the conservatism of the state's opponents. This was, as its leadership always insisted, a national, not a general strike.

In these circumstances the repeated tinkering with special emergency forces, unique in modern British history, remains as testimony to the underlying doubtfulness of the system. The non-deployment of the Territorial Army in these crises calls for some explanation, since it had been authoritatively stated (by the Home Secretary) in 1920 that

it was and is clearly intended that in the event of a grave national emergency such as an attempted revolution endangering the fundamental peace and safety of the entire country, and necessitating calling out the reserves of the regular army, the Territorial Army should be embodied and should be used in every way necessary to maintain order.[46]

Obviously, such an extreme emergency was never judged to have arisen, but there is a little more to it than that. The Director General of the TA was intensely concerned that his force should not be employed except as a very last resort, since he recognized the danger of 'a stigma attaching to the TA from its use in civil emergency, and of subsequent antagonism to its maintenance'. He reiterated that 'we are only now emerging from the cloud cast over the TA' by the 1921 Defence Force, and that premature use of the territorials to maintain order might be fatal.[47] He was evidently persuaded that the attempt to create a concept of economic emergency remained potentially contentious.

Secrecy and Sedition

> an Englishman with a deep respect for tradition ought to oppose this
> Sedition Bill because it runs counter to our English tradition
>
> J. B. Priestley, 1934

The ten years from 1926 to 1936 brought the nature and limits of public power into sharper focus than at any time before or since. The moderation of the general strike was largely the product of countervailing fears: the fear of revolution and the fear of provocation. A traditional penchant for avoiding visible change remained strong. There was, for instance, remarkably little systematic evaluation of the way in which the emergency apparatus, and the state mechanism as a whole, had coped with the strike. Some departmental warnings that the outcome might well have been disastrously different seem to have been lost amidst a general (albeit moderate) euphoria. The army took the opportunity to reiterate its conviction that troops should be kept out of such emergencies as far as possible, certainly where public order maintenance was concerned. Though the Adjutant-General thought that 'one of the lessons of the Strike, certainly in the London area, was the moral value of a formed body of troops in a disaffected area even though no actual disturbance has broken out',[48] an acute critique drawn up by the head of MO 1 reverted to the long-held contention that the appearance of soldiers on the streets was as likely to provoke as to deter disorder, and suggested that 'the way in which troops were used was a departure from the principles enunciated by Lord Haldane'. The fact that such provocation had not aggravated the strike was due to 'the sound commonsense of the average citizen and the absence of bitterness, rather than the correct application of force'.[49]

This standing invitation to government to clarify its thinking brought, as always, no audible response. Likewise the Adjutant-General's insistence that the 'need for ... some efficient force of a semi-military character intermediate between the regular police forces and the fighting services was clearly proved' produced no tangible result. As Jeffery and Hennessy comment, the Adjutant-General conspicuously failed to offer any specifications for the construction and operation of such a force; and it was most unlikely that anyone else would step in to volunteer a blueprint in response to his injunction.[50] His earlier complaint that all the GOCs involved in the strike saw as 'a serious defect in the system, the lack of any C-in-C, to use a military term, of the Police forces as a whole in Great Britain or even in a single county', was more likely to be remedied. But the magisterial side of order-maintenance was sliding into oblivion. The War Office under-secretary minuted comfortably, 'I do not think that many magistrates have a clear idea of their rights and duties according to the law. I cannot say that I have, though I have been a Magistrate for 20 years. Also', he added knowingly, 'there are Magistrates and Magistrates.'[51]

After the innocent experiments with the Defence Force and the CCR proved unexpectedly dangerous, the government reverted to the status quo in the field of organized force. But the rules under which its forces operated proved slightly easier to alter. The hangover of war fostered not only the evolution of DORA into EPA, but also the steady growth of official secrecy law. The 1920 Official Secrecy Bill enjoyed that 'inexorable progress towards enactment' which, as David Williams has remarked, 'we have in this century come to associate with Bills justified in the public interest'.[52] Tolerances had measurably shifted. The Aliens Restriction (Amendment) Act of 1919 created a gaping breach in traditional notions of public crime by making it an offence for 'any alien [to] attempt or do any act calculated or likely to cause sedition or disaffection amongst any of His Majesty's forces ... or the civilian population'. The phrase 'or likely to' meant that no intention had to be proved. In time of total war, aliens (enemy or other) might perhaps expect none of the safeguards normal in peacetime, but this was a peacetime statute, and as the law commissioners later pointed out, the continuance of the Act down to the present 'is a remarkable example of legislation which is surely out of date'.[53] Yet it was never repealed, and indeed the authorities showed unmistakable signs that they were in favour of extending such legislation to the rest of the 'civilian population' as well.

The reason was that the cold war had in effect already begun. The place of the Central Powers as the chief threat to national security had been taken by Russian Bolshevism, which had given a menacing shape to the once-cloudy notion of international socialism.[54] Gauging the nature and extent of this new threat was a recurrent prepossession in the 1920s, although its public justification was variously formulated. In 1925 the Attorney-General produced a brief sketch of a new sedition law which focused on (i) the power of the state to punish or prevent the preaching of revolutionary doctrine which might prevent any chance of the peaceful settlement of an industrial dispute, and (ii) the limits within which a general strike in support of the miners' demands was permissible. The utilitarian justification for attacking 'revolutionary doctrine', and the empirical definition of such doctrine, were carefully constructed to avoid any appearance of political persecution. The issue of the 'constitutionality' (which always meant unconstitutionality) of a general strike remained unresolved in 1926. Although the Ministry of Labour suspected that there was 'little in the contention that the General Strike was unconstitutional', it still believed that the government was right to *resist* the strike 'with all the means and powers' at its disposal, and the Cabinet was minded to put the constitutional issue beyond doubt by direct legislation. An Illegal Strike Bill was, at one stage in early May, got ready to be rushed through Parliament. The Prime Minister was plainly in favour of it, even though there was some difference of views about its effects. Tom Jones noted, 'when I pressed [Baldwin] to define the exact scope of the Bill he was not at all clear. He thought it made sympathetic strikes illegal, and a General Strike illegal, but later I was told that it made a sympathetic strike illegal only when it assumed the aspect of a General Strike'.[55] On his own account, Jones single-handedly steered Baldwin and Churchill away from their determination to push the Act through with the argument that 'it had taken some time to get the country to appreciate what the General Strike was, but this new Bill would come as a thunder-clap on the country which was utterly unprepared for it, and would greatly confuse its mind'. If Jones did so, it is interesting that this lesson in national culture was handed out by a Welshman to two paramount exponents of Englishness.

The mind of the country had, by coincidence, just at that time been subjected to public scrutiny by Baldwin in his collection of essays—or rather, tidied-up speeches—*On England*, published in April 1926, and reprinted twice during the general strike. Jones, as he wryly noted in his diary, had 'written about half of this volume, I suppose, and something of the other half'. But the Prime Minister's speechwriter was careful to add, 'of course S. B. knows how to write'. The linchpin of the essays was Baldwin's deep Englishness—'I think (for a Welshman) I've played that up very well!'—and there was no doubt which country he was talking about. The address 'on England' opens clannishly with 'a feeling of satisfaction and profound thankfulness that I may use the word "England" without some fellow at the back of the room shouting out "Britain"'.[56] Amongst his stock list of national characteristics—staying power, kindness, sense of humour (though not, for some reason, love of animals or children)—he highlit his conviction that 'the Englishman is made for a time of crisis, and for a time of emergency'. While this may have provided grounds for confidence, Baldwin also displayed the suspicion of industry and urbanization long visible in the establishment. 'Love of home' was 'one of the strongest features of our race', and that home was unquestionably rural and antique. 'England is the country . . . the tinkle of the hammer on the anvil in the country smithy, the corncrake on a dewy morning, the sound of the scythe against the whetstone, the sight of a plough team coming over the brow of a hill . . . for centuries the eternal sight of England.'

It was an eternity that was suddenly coming to an end. What had the Transport and General Workers Union, much less one-and-a-quarter million unemployed, to do with this bucolic stage set? Nothing, unless they could re-learn the brotherhood of the village community. 'Who was it said of Rousseau that he was a lover of his kind, but a hater of his kin?', the Prime Minister mused. 'The children of such a philosophy can only bring damnation to this country.'[57] But which country, again? Politically, of course, Baldwin could not persist in confining his community to England, however much his *volkisch* philosophy was rooted in such confinement.

We have confused ourselves in Great Britain of recent years by a curious diffidence, and by a fear of relying upon ourselves. The result has been that many who have been eager for the progress of our country have only succeeded in befogging themselves and their fellow-countrymen, by filling their bellies with the east wind of German Socialism and Russian Communism and French Syndicalism. Rather they should have looked deep into the hearts of their own people, relying on that common sense and political sense that has never failed our race, from which sufficient sustenance could be drawn to bring this country once more through all her troubles.[58]

Thus modern socialism was damned for its foreignness, and it does not seem likely that Baldwin was preaching a return to native socialism either. Rather, English (or British) common sense dictated acceptance of the primal logic of capitalism, 'that driving force of necessity that makes people combine together for competition'.[59]

This insistence on the symbiosis of capitalism and the British public power was a salient feature of the official attitudes which went on to produce the Incitement to Disaffection Act eventually passed in 1934. The struggle over this law, inside and outside Parliament, was more intense and pungent than over any of the Emergency Powers or Official Secrets Acts. Its intensity was generated by the clash of two 'common senses'. The opposition saw the 'Sedition Bill' as a dangerous redefinition of political crime. The government saw it as a vital defence of the British way of life. The origins of the law lay in a fusion of the fears expressed in 1920 by Sir Henry Wilson about the dependability of the army in a civil emergency ('we had a well-disciplined and ignorant Army [in 1912], whereas now we have an Army, educated and ill-disciplined'[60]) with the distinctive post-war fear of deliberate ideological subversion.

The first draft Sedition Bill was justified to the Cabinet in 1921 on the grounds that 'direct and explicit incitement to the unlawful use of force or violence . . . ought not and cannot safely be left unchecked', and with the warning that 'the effect of inaction is cumulative'. The draft, in fact entitled an 'Act for the Preservation of Public Order', was explicitly constructed to replace powers once available under DORA, and showed that the EPA was not, in the official view, enough.[61] When the draft was reactivated at the beginning of the general strike, the Lord Chief Justice, Lord Cave, pointed to 'the archaic character of much of the law regarding sedition and mutiny'—the leading statute was the 1797 Incitement to Mutiny Act—and 'the difficulty of deciding whether any particular language is or is not seditious owing to the absence of any statutory definition of that offence'. Since the Cabinet was aware that 'the passage through parliament of proposals for dealing with sedition presents exceptional difficulties', it did not try to solve this particular problem. Though the draft law remained entitled 'Incitement to Sedition' until shortly before its first reading, it was finally renamed 'Incitement to Disaffection', and during the debates ministers pointedly objected to the opposition practice of calling it the 'Sedition Bill'. Its text, however, made no mention of either sedition or disaffection.[62]

The law created two offences, first that of 'maliciously and advisedly endeavouring to seduce any member of His Majesty's forces from his duty or allegiance to His Majesty'. As first presented to Parliament, the clause lacked the phrase 'maliciously and advisedly', thus extending to British subjects the usage established in the Aliens Restriction Act. Under fierce criticism the Attorney-General, Thomas Inskip, consented to restore the traditional requirement of *mens rea*, the need for proof of intent, but on the substitution of the looser 'duty *or* allegiance' for the old Incitement Act's 'duty *and* allegiance' the government would not budge. The exact import of this shift has never been tested in the courts, but legal analysts have agreed that it is potentially large.

The second offence was possession 'with intent to aid, abet, counsel, or procure the commission of an offence under Section 1' of documents 'of such a nature that dissemination of copies thereof among members of His Majesty's forces would constitute such an offence'. Again, the original wording was markedly wider cast: 'without lawful excuse', rather than 'with intent'. In this clause the presumption of innocence was effectively reversed, and though the underlying intention—to punish the organizers of sedition rather than merely their agents—was broadly approved, the means by which documents could be secured by the police raised strong objections. Ivor Jennings, then Reader in English Law in the University of London, alleged that the whole bill was really about the power of search: seeking the undisclosed 'source of the suggestion to "strengthen" the Incitement to Mutiny Act', he concluded 'the simple answer is that the Home Office advisers knew that the powers which the police claimed were probably illegal and they wanted to make them legal at the first available opportunity'.[63]

The government's line of argument was that the new law really contained nothing new, and was simply a restatement of existing law. When, in Parliament, Harold Laski attacked the proposal in Section 2(2) that 'any person who does or attempts to do any act preparatory to the committing of an offence' under the Act 'shall be guilty of an offence' as an 'astonishing' piece of drafting, Inskip defended the clause against Laski's charge of novelty on the ground that it appeared in the 1920 Official Secrets Act—an interesting example of the process of legislative penetration.[64] Against the objections of Laski and Lloyd George that the new power of search 'seems to be based on the principle that the search will be made first in the hope that there will be found something on which a charge can be based'—which

Lloyd George drily described as 'a new idea of justice in this country'—
Inskip contended that the warrants were not 'general warrants' (which had
been ruled illegal in the grand constitutional law cases of the eighteenth
century) but the same provisions as in several statutes such as the Obscene
Publications Act 1857 and the Official Secrets Acts.[65] Ivor Jennings tartly
commented, 'Bad precedents ought not to be followed. But in truth the
precedents are not similar or even (since the Attorney General insists that
he has been misrepresented, we must give his own words) analogous.'
Jennings contended that the Act did in fact amount to 'the return of
general searches', and gave 'an entirely new, unprecedented, and dangerous
right to search for documents of a controversial character'.[66]

The need for these new powers was never argued by the government.
Critics then and since have pointed out that evidence of increased attempts
to cause disaffection or sedition was never adduced.[67] It is still not clear
whether there was actually as little as appeared. The army's internal
documents demonstrate a consistent anxiety over a long period, an anxiety
unsurprisingly couched in the terms of conservative political logic. No
distinction between Bolshevism and anarchism was recognized in practice
(or thought important in principle); both were germs spread by ruthless
and power-hungry agitators, by their nature invisible. Thus large significance
would be attributed to the discovery in a barracks of a single copy of the
'Spur' Library print of Bakunin's *God and the State* (eightpenny edition,
1920), or to the crude handbills urging pay increases ('How about a bit off
the top?').[68] The Adjutant-General warned the Secretary of State for War
in 1925 that 'Although this propaganda has probably had no material
effect at the moment, it is very insidious and its ultimate effects may well
be far reaching.' Four years on, he was lamenting that

we seem to be going round in a vicious circle... When an emergency does arise
'offering a favourable opportunity' for introducing legislation on the subject, the
evil may have grown to such a pitch that not only may more drastic provisions be
required, but the harm done by the continual spreading of this literature may be
difficult to arrest. A fire is more easily put out when it is first lighted than when it
has 'caught' and spread![69]

The triumphant flourish of this most banal metaphor of revolution measures
the limit of military reasoning; even less impressive arguments were deployed
in the army's *Internal Security Instructions* issued in 1933. (It must be
noted that 'internal security' was used here in a purely military, rather
than a general domestic context.) These began with a section called
'Communism at a Glance' which confidently diagrammed the link between

Moscow and the Communist Party of Great Britain, together with a sequence of political modes as follows:

Activities
Propaganda
Agitation—Strikes
Civil Disturbances
CIVIL WAR

culminating in the revolutionary overthrow of the state.[70] The instructions went on via an explanation of the need for this co-ordinated threat to be countered by a tightly organized Security Service, to an exhortation to general alertness in terms congenial to regimental officers: 'It is the missed catches which help the Communists to score'; 'Some half-educated people will believe anything.' Yet if there was a hint of alarmism in all this, it was balanced by the obvious fact that, as the Adjutant-General fretted, 'in the past there has been a tendency to regard subversive propaganda as a subject for amusement rather than for serious thought'.

Inskip's presentation of the bill side-stepped such issues by claiming that since the war, 'a somewhat sly and almost skulking breed of inciter has come into existence'—apparently so sly as to leave very few traces of its activity. All the instances of incitement he cited in Parliament, culled from anonymous pamphlets called *The Soldier's Voice* and *The Red Signal*, urged the forces to oppose 'capitalism', without any reference to the king, the state, or the government. The Attorney-General contended that these none the less attempted to seduce servicemen from their allegiance by inviting them to take part in 'a number of offences which are abhorrent to anybody'—even pacifists.[71] But no definition of 'disaffection' was offered, either in the bill or in debate. Lloyd George observed that 'you cannot avoid bringing politics into a Bill of this character', and 'it will boil down in the end to what the Government of the day consider subversion to be'. It was obvious, he held, 'that what some people think to be subversive of the Constitution, other people equally honestly believe to be in the best interests of the State'.[72]

'What is sedition?', probed the Liberal Sir Donald Maclean. 'We are told that if we indulge in a strike which is larger than a small local strike, that becomes a political offence and is therefore sedition because it is a blow at the State.' The Solicitor-General headed off this awkward line of investigation by reasserting that 'this Bill has nothing to do with sedition'; Lloyd George had confused sedition with seduction (an allegation which seems to have been made without a hint of humour).[73] Yet criticisms continued to erupt from all sides. One Labour member protested that if the bill went through, 'the old proverb that the Englishman's house is his castle will be dead and buried, and we shall have no further right to use it'. Even more vehemently, the Conservative Sir William Holdsworth, the most eminent public lawyer of his day, described the law as 'the most daring encroachment upon the liberty of the subject which the executive government has yet attempted at a time which is not a time of emergency'. He added the penetrating observation that the government's surprise at the 'storm of indignation' was 'a very disquieting feature of the mentality of the present day' because it showed that 'the statesmen of today are so much in the hands of bureaucrats . . . that they have contracted that limited vision which is the characteristic of the bureaucrat'.[74]

The attempt to delegitimize the incitement bill as unconstitutional was brought to its highest pitch by J. B. Priestley, who had just staked out his claim to be an interpreter of the national psyche through his *English Journey*. Opposition to the bill, he contended, was not a matter of 'continental political terms' like right and left, but of the national—and specifically English—mainstream.

Indeed, an Englishman with a deep respect for tradition ought to oppose this Sedition Bill simply because it runs counter to our English tradition; our grandfathers would not have tolerated it for a moment. They held that the House of Commons existed to protect us against such repressive measures and not to further them. If we allow this ugly tangle of searching and spying and denouncing to be forced upon us, we slip back hundreds of years, and the very ghosts of the staidest old Whigs would regard us with contempt.[75]

Faith in liberal democracy, Priestley observed, had been in decline in Europe since the war, but it needed to survive in England. He saw this new law as a portent of the tribalism that was now the fashion: the powers of arbitrary police action it created were, simply, 'un-English'. Under it the English would join the 'tired, bewildered, nervous folk' who thronged Europe and who had given up on democracy. It was 'a savage piece of irony' that 'a ministry calling itself a National Government should attempt such a fundamentally anti-national piece of legislation'. 'The men who wish to make it law are traitors to the real spirit of the country.'[76] The same charge, almost certainly more penetrating than the protests against 'dangers to freedom', was levelled by E. M. Forster, who also labelled the law 'un-English. It is an attempt to Continentalize us. Our so-called National Government is trying to do an un-national thing, and I don't believe the nation will stand for it.'[77]

In the light of, and perhaps in part as a result of such heated warnings, the subsequent history of the Disaffection Act has so far been oddly tepid. As Street noted, it did not prove a serious threat to liberty. One unfortunate university student suffered exemplary punishment for suggesting to an airman whom he met in a station café that he should go and help the Republicans in Spain.[78] But otherwise the main effects of the new law were generated indirectly, in the form of self-censorship (which is, by its nature, impossible to gauge),[79] and more obviously by way of public protests against it. The most far-reaching result was the ruling in the case of *Duncan* v. *Jones*. The police prevented Mrs Duncan from speaking at a protest meeting on 30 July 1934, and arrested her; 'her arrest was justified on the ground that she might have said something, had she been allowed to speak, which would have led to a breach of the peace'. The *New Statesman* commented that

Boiled down, the police case came to this: Since Mrs Duncan's views were likely to make the unemployed less contented, she should be prohibited from speaking, lest some of her more irresponsible listeners might at some future date commit a breach of the peace. Since Sir Herbert Wilberforce, the Deputy Chairman, did not give the reasons for the magistrates' decision, it is difficult to say how far-reaching it is. But it appears to justify the police in prohibiting any meeting at which some speaker might in their view say something which might lead to a disturbance somewhere else.[80]

After the police case was accepted in the magistrates' court, Duncan's appeals to quarter sessions and the divisional court, sponsored by the newly-founded National Council for Civil Liberties, failed on the ground that 'it is the duty of a police officer to prevent apprehended breaches of the peace' (Humphreys J). This ruling has been described by one modern writer as 'a miserable decision for civil liberties', and by others as 'less than impressive' or 'highly unsatisfactory'.[81] Brownlie points out that this radical extension of police discretionary power was made by the instinct of the judges: 'the cursory judgments contain no citation of authority of any kind. They regard certitude as a substitute for authority.' The ways of common sense do not invariably lead in the direction of liberty.

The gentle application of powers like the Disaffection Act may be taken to bear out Clinton Rossiter's sanguine view of the EPA in operation between the wars, composed in 1947: 'The sincere and successful use of crisis authority . . . calls for statesmanship of the highest quality.' Or it may bear out the less flattering view of Holdsworth and Priestley, that this was an unnecessary panic measure by weak and misguided statesmen who—

wittingly or no—began the process of undermining a central bastion of English freedom. Isaac Foot's warning that 'it is when you have a reactionary government in a time of fear and apprehension that this measure may be used for the destruction of our liberties' remains unfulfilled. Yet the force of Aneurin Bevan's insistence on the inadequacy of British tradition to govern the burgeoning power of the police is hardly diminished. 'The whole essence of democracy', he contended, 'is that when you give people power, you surround that power by all sorts of restrictions and safeguards in order that that power may not be abused. You do not [say] that the man who is going to exercise this power is a good and upright and scrupulous man, and therefore you do not need to have any safeguard.'[82]

The First Public Order Act

> This Conference . . . condemns the provocative tactics of the Fascists; and records its view that whilst freedom of speech must be preserved, the encouragement of civil disorder, racial strife, and parade of force and militarized politics, and the use of political uniforms should be forbidden.
>
> Labour Party Conference, October 1936

At the same time as the government fretted over the threat to national security posed by the sly and skulking breed of inciter, it faced up—rather less enthusiastically—to the growing problem of public violence. One element of this was industrial. Picketing has always, as Jane Morgan shows, been 'seen by the police essentially as a problem of public order, and treated as such'.[83] In 1922 the Chief Constable of Sheffield suggested that 'so-called "Peaceful Picketing" indulged in by gangs of aggrieved persons, accompanied by hooligans etc.' permitted under the 1906 Trades Disputes Act, was 'a grave danger to peace and good order' and should be 'made amenable to the law'. The government turned a deaf ear to such demands, even after the general strike, and the Trades Disputes Act of 1927 did not give the police the enlarged powers they wanted, though it had an unattractive reputation during its eighteen-year life (A. J. P. Taylor roundly denounced it as 'a futile measure'), and Morgan finds that its mere existence 'encouraged the police to more vigorous action'.[84]

A further dimension of industrial conflict opened up with the appearance of hunger marches and other demonstrations against mass unemployment in the 1920s. According to Morgan there was 'vigorous debate' within the Cabinet and other administrative bodies about the control of unemployed marches and demonstrations, though few records of this survive and most of the debate was very far from public. In April 1932 the Commissioner of the Metropolitan Police found that two memoranda on the subject had not been classified as confidential, and catechized his deputy on the need for secrecy:

I do not want this sort of information to leak into the press, and see flaming headlines to the effect that the police are seriously alarmed that very hostile demonstrations may take place. In my opinion it will only encourage numbers of people to take part in these demonstrations (which they may look upon as a chance for rioting), when they would not otherwise do so.[85]

To this interesting view of the people, he added the particular need to maintain the absolute secrecy of the political police: 'I do not want the actual language used in the Special Branch reports to be repeated in such memoranda.'

Even behind closed doors, the debate remained unresolved. At the most basic level, the problem of defining the law of public meetings and demonstrations continued to nag the police. When Trenchard asked for a 'Child's Guide' to the law to be prepared by the Home Office, Frank Newsam came up with what might have been predicted: a document which suggested, for instance, that 'anticipatory action' to disperse or block a procession 'must be taken very sparingly', since it was 'not a matter on which any general rules can be laid down'; while 'as a general principle forcible interference should be delayed as long as possible, until in fact it becomes clear that further forbearance on the part of the police would result in aggravating the gravity of the situation and increasing the risk of disorder'.[86] Trenchard's comment was equally predictable:

I have told him that it is not quite what I wanted for Chief Constables, Superintendents and Chief Inspectors, as it is really nothing more than what is laid down in the book, and does not give them an easy guide. It may be that it is impossible to write a Child's Guide and we shall have simply to rely on people's common sense.[87]

Common sense impelled him to push on the frontiers of police discretion. The 'Trenchard ban', issued in 1931 under the 1839 Metropolitan Police Act, prohibited future meetings by the unemployed at any Labour Exchange, since such meetings had been found to be liable to lead to breaches of the peace.[88] In this respect, *Duncan* v. *Jones* neatly confirmed for the whole country this prophetic power of the London police. But the extension of police power could still be resisted by ministers on grounds reminiscent of the previous century. When the Home Secretary, the Conservative Sir John

Gilmour, brought draft public order legislation to the Cabinet in July 1934 (while the Incitement Bill was still in committee), his colleagues decided that the proposed powers to control open-air meetings and processions militated against the poor, and were

much too wide to be placed in the hands of Chief Constables, who would probably fail to realise for instance that the route of many processions was devised rather from the point of view of filling the subscription boxes than of political considerations.[89]

This dim view of police intelligence, and easy assumption of political superiority, however, was rapidly receding into the past.

Two years were to pass before the Public Order Bill was eventually exposed to public scrutiny. Throughout this time, the Home Office tried to gauge the likely public reaction to the planned restrictions on ancient liberties. The question 'was whether to let the question drift or to tackle it'. By focusing the issue as one of 'private armies', Gilmour 'thought that public opinion was prepared for the view that the wearing of uniforms was a matter for the Government'. The problem of political uniforms was certainly important, and, in the form that it took in the 1930s, a novel one in England. (The Statute of Liveries, which had removed it from the public arena since the end of the Wars of the Roses, had unfortunately been breached on a massive scale in Ireland during the crisis of 1912–14.) The leading exponents of the new style were the Fascists, and the Home Secretary observed that wearing uniform 'intensifies their aggressive behaviour and gives to what would otherwise be harmless evolutions a semi-military appearance which causes considerable resentment'.[90] The number of incidents was increasing, and Gilmour's supercilious phrase 'harmless evolutions' masked an uncertainty about the ultimate size of the problem—much like his Liberal predecessors in face of the Ulster Volunteer Force.

The Home Office recognized that 'rowdyism at public meetings is no new feature in English life'; but tolerances were changing. The existing law, principally incorporated in the 1908 Public Meetings Act, was 'only defensible on the supposition that the organizers of meetings will be ready to invoke police assistance'. Fascist refusal to do this created a new situation, requiring an amendment of the law to enable police to enter private premises where a 'public meeting' was taking place, if the Chief Police Officer believed that disorder was likely to occur. (The oddities of definition of 'public place' and 'meeting' have never been wholly sorted out.) Wider controls on the 'so-called right of public meeting'—which the

Home Office reiterated was 'nothing more than the right of all men to come together in a place where they may lawfully assemble for any lawful purpose'—were admitted to be politically sensitive. Gilmour recalled that

the difficulties caused by open-air meetings have frequently been considered by the Home Office . . . but the habit of holding open-air public meetings, especially for political purposes, is so deeply engrained in English life that it appears to me to be impracticable to propose that the holding of such meetings should be made subject to the sanction either of the police, the magistrates, the local authority, or of any other body.[91]

The Cabinet decided to take no action in 1934, but to plant a Parliamentary question to show that there would be 'no toleration of a menace to public order'.

Two years later, the same problem remained. Gilmour's successor as Home Secretary, the former Liberal (and former Attorney-General) Sir John Simon, reported to the Preservation of Public Order Committee that the provisions of the draft bill dealing with the 'private armies' issue were fairly straightforward. Though no definition of 'uniform' had been worked out, the 'question whether a garb amounts to uniform' could be left to the magistrates. If organizations were to arouse 'reasonable apprehension' that they were trained in exercises of a military character 'with a view to usurping or supplementing without lawful authority the functions of the armed forces of the Crown or Police', that would form sufficient evidence that such a purpose was intended. However, the regulation of processions was a much more difficult part of the subject. Some provision would certainly have to be made, and Simon thought that 'proper authority should have the power to regulate the routes to be followed by processions, and to give special directions and to impose conditions where obstructions or breaches of the peace are likely to arise'. In the nature of things, such authority would now be the chiefs of police, who should also be able to regulate public meetings if two or more were happening near to each other and likely to cause serious disorder.

On this basis, he thought the Cabinet could face the country with the Bill: 'notwithstanding certain criticisms that would be raised, if the Government were to make clear that they would not allow minorities to be attacked, and public order disturbed, they would be supported by a strong public opinion'.[92] The difficulty was that the transition from general rhetoric of order to specific provisions for controlling political organizations and meetings opened a form of constitutional debate which the authorities were usually careful to avoid. It was not, indeed, that the Public Order Bill ran into the 'storm of indignation' that had greeted the Incitement Bill. But it is probably fair to say, as George Lansbury did with weary resignation during its third reading, that 'no Bill has ever been passed, as this will be passed, without a vote against it, which was so intensely disliked'. To that extent its attempt to define and defend the cardinal virtues of British public life was not successful.

Un-British though such an attempt may sound, the Act was undoubtedly projected at the level of grand principle, rather than merely answering the need, as the King's speech had promised, for 'dealing more effectively with persons or organizations who provoke or cause disturbances of the peace'. The terms in which Simon launched the main debate could hardly have been more resonant: 'the grand characteristic of British political life is its tolerance. All the things which we prize—freedom of opinion, freedom of speech, and freedom of meeting—are all based on our conception of political and civic toleration.' He asserted that 'the interests of the general public' in the maintenance of this culture must be upheld. He presented 'the unanimous view of the Chief Officers of Police ... that the wearing of political uniforms is a source of special provocation', and backed it with the endorsement of Sweden, Norway, Finland, Denmark, Switzerland, and Holland. (The Cabinet, however, had questioned whether the invocation of foreign models might not damage the simplicity of the 'established principle of the British constitution that there is only one authority for the maintenance of law and order'.) He copper-fastened his case with the declaration that 'The foundation of all ordered government in this island is that the only instruments of force should be those of the properly constituted authorities.'[93]

But the specific targeting of the bill on the wearing of political uniform brought up all the problems of definition that the Home Office had already side-stepped. After remarking that the term must be linked to 'the promotion of a political object', thus excluding such worthy phalanxes as the Salvation Army, the Church Lads' Brigade, and of course the nurses, Simon attempted the most brazen side-step yet. Assuring his audience that 'uniform' was 'a perfectly well known English word', he generously promised 'I shall not yield to the temptation of describing to the House my own idea of what a uniform is, although I have several phrases at the back of my mind.'

Most contributors to the Parliamentary debate accepted the broad aim of the bill, seeing the use of uniforms as the 'military manner and spirit' in politics, as symbolizing force, and as 'inimical to the safety of the State'. Herbert Morrison thought that 'the uniform in politics is an attempt to evolve a new authority ... rival to the State', and acknowledged that the purpose of the bill was 'to prevent the existence of political organizations on the lines of certain organizations abroad which have destroyed the liberties of whole nations'.[94] Still, the question of definition haunted the debate. Suggesting that words like 'sedition' could not be defined because 'most definitions would prevent all political discussion', one member pointed out that the safeguard 'is that you will not go to prison for sedition unless twelve very ordinary men think you ought to go there'; what safeguard, he asked, would apply to the 'properly undefined words in this Bill?' The Conservative barrister R. H. Turton protested that failure to offer a usable definition of uniform, on which the whole law would hinge, would be 'shirking our plain duty'. Any uncertainty in Parliament about the meaning would be dangerously amplified in the magistrates' courts. In committee he urged that 'we are framing a new law, a very strange law, a complete innovation, and it does not rest with us to say that the courts will find a way of getting out of the difficulty. We must show what precision we can.'[95]

The problem was not confined to political uniform. Vital conceptual terms like 'usurpation' and 'provocation' were the stress-marks etched on 'tolerance' by race tension. 'After all, what is the nature of political liberty?', the Liberal Kingsley Griffith enquired. Tolerance must be distinguished from mere indifference. Dissent was its essence. 'Liberty only arises when people are saying something which is very provocative.' Stafford Cripps agreed that certain difficulties must be accepted:

If we are not going to have any difficult times, we are not going to have democracy at all in this country, because, if you are going to allow the free play that is necessary for political demonstration and discussion . . . you must then have the liability of some public disorder taking place.[96]

But how far could the right to provoke be taken? Bevan insisted that there was 'all the difference in the world between a slogan "down with the Yids" and "Down with the means test"', because 'people do not identify themselves with the same ardour with the means test as they identify themselves with anti-semitism'. Yet 'ardour' was not much more helpful as a precise measure. What the debate was trying to get at was the distinction between provocation and intimidation, but the intimidation of Jews by Fascists could only have been dealt with at the level of collective consciousness, since at street level it was always the Jews and other anti-Fascists who launched the physical violence.

Simon was careful to reassure Parliament that although 'the police may have their faults, they are not complete fools, and for my part I should draw the sharpest distinction between a banner stating a proposition with which I did not agree and a banner with expressions on it which indicated an endeavour to foment a riot.[97]

(However, he was equally careful not to offer examples.) Some of the opposition none the less remained convinced that the general dislike of Fascism was legitimizing a law which would, as the Cabinet had earlier recognized, militate against the poor, or as Stafford Cripps put it now, 'interfere with that type of publicity for grievances which alone the poorer sections of the community have at their disposal'. In other words, the Fascists would indirectly achieve the silencing of protest by the unemployed or disadvantaged, 'striking at the inherent right of the people to demonstrate'. The Liberal Isaac Foot ruefully concluded that though

we have heard a great deal throughout the discussion of this Bill about the preservation of our civil liberties, I am one of the few people in this House who takes the view that the greatest danger of an attack on our civil liberties comes, not from any outside body or faction, but from the growing power of the Executive itself.[98]

A further twist was added by the question of whether public order was aided by organized bodies of stewards at public meetings. While the Attorney-General urged that 'restoring and maintaining order is not a political object', others pointed out that stewards 'would not be there unless they thought they were promoting a political object'. When the government introduced a new clause authorizing the use of organized stewards, on 7 December, Bevan protested that while 'we have been constrained to accept' the bill in order to prohibit private armies, 'we are now re-importing into the Bill the possibility of an organized, disciplined, and semi-military force'. The government made some play with the old story of Captain Moir, who shot a boy stealing apples from his garden, as a guide to the limits of force to be used by stewards; Ellen Wilkinson concluded that 'a steward may do almost anything to a heckler except kill him'.[99]

Altogether, the 1936 Act was traditionally English in its focus on a particular threat to public order. The anti-Semitism of uniformed Fascists was, of course, a threat whose ultimate dimensions could not then be known. With hindsight it may seem to have been overestimated. British Fascism was bled to death by public distaste, generated as much by its obvious 'foreignness' as by the offensiveness of its ideas and behaviour. Clynes picturesquely observed, 'Strange, indeed, it is to us that these new political forces and factors should have turned so readily to alien practices', while the Conservative Maurice Petherick wondered, 'is it not better to allow the good sense of the people to destroy these foolish foreign fanatics than to try to suppress them by the force of law?'[100] Private armies ceased to be a major political problem, despite occasional alarms about organizations such as the Greenshirts, the Woodcraft Folk, the Orange Order, or indeed Securicor, and the more pernicious survival of para-militarism in Northern Ireland. But though the march of Fascism stopped, the Public Order Act soldiered on. Its half-century of life as the central public order statute bore out Cripps's warning that the 'whole tendency in the operation of the Act by local authorities' would be to 'make certain of the "safety first" point of view'. The balance between democracy and public order, contrary elements of the public interest, was struck by Simon thus: liberty meant 'not only the rights of those who wish to demonstrate or protest, but also the rights of the general public, who have their interests in being protected from suffering from serious and illegitimate disturbance'. More would be heard of these new rights in the future.

6

The Ultimate Emergency

Total war cannot be won by a doubtful nation, by a disunited nation, by a nation in which there is any considerable part that is unreliable . . . The necessity, therefore, of concentrating immense powers in a government waging total war is beyond discussion.

Harold Laski, 1942[1]

The coy British state came closest to self-definition in the second overwhelming public emergency of the twentieth century. As the novel physical and psychological scale of total war had necessitated novel public powers for the defence of the realm, so the supercharged apprehension of the 1930s raised the stakes even higher. On 24 August 1939 the Home Secretary, Sir Samuel Hoare, introduced the Emergency Powers (Defence) Bill in the House of Commons. The timing of the measure he explained as resulting from the changed nature of war. Once upon a time it had been a simple matter, but

there is now a twilight between peace and war, perhaps the most dangerous of any periods in international affairs, in which it is essential that the Government, not this Government in particular but any British Government, must be armed with emergency powers.[2]

He plainly considered elaboration of these new dangers to be supererogatory, but he offered a further explanation of why the Home Secretary in 1914 had been able to wait until the actual outbreak of hostilities before asking for emergency powers: in 1914 'war was still a slow-motion play', but now, 'the complexity and intensity of the problems that speed creates, and the dangers that confront these islands as a result of the great developments in aviation' called for the fullest possible powers. These powers were not merely essential—they were 'ten times more essential' than they had been in 1914. They were in fact 'quite essential', and had to be 'very wide, very drastic and very comprehensive'.

Hoare explicitly contrasted the new bill, which Rossiter later tagged as 'a rejuvenated and expanded DORA', with its ancestor. He recalled that his predecessor Reginald McKenna had come into the chamber in August 1914 with 'only half a sheaf of notes in his hand', and that DORA had been more or less made up as the government went along. But now, he impressed on his audience, 'we have brought into the scope of the Bill all the powers that we require'.[3] These powers were taken by the enabling clause, 'His Majesty may by Order in Council make such Regulations ... as appear to him to be necessary or expedient for securing the public safety, the defence of the realm, the maintenance of public order, and the efficient prosecution of any war'. Hoare defended the width and flexibility of the powers by reference to the 'comparatively unknown' nature and the 'uncertainty of the kind of problems that may arise'. 'If you leave a gap anywhere in a situation of this kind', he warned, 'your efforts may be frustrated and the country may be faced with a danger the importance of which cannot be exaggerated.' Certainly there was no danger that the government would minimize it.

In spite of the uncertainty, some powers were specified in the bill, first and foremost for 'the apprehension, trial and punishment of persons offending against the Regulations', and for 'the detention of persons whose detention appears to the Secretary of State to be expedient in the interests of the public safety or the defence of the Realm' (S.1[2a]). This provision was to become the centre-point of a large constitutional issue in mid-war. Hoare made two points about the nature and effect of the new law. The first was that it was in essence declaratory, not so much of the prerogative power vested in the executive—though this was a recurrent subject of debate in the Commons—as of the public will. 'We should make it clear to the world', he insisted, 'that we are prepared to arm ourselves with powers to meet any emergency', and that 'we are setting in abeyance the liberties and privileges that we have prized so much in the past ... as an insurance that we shall retain them permanently in the future'.[4] The second point was the assurance that however sweeping these powers might be, 'we will apply them with moderation, tolerance and common sense'.

Both these contentions drew deeply on English conventional wisdom. The voluntary sacrifice of ancient liberties was evidently a forceful manifestation of national resolve, and not, as it might appear, contradictory or paradoxical, since the English way would be to maintain the spirit of tolerance even in the exercise of dictatorial powers under the pressure of a war of national survival. Confidence in this, and in the ultimate restoration of fundamental liberties, was the proof of the resilience of the English way.

From this standpoint the entire argument was self-sustaining and self-referencing. Even so, it did not pass wholly unchallenged in Parliament. Although every speech from this moment to the end of the war was burdened by the tangible fear of seeming less than totally patriotic, some pungent observations about the government's claims were made. The Liberal Kingsley Griffith ventured to suggest that 'the liberty of the subject is so important that even in these times of national emergency we should deal with it extremely tenderly'. The Quaker Edmund Harvey, Independent Progressive MP for the Combined English Universities, saw the proposed powers as 'overwhelmingly large', and demonstrated that the government's central justification for them could be turned on its head: 'we must not, for the sake of winning a victory, lose the very cause for which we are struggling'.[5] Demanding that regulations under the proposed Act must secure the approval of the Commons, the former Labour Secretary of State for India, Wedgwood Benn, likewise urged 'Let us at any rate retain this vestige of Parliamentary democracy for which we are just about to ask others to fight. Let us at least retain that.'[6]

The government's assurances of moderation also encountered a mixed reception. Harvey judiciously observed that though 'the present Home Secretary is one who would exercise these powers with the utmost desire for justice and the utmost respect for the liberty of the subject', the previous powers under DORA had been wielded by at least three Home Secretaries. Amplifying this hint, Arthur Greenwood bluntly asserted that there were 'a good many incipient dictators on the other side of the House'. Labour was unlikely to see the government as virtually representing the people. In fact, Wedgwood Benn—despite his ritual declaration 'I do not want to do anything to disturb the atmosphere of unity'—not only reinforced the doubts about the instinctual reasonableness of the government by referrring to the worthless assurances formerly made about the application of the 1911 and 1920 Official Secrets Acts, but went on to say that the people to whom 'we are asked to give dictatorial powers' were actually 'a small group of men who have led this country practically to the brink of disaster'.

The atmosphere of unity survived even this rude irruption of realism. The underlying question in all this, however, was just what did the authorities most fear amongst what Hoare admitted—or rather insisted—were the 'comparatively unknown problems with which we may be confronted in the event of war'? The fact that 'the maintenance of public order' was ranked equally with the public safety, the defence of the realm, and the efficient prosecution of the war, is obviously significant. Though the long-standing fear of strikes, riots, and looting had not in itself diminished, it had been eclipsed by speculations about the impact of air attack on public spirit. The new philosophy of strategic bombing was that victory in war would be decided by the strength of civilian morale. And in spite of Lord Trenchard's unblinking confidence that in any bombing duel the enemy population would 'squeal' before the British did, the government shared the general belief that large-scale air attacks on cities would create mass panic.[7]

This belief does not seem to have been specifically linked to the wartime emergency regulations. In his study of civil liberties in the Second World War, Neil Stammers traces the evolution of draft emergency provisions from the mid-1920s under the aegis of the War Emergency Legislation Subcommittee and, after 1935, the Ad Hoc Interdepartmental Committee and the War Legislation Subcommittee. He notes that the earlier committee had no brief to consider in general policy terms the kinds of powers and restrictions on civil liberties which might be thought reasonable in a major emergency.[8] All it did was to assess the technical performance of the old DORA regulations and suggest improvements.

Underlying political assumptions certainly entered into the deliberations of the Ad Hoc Committee on DORR 14B, since it argued that there would in future be 'a serious danger that attempts to impede the war effort' might be made not only by enemy aliens or sympathizers, but also by people 'actuated . . . by "internationalist" affiliations or by disinterested opposition to the war'. It went on to suggest that 'if this country is subjected to frequent and large-scale attacks from the air, the need for swift and effective action' against such 'mischievous' people would be 'far greater than in the last war'. But there is no sign that such hypotheses were ever subjected to systematic scrutiny by ministers. Stammers noted that there was, in all the long period during which the emergency regulations were repeatedly redrafted, 'no attempt to discuss the issues involved, either in Parliament or with interested parties outside the government'. His conclusion, 'that public discussion was intentionally avoided until the crisis had arisen and "national unity" became the political order of the day' would seem hard to resist.

The motives for this reticence, however, remain ambiguous. As with the later problem of civil defence for nuclear war, the conscious intention of the officials may have been to avoid causing public disquiet which could, in their view, have no utility. Democratic discussion could not, in the nature of things, generate meaningful choices for such hypothetical circumstances. This benign authoritarianism tends to look very different outside Whitehall: to look, in fact, like the stifling of a debate which might go in directions unwelcome to the authorities; it might even, indeed, favour those dangerous 'persons actuated by disinterested opposition to war'. Once again the question arises: did the authorities trust the people? How far did they expect order to go on being maintained by public good sense, how far by state force?

The gradual erosion of the boundary, once so firmly drawn, between central and local authority, inevitably brought a shift in perceptions of what was spontaneous self-regulatory action, internal to the 'community', and what was external and (perhaps) coercive. Those who argued that the new Emergency Powers Act formed an excessive increment to central public power were implicitly contending that 'the people' were still capable of a high degree of self-regulation, even in an unforeseeably large crisis. The official view was equally clearly—though not explicitly—that patriotism would not be enough. Powerful and elaborate machinery was needed, and only the state could provide it. This was in part a technical issue: exactly what would be the impact of modern war on various functions of the modern social and economic structure? Nobody knew the answer, and the government did not want to take chances. 'Safety first' was a cast of mind which had shaped the entire administrative system.[9]

The technical analysis merged with the psychological when the question of 'subversion' in all its alarming ramifications arose. Subversion is a concept which has become especially meaningful to twentieth-century governments. This is not to say that it can be given an exact meaning: rather the opposite. It is an almost meaningless word. As the Oxford dictionary shows, its old, drastic meanings have become rare or obsolete, but no new meaning can be assigned to it. Yet it is a concept whose political usage, as many observers have remarked, has vastly increased during this century. Its very vagueness signals the enlarged sense of the vulnerability of modern systems to all kinds of covert assault. Subversion has not of course become a legal offence as such. Brownlie's index does not contain a single reference to it. Its most definite (though mainly invisible) product in the executive sphere has been the growth of the once unknown 'security services' since the First World War, and particularly since the Bolshevik revolution. After the Second World War the system of surveillance of 'subversive activities' would be steadily enlarged.[10]

Parallel to this process has been the increasing petrification of the old legal terms which once flagged the terrain of public security. Foremost amongst these was treason. Admittedly, there was always some element of semantic negotiation in this ancient notion, especially in the age of palace revolutions—as Harington's epigram put it, 'if it prosper, none dare call it . . .'—but it definitely related to specific acts of opposition to the Crown. In modern times, however, no attempt was made to mesh it with the processes of social, political, military, and technical evolution. When the Law Commission finally tackled the subject in the 1970s, it found it 'unsatisfactory that the most serious of all criminal offences should turn on the construction of language some six hundred years old, which is both obscure and difficult'. It noted that over the years, through 'somewhat strained' linguistic interpretations, the courts transformed the feudal notion of disloyalty into the modern concept of treason as 'armed resistance made on political grounds to the public order of the realm'.[11] In spite of this recognition of 'the overlap in practice between offences against the State and offences against public order', it believed that 'a clear dividing line can be drawn between them'; but even so it did not offer any definition of 'the State' to replace the body of the monarch.

Such cloudiness extends to the more humdrum terms sedition and dis-affection. Brownlie notes that the most detailed modern analysis of sedition was made (in 1951) by the Canadian Supreme Court, one of whose members commented that 'as is frequently mentioned in the authorities, probably no crime has been left in such vagueness of definition . . . and its legal meaning has changed with the years'.[12] The key to this may be found in the observation by Justice Fitzgerald in *R*. v. *Sullivan* (1868), 'sedition is a crime against society'. Hence the strikingly wide definition offered by Fitzjames Stephen in his *Digest*:

an intention to bring into hatred or contempt or to excite disaffection against the person of Her Majesty . . . or the government and constitution of the United Kingdom, as by law established, or either House of Parliament, or the administration of justice, or to excite Her Majesty's subjects to attempt, otherwise than by lawful means, the alteration of any matter in Church or State by law established, or to raise discontent or disaffection amongst Her Majesty's subjects, or to promote feelings of ill-will or hostility between different classes of such subjects

This could, as S. A. de Smith has seen, 'encompass any forceful criticism of the existing structure of authority within the state'.[13]

The old test, as Brownlie shows, was the real likelihood of a public disturbance ('to incite violence or to create public disturbance or disorder'), but this relatively clear meaning has been lost. It might have been assumed, he adds, that the offence of sedition had become obsolescent since the nineteenth century, but recent experience with offences such as affray, misprision of felony, and conspiracy to corrupt public morals, must lead to caution: 'In time of crisis an uncertain executive might resort to it again, as it has done in modern times in areas of British colonial rule.'[14] The disuse of the offence has been due, he thought, to the uncertainty of definition, the possible distaste of juries for the crime, and its 'unhappy historical associations with a palpably undemocratic past'.

In 1940 that past—like the foreign enemy—was tangibly closer, though the decision to drop 'sedition' from the title of the 1934 Act had indicated that its political value was already verging on the negative. The preference for 'disaffection' was now carried through into the Defence Regulations, but so was the arresting failure to offer any definition of the term. Some clarification was achieved when the government offered a clutch of amendments in November 1939, so that in Regulation 39A the phrase 'to cause disaffection' was replaced by 'to seduce from duty' and 'to cause disaffection likely to lead to breaches of duty'. Duty was a much more exact term, though since it would amount in practice to 'orders', the political shift from a notion of ideal self-obligation to one of simple obedience was noticeable.

The fear of disloyalty seems to have grown in two or three stages for the inter-war generation of administrators. The Great War produced a new level of concern with public support for the 'war effort', and what may without much exaggeration be called an obsession with the power of propaganda in the manipulation of public opinion. This plainly underpinned the Attorney-General's belief that his otherwise less than overwhelming evidence of 'incitement to disaffection' in 1934 would persuade the country at large of the reality of its peril. Ultimately it engendered both the ultra-modern, Orwellian 'Psychological Warfare Executive' on the one hand, and the oddly archaic wording of Regulation 39BA (against the causing of 'alarm and despondency') on the other.

In the interim, the mental atmosphere was supercharged by one phrase above all, imported from the Spanish Civil War—probably the most far-reaching Spanish contribution to the political vocabulary since the word 'liberal'. Coined by General Mola during the Nationalist advance on Madrid in October 1936, 'la quinta columna' may in fact have been given the wrong number, but the 'fifth column' immediately broke through into the imagination of conservatives everywhere. Even the post-war fascination with 'moles' was hardly to rival the thrill of disquiet produced by the notion of organized traitors in our midst. England had formerly been impervious to the 'dismal cry' (as Michael Howard's account of the French defeat in 1870 has it), 'Nous sommes trahis!'. Denis Brogan, penning a by no means uncritical portrait of the English for American consumption in the middle of the war, observed that 'no nation is less subject to the panic fear of internal treason'. In crisis or disaster 'the Englishman does not think he has been betrayed, merely that his affairs have been mismanaged; he does not shout "each for himself" but "stick together" '.[15]

Such sanguine self-images would persist, but the two world wars, commonly celebrated for allowing the English to 'discover hidden though not unexpected sources of national strength in their mutual trust', also elicited hidden fears. The fifth column menace unnerved both left and right, the former for the good historical reason that the original was a Fascist coinage, and Quisling was a Nazi. Thus Harold Laski: 'The perspective of [total war's] psychological basis is set by the threat—in scale a new factor in war—of the Fifth Column and its potential activities.'[16] The potential scale was a matter of guesswork. The spread of the belief in the fifth column was accelerated by the common wartime syndrome of exaggerating the enemy's power. Anxiety bred unfalsifiability. Observing that Lord Ironside was on the brink of rumbling the concept in the summer of 1940 ('It is extraordinary how we get circumstantial reports of 5th column and yet we have never been able to get anything worth having'), A. W. B. Simpson has recognized that the brink was impassable: 'those who believe in the enemy in our midst have minds insulated against evidence; its absence proves the extreme skill of the enemy'.[17]

In February 1940 the Home Secretary reported to the Civil Defence Committee that he was 'receiving from all quarters expressions of concern at the growth of various kinds of subversive propaganda'. The War Cabinet met on 18 May to discuss a Home Office memorandum entitled 'The Invasion of Great Britain and the Possible Co-operation of a Fifth Column'. This was certainly not an alarmist document, and it took a cautious view of the suggested need for drastic action against enemy aliens, British Fascists, or Communists.[18] The Cabinet, however, or the new Prime Minister, Churchill, clearly found this too complacent. Four days later it pushed through Parliament the Treachery Act, a statute which in Rossiter's view redefined treachery 'in the light of the modern standards of the fifth column'. It provided for trial by court martial of enemy aliens accused of espionage or sabotage ('any act which is designed or likely to give assistance to the operations of the enemy or impede the operations of His Majesty's forces'). This minatory statute was followed by a direct move against Mosley's British Union under Regulation 18AA on 10 July. By August, some 750 people were in detention for their connection with the Fascist organization.[19]

A less direct mode of controlling political dissent has been traced by

Stammers. On 14 May a Metropolitan Police memorandum advised that police officers 'should not hesitate to make arrests if in their judgement a breach of the peace is being invited' by speakers at anti-war meetings. Was this merely a prudential move to preserve public order in sensitive areas, or, as the memorandum indicated, a policy with the more general political objective of 'curbing activities of an anti-war character'?[20] For this purpose, as Stammers points out, Section 5 of the Public Order Act was undoubtedly an ideal tool. 'Not only was it part of the ordinary criminal law, rather than a potentially controversial defence regulation, it also required a minimum of proof, without reference to the political activities involved.'[21] Though he suggests that 'the common use of S.5 of the Public Order Act suggests that the strategy had been formulated at governmental level', Stammers sees the difficulty of assessing the attitudes and motives of the authorities from the surviving documents, the most relevant of which remain under closure. And indeed there was no need for superior direction in a matter which had been one of police instinct even before the Public Order Act; the Act, it might be said, was in this respect simply a crystallization of that instinct.

There was not much cause for official anxiety. Public distaste for the new Defence Regulations seems to have been less palpable than during the First World War. As Ronald Kidd admitted, the sharpest criticism was levelled—by the 'popular' press—at the threat of curfew (Regulation 37), but it is not very evident why this provision seemed more objectionable than the rest. Kidd himself thought that the curfew regulation was considerably less important than most of the others from the civil liberties standpoint. Its purpose 'was to deal with possible panic or looting in case of intensive bombardment'; but Kidd believed (optimistically perhaps) that 'if such an order were arbitrarily imposed for any other purpose than to deal with a really grave emergency, citizens would revolt against such a drastic curtailment of their general freedom of movement'.[22] Plainly public order was still, in the public mind, actively negotiated. The pivotal issue was the perception of 'a really grave emergency'.

The threat of invasion was far more immediate and real in 1940 than at any time in the First World War. Eventually, after the invasion and defeat of France, the government turned to the problem of maintaining public order in a situation of actual fighting. It came up with a curious solution which provoked the nearest thing to a constitutional crisis that the constrictions of war would permit. On 16 July 1940 the Emergency Powers (Defence)(No.2) Bill was introduced by Sir John Anderson, Home Secretary since the outbreak of war, now formally responsible for 'Home Security'.

This was the third major enlargement of the Act whose scope, his predecessor had originally claimed, embraced 'all the powers that we require'. Anderson opened on a rather defensive note with the suggestion that the proposed law's purpose had been 'misunderstood in some quarters'.

It is thought by some that the object of the Government is to establish courts-martial, or some other form of military tribunal, for the punishment of civil offenders. The exact opposite is the case. The object which the Government have in view in promoting the Bill is to avoid the necessity for establishing anything in the nature of military courts.[23]

The misunderstanding was to prove hard to correct. Anderson explained that his 'plan' was to establish special war zone courts, to be presided over by 'suitable men of judicial rank', to replace the ordinary courts in areas where active military operations were imminent or had recently occurred. There, 'as part of the process of re-establishing normal conditions', it would be 'necessary to have courts in operation which can deal with grave offences far more speedily than would be possible under the normal processes of justice'.[24]

Anderson, who can hardly have forgotten his experience as the civil half of the civil-military administration of martial law in Ireland in 1920–1, repeatedly stressed that 'there is no question here of any difference of opinion between soldiers and civilians, or of any conflict of rival theories'. Nobody, least of all the soldiers, he said, wanted 'what I believe is sometimes described as martial law' except in the immediate zone of combat. For the army it would be a burdensome diversion of resources, and for the civil population it would be unnecessarily arbitrary. The proposed special courts would administer the ordinary civil law—in effect, of course, the Defence Regulations—but without procedural impediments such as the committal process. There would be no jury, and no appeal.

Anderson's argument ran into a wall of hostility and incomprehension in the House of Commons. Indeed, this day may well have been unique in constitutional history in witnessing Members of Parliament arguing in favour of martial law, which they felt was at least traditional and understood, and even carried more safeguards than the government's proposal. They also argued, more comfortably, for the old common law test, by which the ordinary courts would be superseded only when it became physically impossible for them to operate. Against these objections, the civil-service-trained Home Secretary battled somewhat unconvincingly. 'I wonder', he pleaded, 'whether Hon. Members really appreciate what it is that we are trying to do, and what the situation is that we are trying to face.'[25] The idea that martial law would provide better safeguards than the new courts was based on a (hardly surprising) misunderstanding of the term, and confusion between courts martial and drumhead courts. 'Martial law in this country is a phrase of very indefinite import', Anderson instructed the House, but the common law 'contemplated' a system of military courts 'in cases of grave danger when the safety of the people is the supreme test of action'.[26] The problem—and here he directly echoed his own words in 1921—was how to get back to normality afterwards. 'The sooner you can get back to the processes of ordinary civilian law, in the sense in which I use the term, so much the better.'

But the sense in which these novel courts merited that description was precisely the issue raised by Kingsley Griffith, who protested that Anderson had 'tried to frighten us with the idea that the alternative to the Bill is military rule, but all kinds of military rule are possible under the Bill itself'. The fallen Conservative star Leslie Hore-Belisha, a former Secretary of State for War who had been 'loathed by GHQ',[27] contended that while 'he has produced it as a measure to protect the civilian from a harsh military procedure, in fact the Bill does exactly the reverse, and is expressed to be a measure to subject the civilian to martial law'. On the left, Sydney Silverman fiercely objected that

The real offence which this Bill does to the conscience of the House is that under it it will be possible to make regulations by which every safeguard that the citizen of this country has ever had against arbitrary action by the Executive is removed without possibility of amendment in the House.[28]

The Liberal Sir Richard Acland asked the Home Secretary to spell out 'what is the real problem that is facing him, because I have not been able to make out what it is'. Was it at root a fear of mass disorder? The Labour front bench asked whether the nature of the emergency envisaged could be more clearly specified, to which Anderson replied that this 'may be possible, but I am not quite sure'.

A profound disquiet about the bill (Lees-Smith said it was 'far too vague for the House to accept', Acland that 'this is one of the cases where the Government is asking for just a little bit too much power') focused as before on the trust reposed in the Home Secretary. 'It is all very well', Kingsley Griffith tartly commented, 'for anybody to come before this House and say, "I have a Bill which entitles me to cut off your head, but I can assure you that I am only going to cut your toe nails."' Aneurin Bevan, saying that the time had come to speak in 'a forthright fashion', bitterly alleged that experience during the last nine months had shown that the powers which Parliament had parted with had been 'gravely abused by the Executive'. 'I had hoped—and I say this with great sorrow—that the inclusion of certain persons in the Government would have restrained the excesses of the Executive, but that has not happened.' He and others had been deluged by constituents with 'evidence that we are now slowly degenerating into a police state, and that the liberties of the subject cannot be entrusted to persons who appear to be unable to stand up to their civil servants'.[29]

Opposition came to a head in committee, over Edmund Harvey's amendment inserting a judicial committee to review the sentences imposed by the war zone courts. In a debate lasting two and a half hours—quite long for one amendment to a bill which the government had initially tried to hurry through all its stages in a single day—Harvey and his supporters manifested open disbelief in the capacity of the Home Secretary to review the findings of the special courts. Anderson for his part refused to accept that the advice of the proposed judicial committee could be binding. That the government eventually accepted the amendment was, in the circumstances, a dramatic victory for Harvey, but the revelation of the extent to which the Home Secretary already ignored the opinion of his judicial advisers in exercising the prerogative of mercy—and frankly proposed to continue ignoring the new review committee if, in his view, the public interest so required—made it somewhat hollow.

Overall, there were two sharply contrasting views of the new Emergency Powers Act, and the necessities which would justify it. Opponents branded it as 'repugnant to our instincts and to the desires of the country'.[30] Like the original EPA it was dangerous because it undermined the very cause for which the war was being fought: as Hore-Belisha put it, 'we are fighting for our system of justice against a much harsher system'. The 'essence' of the British constitution, Griffith held, 'the separation of the powers of the Judiciary from the Executive', was being eroded. The shade of the Star Chamber haunted the debate. 'We cannot be expected', protested Acland, 'under a plea of emergency, to grant the executive powers which will enable it to arrest anyone for anything, and try anyone by any secret procedure without appeal'. The government had not shown that the abrogation of traditional procedures and safeguards was either necessary or useful.

The other view saw the necessity as self-evident, and had no doubt that public opinion wanted tough measures. Maxwell Fyfe believed that 'there is an immense desire in every class and section of the community for vigour and action in punishing offences against the State and our war effort'; he claimed that 'in the last few months the country has been amazed by the small and almost unimportant charges which have been laid against civilians for serious offences which in fact amount to treachery'. One Ulster Unionist found the whole debate 'unreal and depressing ... at a time when as a nation we are engaged in such a herculean struggle. One would think we were living in the piping days of peace, and not faced with a life and death struggle.' Admiral Tufton Beamish saw the debate as 'an indication of the astonishingly phlegmatic character of the British people'. 'It is amazing that it should be hinted, to put it no higher, that these courts are to be set up to act as some terrible scourge on the people of this country.' Instead, 'we should trust the Home Secretary and Attorney General'.[31] There was solid support, if not evidence, for the Attorney-General's assertion that 'the important thing, if you get offences of this kind by the civilian population, is undoubtedly speed'. Maxwell Fyfe agreed that 'in the circumstances in which these courts are suggested, deterrent and speedy action is essential if they are to work at all'. The logic was one enshrined by tradition. 'One of the rights for which the Common Law exists is to preserve order, and one of the methods used consistently was the institution of military courts.'

On this view, the enlargement of state power was the natural and ineluctable expression of public insecurity. This argument was indeed advanced as defiantly on the left as on the right. Harold Laski specifically invoked (for American benefit) the experience of Norway and Holland to show that in total war 'a state which is not fully armed against its Quislings is already on the high road to defeat'; such armament meant 'concentrating immense powers in government', though he reassured his American audience that 'the calm commonsense of the British public' had recovered 'a good deal of the ground originally lost' in the ministerial panic of 1940. (Still, it was evidently not calm enough to resist the threat of alarm and despondency spread by 'wild rumors', whose criminalization Laski upheld.[32]) The indefinite scale of the powers assumed was seen as consonant with common law principle. But there can be no doubt that the creation of a new kind of juryless tribunal was a crucial complication of the simple traditional mechanism of emergency power, an acceptance that it had become (if it had not always been) unworkable in practice. Britain was moving, as Rossiter perceived, inexorably though irregularly towards the rival continental version of the state of siege. Though the House of Commons hung on to a more constructive role in the discussion of war policy than its predecessor had in 1914–18, Parliamentary scrutiny of delegated legislation was in apparently irreversible decline.[33] Silverman's sardonic 'we shall be told that in the public interest we cannot be told' expressed a widespread sense of resignation.

Still more decisively, judicial scrutiny of the executive was going the same way. By far the most contentious war emergency law (Kidd's view notwithstanding) was Regulation 18B. This crucial regulation implemented the power declared in the EPA to detain 'persons whose detention appears to the Secretary of State to be expedient in the interests of the public safety'. As originally drafted, 18B provided that if the Home Secretary was 'satisfied' that it was necessary 'with a view to preventing' a person from 'acting in any manner prejudicial to the public safety or the defence of the realm', he could make a detention order or an order restricting that person's business activities or his association with others. This immense and loosely couched power was fiercely criticized, and was substantially rewritten in the batch of amendments issued in November 1939. People were thenceforth liable to internment only if the Home Secretary had 'reasonable cause to believe' that they were of 'hostile origin or association', or had been 'recently concerned in acts prejudicial to the public safety or the defence of the realm'. The replacement of 'is satisfied' with 'has reasonable cause to believe' was to have larger significance than the draughtsman may have intended. There can be little doubt that the rewording helped to head off persistent criticism of the regulation, but the government continued to insist that it made no substantial difference to the power or the mode of its exercise. It merely meant, as the Home Secretary explained, that 'he is required to satisfy himself that it is reasonable that the person should be detained'. No objective examination of 'reasonable cause' by the courts of law was possible under the regulation.[34]

For some time the official interpretation remained immune to public scrutiny. By the end of 1941, nearly 1,800 detention orders had been made, all but 114 of which concerned people of German or Italian origin, or a member of the BUF. Many detainees applied for writs of habeas corpus, but courts always refused them on the basis of affidavits from the Home Secretary. But eventually the left-wing barrister MP Denis Pritt, acting for a detainee named Robert Liversidge (formerly Jack Perlzweig), brought an action for false imprisonment which, he reasoned, should compel the Home Secretary to tell a court the grounds for detaining Liversidge. This manœuvre ultimately failed of its immediate object, but in taking the case on up to the House of Lords, Pritt revealed the extent to which the state had moved beyond the constraints long assumed to be at the heart of the constitution.

In legal terms, the final judgement in *Liversidge* v. *Anderson* was dramatic.

The majority ruled that in the execution of Regulation 18B the term 'reasonable cause' could not be objectively examined by a court: it was a matter for the subjective judgement of the Secretary of State. The Home Secretary, Lord Macmillan of Aberfeldy declared, was

one of the high officers of State, who, by reason of his position, is entitled to public confidence in his capacity and integrity, who is answerable to Parliament for his conduct in office, who has access to exclusive sources of information . . . [and has] both knowledge and responsibility which no court can share.

In Lord Maugham of Hartfield's opinion, the minister was 'not at all in the same position as, for example, a police constable', and 'the suggested rule has no relevance in dealing with an executive measure by way of preventing a public danger when the safety of the State is involved'. The majority took the view that the subjective rather than the objective test of reasonableness was indicated by the 'personal form' of the regulation—'if the Secretary of State has', rather than 'if there is'. Thus, Lord Wright said, 'The reasonable cause can only be material in so far as it is an element present to his mind which determines his own belief.'[35]

But what gave Liversidge's case a permanent place in the constitutional law texts was the tremendous dissenting judgement delivered by Lord Atkin of Aberdovey. Atkin directly repudiated the view that 'the words "if the Secretary of State has reasonable cause" merely mean "if the Secretary of State thinks he has reasonable cause"'. The result of such an interpretation, 'that the only implied condition is that the Secretary of State acts in good faith', Atkin argued, would be 'an absolute power which, as far as I know, has never been given before to the executive'. He surveyed a vast swathe of English constitutional history, all of which, he held, bore out his contention that the term 'reasonable cause' had always up to that moment raised a justiciable issue. He saw no grounds for Lord Romer's notion that in this case 'even the most familiar words and expressions are used in other than their ordinary meaning'. The words could have only one meaning: 'They are used with that meaning in statements of the common law and in statutes. They have never been used in the sense now imputed to them.' With calculated mockery he suggested that 'the only authority which might justify the suggested method of construction' was Humpty Dumpty. This invocation of *Through the Looking Glass*, with its barely concealed charge of authoritarianism ('The question is,' said Humpty Dumpty, 'which is to be master—that's all') stung his fellow barons no less than his provocatively phrased expression of 'apprehension' about 'the attitude of judges who on a mere question of construction when face to face with claims involving the liberty of the subject show themselves more executive minded than the executive'.

What strikes one modern legal commentator as the 'passionate, almost wild rhetoric' of Atkin's closing paragraphs, may equally strike the lay reader as a mordantly rational assertion of traditional views of the public power.[36] ('I protest, even if I do it alone, against a strained construction put on words with the effect of giving an uncontrolled power of imprisonment to the minister.') And though most legal opinion at the time aligned itself with the majority, the judgement has been conspicuously lacking in support since the end of the war. Wade and Phillips typify modern legal views in observing with evident disapproval that 'the House of Lords appeared to go very near to upholding the doctrine of State necessity so decisively rejected in the eighteenth century in *Entick* v. *Carrington*'.[37] The consensus seems to be that Atkin's dissent won the day in the end—or at least saved the spirit of the law. But this characteristically English reading may be the product of an ingrained optimism less justifiable than once it was.

The outstanding critic of the House of Lords' interpretation of Regulation 18B, and of delegated legislation as a whole, was Sir Carleton Allen. At the time of *Liversidge*, 'C. K.' took issue with the leading jurists, such as Holdsworth and A. L. Goodhart, Allen's successor as Professor of Jurisprudence at Oxford, and editor of the *Law Quarterly Review*, who lent their authority to the assertion that it was impossible to apply an objective standard. Holdsworth, for instance, wrote that 'the Secretary of State's statement that he had a reasonable cause must be conclusive'. Allen's line was radically different. Fixing on the point repeatedly stressed by the majority, that 'a Secretary of State occupies a different position from an ordinary citizen', he argued, 'Surely the omnipotence and omniscience of Cabinet rank have seldom received so much deference as in this case!'[38] This aspect of the decision was 'perturbing to those who are unable, whatever may be the exigencies of war, to divest themselves of certain old-fashioned constitutional doctrines'.

'Generations of Englishmen' had been brought up to see equality before the law as a vital component of the 'Rule of Law', and to believe that for any unjustified infringement of the liberty of the subject the liability of a high officer of State was 'in no whit different from that of the meanest of the King's subjects'.

If we are to understand for the future that executive office, dignity or responsibility, whether in peace or in war, exempts the incumbent from inquiry into the reasonableness or arbitrariness of his conduct, when it affects the elementary rights of a citizen, then we must revise all our ideas. Far from sharing Professor Goodhart's enthusiasm for this vindication of executive power, we submit that *Liversidge* v. *Anderson* has put back the clock to a day when Englishmen found it necessary to declare that the power of the executive had increased, was increasing, and ought to be diminished.[39]

Behind this rhetorical trumpet blast, Allen's critique moved through the 'deep and treacherous waters' of psychology into which the majority had—unnecessarily, he thought—entered. He countered their reading of the ministerial mind with his own reading of the Parliamentary mind. Being himself a vocal critic of 'rigid liberal interpretation', he was bound to applaud the court's attempt to give effect to what Parliament 'really intended', but, as he said, such a mode of interpretation was an astonishing departure on the majority's part from 'the orthodox doctrine of English law today'. It was mysterious that the orthodoxy had been 'so suddenly and so emphatically rejected in this case'. At the root of this, surely, was the 'question of policy': references had been repeatedly made in the judgements to 'the *suprema lex* of the security of the realm'. Allen conceded that it would be mischievous for courts to 'shut their eyes to the necessities of a perilous situation, or allow mere technicalities to prevail over the demands of public security'.[40] But the essential question was—what were those demands, and who was to interpret them?

Allen insisted that 'we are here dealing, not with a mere technical obstacle to substantial justice, but with a fundamental right of the citizen, which has been more jealously preserved than any other'. The definition of the *salus populi* was perhaps too important a matter to be left to the government. Like the Parliamentary critics of Regulation 18, he saw this matter as intimately linked to the country's claim to be fighting a war of principle, and he surmised that Lord Atkin 'considers that the principle for which his voice has cried in the wilderness is of more *ultimate* importance to the health of our society than the arbitrary imprisonment of certain enemies within the gates'.[41] He held that the courts which had granted writs of habeas corpus to Wolfe Tone in 1798 and to Art O'Brien in 1923, by extending the common safeguards of liberty 'to these open and declared enemies of the State . . . did far more for the true safety of this realm than was ever done (again, and in all honesty, in the name of public order and security) by the Star Chamber in the exercise of its summary powers'.

The core of the dispute was thus the interpretation of public culture. The baronial majority, and their supporters both expert and lay (like the *Daily Telegraph*), saw the assertion of executive power as an expression of public will to win a 'life and death struggle'. Allen, by contrast, urged that the spectacle of dispassionate justice and of calm adherence to the law of the land, even in the face of imminent danger, will always be more admired by Englishmen than the immunity of executive action on any grounds of temporary urgency.

Such clashing images could not be easily harmonized; both were rhetorical distortions. Certainly many great crises in national history—or what in this kind of debate is more expressively called 'the nation's story'—had been ridden out by such restraint as Allen preached, but whether his belief still held true in 1942 is open to question. The 'English way' was at a crossroads.

Clinton Rossiter admired in retrospect 'the scrupulous and consistent regard for the civil liberties of the people maintained throughout the conflict', though he also described Regulation 18B as 'a severe break with the traditions of British liberty', and hinted that 'the lessons of the fifth column were a bit too thoroughly learned by the government'.[42] Overall, he found encroachments on the freedom of the individual 'were in fact rather trifling' (the total number of 18B detainees—1428 'at any one time'—he also described as 'trifling'). Another American commentator, Cornelius Cotter, charged that Allen was 'mistaken in assuming that the imposing list of abuses of the detention power which he marshals . . . indicates that the issue of detention should be a justiciable one'. Cotter held that even if the courts confined themselves to procedural matters, they 'may play a vital role in curbing any tendency towards capricious or arbitrary governance and yet avoid reviewing the necessity for particular governmental action in terms of the national security'.[43]

Such optimism was lost on Allen, who mocked Lord Macmillan's opinion that arbitrary imprisonment was a 'relatively mild' precaution, and refused to accept that the breach of tradition was merely temporary. Where Rossiter detected 'an all-time record for the swift abandonment of instruments of constitutional dictatorship' at the end of the war, Allen maintained, in his celebrated study *Law and Orders* published in 1945, that the Liversidge decision would give 'executive discretion an almost unlimited charter for all time . . . We shall not have heard the last of this case when the war is ended.'[44]

Thus two views can be taken of the enlargement of the public power to meet the supreme emergency of total war. One, most coherently expounded by Rossiter, saw the infringements of liberty as trivial and justifiable. Whether these qualities were interdependent is a question that his analysis tends to side-step. On the measurement of triviality, one can detect a certain ambiguity in his assessment of the long-term significance of the

Second War emergency powers: 'It remains a debatable question which feature of this most recent British venture in constitutional dictatorship was the more remarkable—the scope of the autocratic power handed to Churchill or the democratic and restrained manner in which that power was employed'.[45] Pointing to the fact that Herbert Morrison, one of the principal critics of Regulation 18B while in opposition, 'clung to this power like a bulldog' once he became Home Secretary in October 1940, Rossiter observed with a touch of complacency that 'the bitter critic of emergency powers always seems perfectly willing to use them himself when he in turn gets the responsibility for defending the nation in crisis'. (It is not clear whether Rossiter saw this iron law as a justification or simply an explanation of such use of power.) He also noted the persistence of public political activity in spite of Regulation 39E, which authorized the Home Secretary to prohibit any processions or meetings 'likely to cause serious public disorder or to promote disaffection', a provision which, he notes, 'the American people would have regarded as a shocking violation of their liberties'. In the spectacle of soap-box orators in Trafalgar Square demanding a second front he found 'conclusive proof that British democracy was still very much of a going concern'.[46]

The alternative view is that the real importance of the emergency powers lay not so much in the issue of whether the particular abrogations of liberty during the war were trivial or spectacular, as in the less visible but more thoroughgoing extension of bureaucratic immunity; it was an instance perhaps of Justice Davis's suggestion in 1866 that there comes a point in the course of increasing governmental powers over individual liberty at which a qualitative change in the nature of the state occurs.[47] As the invocation of the public interest grew, its definers were becoming less identifiable. A modern re-examination of the Liversidge decision by the constitutional lawyer R. F. V. Heuston, who is noticeably more sympathetic to the majority than has been fashionable since the end of the war, finds that the material so far available concerning the administration of Regulation 18B 'certainly suggests an alarming degree of official carelessness'. He accepts that if the information leaked to D. N. Pritt himself about the actual grounds for Liversidge's detention was correct, 'it was fortunate for the executive that the courts held that they had no power to inquire into the matter'.[48] A. W. B. Simpson has traced most of the detention documents—most important are the 'Reasons for Order' notes which were supplied to the Advisory Committee—and revealed the special logic employed by MI5. Liversidge (formerly Jack Perlsweig), who was a wealthy businessman with a chequered past, made his biggest mistake when he joined the RAF under his new name (once upon a time the stuff of romance, but now the stuff of suspicion). The Home Office moved from the argument that 'Liversidge has apparently associated with certain enemy aliens who are now interned . . . and this is strictly "hostile associations" . . . and his history makes it clear that he might be tempted by the offer of money to perform hostile acts' to the conclusion that his 'record shows that he is completely unscrupulous and it may well be that he has been recently concerned in acts prejudicial to the public safety, though we have no direct evidence of this'.[49]

The research of Neil Stammers amplifies this picture by illustrating the multiple encroachments of departmental and police powers. There is no direct evidence for his view that these were deliberate, much less for his radical condemnation of British 'democracy' as no more than a disguise for the underlying authoritarianism of the state. But in the end it is hardly less—it is perhaps more—of a public problem if the encroachments were thoughtless and opportunistic. The drift was steady and unilinear. Stammers rightly points to the intimidatory character of the EPA and Defence Regulations: their threat far outweighed their actual application. But that is in the nature of intimidation; and intimidation is surely in the nature of the state.

7

The Last Postwar

You may think you're being efficient in enforcing your laws ... but look at it, the place is burning around you

John Alderson, 1981

Fortunes of Peace

Apart from violent demonstrations in the pre-war years and the anti-Vietnam war disorder in the 1960s, the Metropolitan Police had, until recently, to contend with a relatively low level of public disorder although they frequently policed vast demonstrations.

Metropolitan Police Public Order Review, 1986

The half-century between the two Public Order Acts, 1936 and 1986, seems to divide into two very unequal parts. Crudely, from the standpoint of the 1990s, the history of English public order turns on the year 1981. 'Before Brixton', England basked in the Indian summer of the Victorian 'conquest of violence'. After it, as the montage of the Southall, Toxteth, Handsworth, St Paul's, and Tottenham riots made it impossible to see Brixton as a mere freak, the English rearranged their laboriously constructed self-image of orderliness. Two legal analysts recently observed, 'it is a rather grim statement on our own times that the power to ban marches was resorted to in March 1981 on as many occasions as in the entire period of 1951–80'.[1] For a decade war fever, terrorism, football hooliganism, and strike battles fed into a crescendo of alarm which culminated symbolically in 1990 in a tax riot in the grand manner.

In reality, the division is naturally less clear-cut. Brixton was the accelerator rather than the initiator of a sense of crisis which had already been sufficiently acute in 1977 for one of the country's more excitable writers on political violence to produce a book called *Britain in Agony*.[2] Clutterbuck's anguish was primarily the product of the 1972 miners' strike—above all of Arthur Scargill's 'battle of Saltley'—and of the 1974 Red Lion Square clash. As we can now see, worse was still to come, and as with the radical orthodoxy of a systemic 'crisis' dating from the 1960s (if not, indeed, the 1860s), there are grounds for wondering whether there may not be a mismatch between concept and reality.[3] In the sphere of public order and security, still more than in that of 'the economy', the process of crisis is evidently a matter of collective psychology as much as of objective reality. The grounds on which public awareness and anxiety feed into public policy making are especially indefinite here, and the warp between the popular and official senses of the word 'public' especially significant. Whose fears really count?

It is possible to demonstrate, as Geoffrey Pearson did in his acute *History of Respectable Fears*, that the public sense of recent sudden deterioration in security—or sudden growth in violent crime—is a recurrent one.[4] There seems always to have been a 'golden age' about twenty years ago. It may be on the basis of this perennial belief that the report on public order produced by the Society of Conservative Lawyers in 1970 started from the assertion that 'during recent years things appear to have changed, and any sense of complacency has been rudely jolted. Violence and disorder have become much more frequent.'[5] Pearson's history was a useful reminder to the people of the 1980s of how alarming the 1950s had seemed. But comparisons cannot be precise. Is all this, as Pearson implies, no more than a quirk of mass perception? It would be absurd to conclude that objective deterioration of public security does not happen. Yet it is profoundly difficult to specify what is to be measured. An individual's sense of vulnerability is conditioned by an interpretation of statistics (at best; at worst by rumour) rather than by direct experience. Interpretations can differ very greatly—hence the traditional requirement that public order offences should be such as to alarm persons of 'reasonable firmness'.

To take one offence: what are we to make of the fact that the first prosecution for affray since 1845 was brought in 1957? Does this mean that in the previous 112 years there had been no fighting 'in some public place to the terror of the King's subjects'? Or does it mean only that the profusion and looseness of common law concepts had facilitated the use of other charges for the same offence? But if so, why the shifts? And are such shifts in any way regular or linear? The view of student unrest, say, taken in 1970, when books such as Crick and Robson's *Protest and Discontent* were trying to grapple with its significance,[6] would have been unrecognizable to the writer who, casting about for reliable elements in society at the time of the general strike, noted with evident relief that the undergraduates, at least, could be relied on since 'they have no loyalty which conflicts with their loyalty to the state'.[7] Again, there looks to be an objective difference between the operational methods and assumptions of the lone police constable (with perhaps an apprehensive newly-sworn-in Special in tow) robustly confronting a crowd engaged in burning a bus during the 1926 strike, and those of the police confronting anti-poll tax demonstrators in Whitehall and Trafalgar Square in 1990.[8] Underlying expectations had markedly shifted, as had those of the London bus drivers who nowadays have to be shielded from violent assault and robbery in the same way as bank cashiers. Yet it remained possible to contend, as do Stuart Hall and others about the 'mugging' panic of 1972–3, that the change was fundamentally subjective.[9]

Subjectively, at least, there can be no doubt that the post-war decade was perceived as a time of remarkable internal peace. After the experience of total war, international peace was a moral necessity which overrode the awkward persistence of actual war from Palestine to Korea, and the cold war conducted across the iron curtain. Domestic peace had reached its apogee in the cohesion of the war effort, and the writ of the authorities had never run more extensively or more freely. A study carried out after the war by two American political scientists, Hubert Wilson and Harvey Glickman, provides an interesting perspective on British attitudes to internal security at this time. Their heterodox focus seems to have attracted little attention in Britain, maybe because it largely bore out cherished national assumptions. Wilson and Glickman found that the British people had very strong convictions about the 'British way', which were reflected in the popular attitude towards the problem of reconciling liberty with security.[10] They recognized also that there had been measurable shifts in judicial tolerance—most obviously as between *Beatty* v. *Gilbanks* and *Duncan* v. *Jones*—so that 'free assembly depends...on the prevailing climate of opinion, the spirit of the times'.[11] They marked out the distance separating British practice from the sort of abstract notion of democracy which, as we have seen, radicals such as Aneurin Bevan (himself by then in charge of the emergency organization) had been wont to invoke, and which Americans believed in trying to make real. 'The extent to which political freedom and individual liberty are dependent on the discretion and restraint of enforcement officials' must, they pointed out, strike Americans as the most remarkable aspect of the British system. There was no guarantee of individual rights; rather a continuous negotiation, the outcome of which was that 'by 1948, most British people were agreed that the civil service security program, though nasty and unpleasant, was necessary for the safety of the nation'.[12]

Wilson and Glickman fenced intelligently with the apparently paradoxical British synthesis of class-consciousness with tolerance, which they saw as lying at the core of the 'British way'. They were under no illusions about the manipulative nature of what was shortly to be christened the establishment, though some of their incidental observations indicate the extent of later changes in the modes of hegemony. (Explaining, for example, that 'the British governing classes have always felt ... that there was no better testing ground for ideas than in the sheltered confines of the lecture hall or tutorial', they held that 'a great segment of the tradition of freedom of speech and ideas centers on the universities', adding for good measure that 'the professional pride of teachers is high, certainly a reflection of their community prestige as well as of the high standards of appointment'.[13])

In pointing contrasts between the British and American experiences, Wilson and Glickman were plainly concerned to demonstrate that British tolerance provided a more resilient cushion against Communist 'subversion' than did McCarthyite witch-hunting. (Their warning that 'it is an extremely dangerous luxury for a democratic society to foster an uncritical admiration for any police agency' was aimed at the FBI rather than the Special Branch.[14]) In so doing, though, they were impelled to conclude, like Rossiter, that the secret of the British way was the combination of 'the strength of public devotion to democratic principles ... and the shrewdness of those who govern'. What would happen if the first of these declined? They could not help but recognize that 'there actually are no formal institutional obstacles to the establishment of a police state', and that 'there are few more potentially repressive statutes to be found in any nation than those presently on the books in Great Britain'.[15] The question henceforth was whether this dependence of the system on diffuse political culture was to be viewed with the traditional complacency or with a new anxiety. Was the absence of institutional guarantees a strength or a weakness in the British constitution?

C. K. Allen voiced an early warning that the expansion of state power under colour of war emergency might never recede. Emergency was the chink in the flexible armour of English liberty: a system which relied on, and indeed gloried in, the absence of formal definitions was particularly vulnerable to the incremental rewriting of the terms of public security by the authorities. In his major work *Law and Orders*, he charted in brilliant style the growth of delegated legislation down to 1945 on a scale which undermined if it did not demolish one of the central pillars of the Diceyan constitution. Later editions, in 1956 and 1965, showed that his apprehensions were only partly allayed by the following two decades of peace.

Twenty years on, he insisted that 'the whole history of the subsequent years shows that government by decree, once made, is extremely difficult to unmake and that "emergency", once it has taken hold, is a very tough plant to uproot'.[16] He began his chapter on peacetime emergency powers with the heading 'Liberty in Pledge', and displayed no confidence that it had been, or was likely to be, fully redeemed.

Allen's sardonic treatment of the slow process of 'overhaul', as the 1953 White Paper put it, of the war emergency legislation, sharpened at particular points such as the Labour administration's Emergency Laws (Miscellaneous Provisions) Act and the Supplies and Services (Extended Purposes) Act 1947. The 'bewildering variety' of powers taken under such laws amounted to 'the high-water mark of governmental powers in the whole history of English legislation' giving virtual *carte blanche* to executive discretion. Allen fixed on the somewhat lame defence of these powers put up by the Lord Chancellor, Jowitt, who admitted that they were not strictly necessary but stressed that they had never been exercised. Jowitt's remark that their mere existence 'in the background makes it possible to arrange things by agreement'—a disturbing echo of Lloyd George's wielding of DORA in industrial disputes during the Great War—was excoriated by Allen as 'legislation by intimidation', 'a conspicuous example of the fallacious and dangerous argument so often heard in defence of exorbitant governmental powers'. He did not fail to point out that Jowitt was later to attack the Conservative government for maintaining such powers, with the argument that

it is quite intolerable that the Government should ask us to pass these immense powers unless that Government can make out a case to show that they are necessary ... We ought not to go on letting the Government get away with them every year as though it were simply a matter of course to make those regulations, making profound changes in the law of the land.[17]

Despite his crushing opinion of Jowitt's 'intellectual versatility', Allen attributed the core of the problem not to governmental tyranny, or even stupidity, but to bureaucratic psychology. He quoted a remark of the Financial Secretary to the Treasury at the time of the 1953 White Paper: 'anybody who knows anything about the work of a Department of State knows how much easier it is to retain powers than to give them up. There is always the argument that we would perhaps be well advised to keep a particular power for a rainy day.' Commenting that, ten years on, there were still 'a formidable number of "particular powers" and still many rainy days which they seem to anticipate', he could not resist adding, 'Possibly the physical climate of our island has reconciled us to this dank prospect.'[18]

Whether the culture was geophysical or political, there could be no doubt that the public had ceased to be much exercised over such issues. 'Liberty in danger' had lost whatever power to mobilize opinion it had once had, even amongst the middle class, as Tony Benn was to find when he began to campaign for open government within the Labour administration of the 1970s. The Labour Party's disappointing record in this area is glancingly acknowledged by Kenneth Morgan in his recent study of the Attlee government, when he admits that the 'agreement' to renew the EPA (implying that the initiative came from the officials) was 'ominous'. But the force of this criticism is immediately softened by the observation that Labour's lack of interest in altering the adversarial nature of industrial relations, 'while Britain was encouraging moves towards *Mitbestimmung* in western Germany at precisely this period', was merely ironic.[19] Maybe the national propensity for irony has indeed been growing.

Certainly the 1950s demonstrated a striking reversal of old priorities. The class which had once accepted violent crime as the price of avoiding a national police—the victim of highway robbery exclaiming 'At least we have no Marshalsea!'—now expected an unprecedented degree of security. Had the expectation become impossibly high? Pearson's chastening account of the Teddy boy scare suggests that it had. Threats to public security were magnified out of all (retrospective) recognition. The salience of 'law and order' at the Conservative Party conference preparing for the 1979 general election, widely seen as a key element in the emergent 'Thatcherism', was directly prefigured twenty years earlier, when the conference addressed the 'sudden increase in crime and brutality which is so foreign to our nature and our country', and was asked 'Is it not a fact that our wives and mothers, if they are left alone in the house at night, are frightened to open their doors?'[20]

If the public peace were to be tightened beyond even the pitch achieved during the 'conquest of violence', something beyond the much-lauded system of police then perfected would be required. In fact, the system had never been perfected in the view of its practitioners, whatever the press and public opinion may have been. A tendency towards centralization in the interests both of general efficiency and of maximizing resources for public order maintenance had repeatedly surfaced in the past; from now on it was to be given corporeal shape.

The Chief Constabulary

> It is wrong for policing to be in any way either directly controlled or
> substantially influenced by a party political view. That is why I would
> much prefer to see the introduction of the Northern Ireland police
> authority pattern.
>
> Chief Constable, *c.*1986[21]

Few changes in the make-up of the established authorities in twentieth-
century Britain can be more significant than the steady enhancement of the
power and prestige of chief officers of police. Ministers once regarded
Chief Constables with much the same condescension as Sherlock Holmes
regarded Inspector Lestrade (and for much the same reasons); now they
concede them virtual parity. Indeed, it would not be too hard to argue that
the extraordinary achievement of the chiefs in securing working independence from both local and central government has effectively reversed
the relationship. As in so many other cases, the shift has stemmed not from
a deliberate pursuit of power but from the absence of constitutional
definitions and constraints on a tendency that was mechanical, inevitable,
and predictable from the outset. Fear of such a tendency, in fact, had been
the root of the protracted resistance to the whole concept of a professional
police. In the event, the tendency has been rendered more irresistible by the
steadily increasing difficulty of grasping and operationalizing the police
function in a society more complex than ever before.

This evolution has been markedly at variance with the traditional rhetoric
wielded by the system's operators. It will be remembered that the long-
serving Home Office head, Sir Edward Troup, was still insisting in the late
1920s that a police force 'impervious to public opinion' (such as the
German) would be 'intolerable in England' and 'contrary to the genius of
the English people'. At that time, the police themselves had been enthusiasts
of this cause: when the Central Conference of Constables debated the issue
of the 'nationalization' of the police in 1922, they expressed themselves as
convinced that 'it would be contrary to the constitutional basis of the
police system and the peculiar and perhaps the best traditions of the local
government of our country'.[22] (With hindsight one may be inclined to read
more into that 'perhaps' than was intended.) Since then, general enthusiasm
for local government has eroded, followed by the public rapport with the
police. The police were still thought to be 'viewed with respect and an
admixture of affection' in 1974.[23] But by the late 1980s it would be a
daunting task to select a manageable sample from the spate of books,
television documentaries, and newspaper articles exploring what one of

them called the 'spiral of mutual mistrust between the police and the people'.[24] This perception of possible if not imminent catastrophe struck right at the heart of the English conception of public order. The complex and continuous—in a sense inconclusive—negotiation was bending under an attempt to impose a one-sided solution.

Though the steady homogenization of the English police has played an important part in creating the version of alienation which has caused most concern, there have been strong arguments that the connection is illusory. The Royal Commission in 1960 believed that the creation of a national police force would not be either constitutionally wrong or politically dangerous. And indeed it may be that if any government had been prepared to adopt the commission's line, and radically reorganize the police, there would have been no danger. More dangerous, because more disguised, and subversive of convention, was the 'typically British compromise' (as one scholar calls it) which was actually implemented.[25] The 1964 Police Act, forthrightly described by another as a 'lurch towards a non-accountable professional police', mauled the traditional powers of the police authorities. It led to a rapid acceleration in the amalgamation of forces, a process which had really begun under the wartime Defence Regulations.[26] In 1966 there were still 117 separate forces; twenty years on there were 42. But the most striking feature of the 1964 Act was its attitude to the authority of Chief Constables. The language of section 5(1), which declared that each police force shall be 'under the direction and control' of its chief officer, is, as a recent legal writer points out, not found in any of the earlier statutes governing the police; it is, in addition, 'quite different from the definition of the position of other directors of local government services'. There appears to be little doubt that 'Parliament well knew how to subordinate the chief constable to the police authority, but chose not to do so'.[27]

The result was the special British 'doctrine of police independence'— incomprehensible to Europeans—which insists that no political body should have the power to direct those in charge of the police to use or refuse any particular policy or method.[28] Geoffrey Marshall traces the origins of this dogma to the 1930s, acidly observing that it was instantly subsumed into the panoply of ancient liberties, as 'a thing of antiquity with its roots alongside Magna Carta'.[29] This example of the marked British propensity for the invention of tradition, like others of its kind, says a good deal about the public culture which embraced it. Plainly enough it rests on the wish to give allegiance to 'the law' rather than to 'the state', and the hope that the police system could share the law's unique eminence and presumed neutrality. As a camouflage, this could not but be useful to the authorities—albeit they have, no doubt, not deliberately used it as such. At some point, however, there would arise the possibility that the sheer weight placed on this dogma would increase the subversive potential of fundamental dissent. The extent of such dissent can be measured in the confident assertions of two recent writers: according to Richard Clutterbuck (1978), 'the police act in the name of the law, not of the state', while to Maureen Cain (1982) it is evident that 'the police I am discussing are, after all, a state agency'. Dennis Kavanagh adds a significant notion through his—undocumented—confidence that 'Most people regard the police not as the agent of government but as the upholders of a concept of law and order in which the rights and liberties of individuals are balanced with the requirements of public order.'[30]

Lustgarten's *Governance of Police* elaborates a penetrating argument that, in quintessentially English style, the authorities managed to have it both ways. Only after the Great War, when local government began to pass into Labour hands, did the possibility of an open breach between watch committees and Chief Constables become serious. The doctrine of police independence emerged as 'a godsend to the Home Office'. Chief Constables would still share mainstream assumptions, so could be trusted with autonomy. 'Intervention by meddlesome Socialist local bodies could be constitutionally precluded, yet the centre would not incur any opprobrium for politically controversial policing.'[31] Lustgarten and Marshall may exaggerate the extent to which nineteenth-century Chief Constables were, as Redlich and Hurst wrote of the borough forces in 1903, 'entirely subordinated to the Watch Committee'. The analogy then drawn with military command (the Chief Constable 'has as it were' the military command of the police) suggests that the operational sphere was early accepted as quite distinct; and of course most recent dissent over the control of policing has hinged on the limits of the term 'operational'. The Great War solidified public acceptance of military autonomy, and hostility to political 'interference', at the operational level.

In any case, the role of watch committees in the definition of police functions remained somewhat mysterious in the first half of the twentieth century. When 86 Southampton policemen petitioned in 1902 against the borough council's instructions that the police should turn off gas and water in public urinals at night, on the grounds that this was (i) degrading and (ii) not a police duty, they were backed by the watch committee. The Home Office confirmed that the council was not competent to override the committee, but left it unclear whether the committee would have had the power to issue such instructions if it had wished.[32] Asked to arbitrate a dispute in Grantham in 1940, the Home Office advised the town clerk that 'on the status of the Watch Committee . . . the Secretary of State can only refer you once again to standard works on local government and police administration'. When the Birmingham Watch Committee was 'somewhat disturbed' by a remark of the Chief Constable of Staffordshire in September 1941, which 'had been interpreted as meaning that the Chief Constables take exception to any interference by Watch Committees', the Inspector of Constabulary noted that it was 'difficult to lay down any hard and fast line'; 'when a Watch Committee had a good Chief Constable, the less they interfered with him the better, but he recognized that a Watch Committee must be able to feel that they had a responsible duty to perform'. It would be hard to find a better example of the patronizing reasonableness which coursed through the process of police evolution.

Another tone was also present, if muted. The Derby Chief Constable who fulminated to the Home Office in 1942 against the interference of 'political groups' on the city council in the matter of police promotions ('I think it is high time that some of these folk got a real good rap across the knuckles') would certainly have been supported by the solid citizen of Hull who complained—'As one who was born humble and endeavoured to retain that spirit throughout fifty years of life in this city'—that open criticism of the Chief Constable was not 'conducive to the spirit of good law and order'.[33]

By this time it is clear that the special position of the police service meant that it could not be bracketed with other local government services. Chief Constables whose offices had once been housed in town halls would get their own separate headquarters; and 'In a disciplined service like the police the scope of discussions between the Branch Board and the Police Authority would, for convenience, have to be restricted in some ways.'[34] The ways that were most convenient, of course, involved excluding operational matters and, by steady extension, everything to do with internal economy, discipline, and management. By 1949 it was public orthodoxy that

The Police Authority have no right to give the Chief Constable orders about the disposition of the force or the way in which police duties should be carried out, and he cannot divest himself of the responsibility by turning to them for guidance or instructions on matters of police duty.[35]

When one expert commentator wrote in the mid-1970s that it was 'almost impossible to discover where the line would be drawn' between operational and general policing policy, he was certainly understating the problem; but he was no doubt right on the police view of it: 'To chief officers, in particular, the idea of decisions affecting the police being influenced by the political make-up of the council is abhorrent.'[36]

The shadowy path by which the police chiefs came to their present eminence is reflected in the fact that, though there were many histories of policing, no study of the Chief Constables as a group was made until the late 1980s. The conclusion of the experienced legal sociologist who carried out this pioneering research was that

what the Inns of Court Conservative and Unionist Society, Professor Goodhart, and others forecast in 1962 has come about. Rejecting a *de jure* national police force, we have ended up with the substance of one. But without the structure of accountability which the explicit proposals embodied. You cannot have accountability for something that is not supposed to be there.[37]

This very English mode of progress plainly has wide ramifications, possibly even justifying the alarm sounded by E. P. Thompson in 1979: 'the police are attaining to a position in which they can actually manufacture what is offered as "public opinion", and they are offering their occupational needs as a supreme priority'.[38]

The indirect centralization of the police service presents a classic instance of the hegemonic process, and no aspect of it is more emblematic than its central institution, the Association of Chief Police Officers (ACPO). The curious position of this body, indefinite even by English standards, locates it in what Carleton Allen christened 'the Ghost-land of the "Quasi"' (though when he began to map this land out, ACPO looked very insignificant, and the quasi-Orwellian undertones of the word 'Quango' had barely started to disturb the public consciousness). If its significance is still in dispute—and some of its members continue to regard it as merely a private club—that is all part of the 'lamentable confusion' generated by the 'question-begging . . . evasion' inherent in the proliferation of 'quasi' authorities.[39] In 1988 it still appeared that 'the exact relationship between the Home Office and the ACPO exists in a twilight world of speculation, charge, counter-charge and denial'.[40]

ACPO's significance is certainly altering by the year, and at an accelerating rate. T. A. Critchley's semi-official *History of Police* could still portray it as no more than the senior management's equivalent of the Police Federation, a professional association mainly concerned with negotiating pay and conditions. In fact, though his index listed only this reference to ACPO, his text contained another, less benevolent view: that of the minority report of the 1962 Police Commission, which referred to the role of ACPO in forging a certain historical lineage of the constabulary. Critchley implied that the operational connection between forces was made not through ACPO but through the Central Conference of Chief Constables, established in 1918–20.[41] If this was still true in 1967, it plainly was not by the time that ACPO prepared its *Public Order Manual of Tactical Options and Related Matters* on its own authority and under its own name in 1981–3. The comment of the BBC radio editor Gerry Northam that this manual marks 'the most significant shift in police strategy Britain had known for a century and a half', is hardly an exaggeration.[42] It is likely to be seen as a landmark constitutional document, as much for the secrecy in which it was prepared and issued as for the style of policing it assumes. It was restricted to officers of 'ACPO rank'; that is, Assistant Chief Constables and above. 'The matter is worrying enough', Lustgarten remarks, 'but the manner raises the more fundamental questions.' In his view it looks like another example—maybe the most subversive so far—of the concealed aggregation of Home Office control, and the deliberate avoidance of public scrutiny. 'Blurring of responsibility becomes irresponsibility.'[43]

Storm and Stress

> There is less that is nice about the British police today than at any time I can remember. I am told by the Post Office that what the handsome bobby is whispering to the blonde little girl and the darkie toddler on the ten pee stamp is 'sus-sus-sus'.
>
> E. P. Thompson, 1979

ACPO's initiative did not come—altogether—out of the blue. In September 1977 it had made a remarkable statement that 'the police can no longer prevent public disorder in the streets', and called for a 'new Public Order Act giving the police stronger powers to control marches and demonstrations, similar to police powers in Ulster'. This definite expression of preference for preventive stifling of public protest was plainly the product of a real alarm, a fear that Britain was becoming as explosive as Northern Ireland. What was the evidence for this, and who interpreted it? Compared with what was to follow in the 1980s, the evidence from the 1970s may look oddly inconclusive. (And it needs hardly be said that at no time so far in Britain has there been anything resembling the systemic connection between 'marching' and public violence that has been part of the fabric of Ulster life for over a century.) But the tempo of events has to be measured against the uncannily calm *andante* of the 1950s, when political violence was no more than a distant echo of the Fascist epoch. Between 1951 and

1960 only two processions were banned in London under the Public Order Act, and outside London only two were banned before 1964. Sensitivity to subversion, however, had hardly died away, as the tough police reaction to CND protest showed. Indeed the tightening linkage between the concepts of public order and national (i.e. state) security is vividly illustrated by the perceived threat posed by anti-nuclear demonstrators such as the 21-year-old student Adam Roberts, who later wrote an important book on non-violent civil resistance.[44] And whilst acute anxiety about the possible implications of political violence was certainly not new, it was tremendously magnified by the events of the mid-1970s.

The most tangible change came in 1974. The first person to be killed in a political demonstration since 1919, Kevin Gately, died in Red Lion Square in London on 15 June. In the previous month, the Ulster Workers' Council strike had screwed the 'ungovernability' of Northern Ireland up to a pitch sufficient to strangle the most daring constitutional innovation of the century, the Sunningdale 'power-sharing' executive. On 21 November, the most destructive IRA bombing so far carried out in Britain massacred 21 people in Birmingham. Within a week the Prevention of Terrorism (Temporary Provisions) Act was on the statute book, where it was to stay. (see Chapter 8). This was 'England's most violent year', with 45 people killed in political conflict. What did it all signify? Clutterbuck believed that 'compared with the mighty confrontation at Saltley, which had great political, social and economic significance, the events in Red Lion Square were little more than a sordid scuffle'. He was also confident that 'in the broader context of Britain's agony' the burst of terrorism in 1974 drew the people together'.[45]

This perspective owed a great deal to Clutterbuck's fascination with Arthur Scargill, who for ten years stormed about the political arena as the most convincing British incarnation of class war. The battle of Saltley raised the stakes in that somewhat mythical conflict, but the showdown was to come several years after Clutterbuck was writing. Another half-decade on, the largest significance of the 1972 miners' strike seems to be the invigorating impact it had on the defenders of public security. Jeffery and Hennessy noted that five out of the twelve proclamations of emergency issued since 1920 were generated during Edward Heath's administration of 1970–4. A system which had gone into suspended animation in the 1950s and 1960s was brought back to life. Certainly the authorities were shocked: they 'looked into the abyss and saw only a few days away the possibility of the country being plunged into a state of chaos not so very far removed from what might prevail after a minor nuclear attack', the gradations of chaos being quite carefully measured in war planning at least.[46] Secondary picketing gave the NUM the power to do what the Triple Alliance and the general strike had been unable to do in the 1920s. At the time, the victory was famous, but ten years later Jeffery and Hennessy offered the prophetic comment—more than a year before Orgreave—that the miners' triumph was 'a demon still to be exorcised in the contingency planning community'.

The service of exorcism has been conducted with both rhetoric and action. The Red Lion Square affray acted as a trigger for this process, focusing a diffuse alarm about the decline of public security. This was its principal importance, since it was in itself a marginal event, whether or not one wishes to brand it as 'sordid'. It was a special kind of riot, a faction fight or *Zusammenstoss* whose ancestry lay in the Fascist period, and whose location was determined by the National Front's habit of holding an annual anti-immigration meeting in Conway Hall. When a broad left organization (Liberation) was formed with the purpose of mounting a counter-demonstration in the same place, violence was widely anticipated, even though it seemed, when it began, to take the police and even some journalists by surprise. This undoubtedly magnified the sense of shock which is otherwise, in historical perspective, rather hard to explain. For all Bernard Levin's supercilious dismissal of 'rival gangs of totalitarians flexing their weedy muscles', Red Lion Square opened a wound in the body politic. The mainstream perception of an 'orchestrated element of malice and hate' became widespread in the street violence of 1976 and 1977. One lawyer indeed traced as far back as the 'three purposeless riots' of 1968 the public realization that 'the cherished conception of the citizen constable' had been 'rendered obsolete by the savage instincts of the age'.[47]

The measurement of insecurity was as usual made most plausible by the display of criminal statistics. The police pressure for procedural reform—in plain language 'larger powers'—which fed into the Royal Commission on Criminal Procedure, derived from the comparison of the 2.5 million crimes reported in 1977 with the 1960 total, less than one-third of that figure. The argument ably made out by the editor of *Police* in 1978 was that the police effort to contain this explosive growth was crippled by procedural rules designed to protect the innocent, which drove the police—as the Metropolitan Commissioner had admitted—to 'bend the rules'.

If the police are obliged to resort to subterfuge and, in consequence, be less than frank when giving evidence about their actions during investigation, the possibility of the conviction of the innocent is greater than if the rules allowed them to do what reasonable men expect them to do.[48]

This was obviously an intelligent approach, even if it might still be anyone's guess what reasonable men expect.

But the apparent common sense of the contention that the police were 'obliged' to bend the rules concealed the crucial question of just how they arrived at their definition of the task they were expected to accomplish. The publication next year of John Alderson's *Policing Freedom* helped to focus attention on this question, as did Jack Straw's private bill to amend the 1964 Police Act 'to extend the powers and duties of police authorities in respect of the operation and organization of police forces'. The home affairs correspondent of *The Times* pertinently linked a report that the chairman of the Police Federation had said that 'people who got hurt while attending demonstrations which turned violent had only themselves to blame' with the view of Councillor Margaret Simey, Labour spokeswoman on Merseyside Police Committee, that while a new breed of 'extremely quick' Chief Constables had emerged, 'the Police Committee has become more and more of a prestige committee that doesn't do anything... so that we have opted out as they have become more efficient. The result is that they've taken over all the policing field and the whole field of political responsibility.'[49] Straw likewise charged that 'some of the Chief Constables have not confined themselves to policing policies but have been willing to engage in explicit political controversy'.

Straw might have gone much further in suggesting that the traditional distinction between operational policy and 'politics' was untenable, and that in volatile inner-city areas the style of policing was in very large part its substance. The 1977 Notting Hill carnival provided an ominous warning of this. The street carnival itself was an institution rather marginal to the tradition of English public assembly. A straightforward—as the police thought—public protection operation, aimed against pickpocketing, blew up into a street battle. The London police were astonished that an ostensibly neutral action (albeit one which put a lot of blue coats on the streets) could be so provocative, and became more careful in their handling of such events. But bigger surprises were in store. The violence in Southall in April 1979, though it was triggered by the kind of National Front action and Asian reaction which seemed familiar, and was legally containable within the framework of the 1936 Public Order Act modified by Race Relations laws, was disturbing in its scale and intensity.[50] A police deployment as large as the crowd itself on 23 April proved insufficient to stifle the violence which led to the death of Blair Peach in confused circumstances, associated in the public view with the dubious image of the Special Patrol Group.

But the most shocking outbreak before Brixton came in Bristol, widely thought to be an amiably quiet place. A police raid on the Black and White Café in Grosvenor Road, St Paul's, early in the afternoon of 2 April 1980, led to an escalating confrontation between a crowd which gathered outside the café and the police raiding party, eventually reinforced by men with riot shields. The pattern was still unfamiliar, though it was to become less so. The Bristol police were so shaken by the unanticipated clash that at 6.30 p.m., despite the arrival of reinforcements from as far afield as Yeovil and Taunton, the Chief Constable decided that the riot was uncontrollable, and ordered a withdrawal from St Paul's. He does not seem to have considered the possibility of calling for military aid. The outcome was a night of looting and destruction as extensive as anything seen for two centuries.

This was a tremendous blow, above all to the familiar means of explaining English consensus. After the riot a *Guardian* writer pointed out that 'the Bristol disturbances have drawn out a traditional British reluctance to attribute trouble to tension and fear between the races'.[51] There had already been a number of confident assertions that this was not a 'race riot', an assertion that was to be repeated by *The Observer* on the ground that 'white people were left entirely alone'. The eminent Sunday paper took this line in spite of recognizing that 'Black Britons do not begin to believe that they belong in British society. And they loathe much of it.' It added that 'they have bottled within them an immense aggression against all authority', and went on to quote testimony that 'It is a widely held view among the police that black people here are not prepared to accept the laws of this country': whatever public-relations-conscious senior officers might say, 'Some constables and sergeants regard blacks as "coons", intellectually subnormal and inbred criminals, and treat them accordingly.'[52] In face of all this, the paper held to general orthodoxy in insisting that since 'disadvantaged white youths' shared the same aggression against authority, the real problem was an economic one. The *Guardian* took a more complex view by noting that 'There is no form of the perfect race riot, although in their different forms they usually contain a confrontation with authority in the form of the police'; 'racial but not racist' was its headline verdict.

The sheer difficulty of establishing the objective 'causes' of public disorder tends to confirm the beliefs of those who sense an underlying erosion of civilized values. A representative view is presented by Clutterbuck, and is worth analysis: 'the threat [represented by the violence of the mid-1970s] was not so much to life and property as to the public tranquillity and tolerance on which the stability of a democratic society is based'.[53] Working backwards through this skein of assertions, it is obvious that there is nothing inherently 'stable' about democracy as such—if anything the reverse—even though the principal appeal of democracy to conservatives may be that democratic societies tend to avoid the grosser instabilities which erratically afflict less legitimate regimes. The particular stability which was regarded as the chief glory of the English version of democracy may indeed be said to have been characterized by 'tranquillity and tolerance'. But did this tranquillity really derive from active tolerance, if such may be distinguished from its passive form, apathy? The stress of the 1970s made it hard to maintain the old notion of a (specially English) synergy of these rather disparate qualities. In its place appeared the more mechanical notion of 'balance', a notion most closely associated since 1974 with the public judgements of Lord Scarman.

The Scarman Effect

> Lord Scarman hit on beautifully written reports if I may say so. But the preservation of public tranquillity can't be achieved by failing to enforce the law, because if they are mugging, using drugs or whatever, they will bring the law into disrepute and therefore there will be a breach of public tranquillity whichever way you go.
>
> Chief Constable, *c.*1986[54]

Leslie Scarman became for the 1980s the hopeful symbol of judicial (and judicious) liberalism on the issue of public order. This reputation was established by a sequence of official reports on acutely sensitive public events, running from the 1969 'civil disturbances' in Northern Ireland, through the Red Lion Square 'disorders', and the mass demonstrations of the APEX dispute with Grunwick film laboratories in 1977, to the Brixton riots of 10–12 April 1981. Each of these 'Scarman reports' was distinctive in its apparent readiness to grasp painful nettles and grapple with recalcitrant constitutional problems of policing.

The most influential of his judgements was launched at the beginning of his second report. A paragraph setting out—unusually in itself—'first principles' stated that 'our fundamental human rights' include 'without doubt, the rights of peaceful assembly and public protest and the right to public order and tranquillity'. There followed a persuasively cast argument: 'Civilized living collapses—it is obvious—if public protest becomes violent protest or public order degenerates into the quietism imposed by successful oppression.' (So much, one is impelled to reflect, for the fond delusion that Georgian England was civilized. But is it really a delusion? The implication that we are presented with a choice between civilization and barbarism crumbles on closer investigation into an assumption that 'civilized living' is a function of the avoidance of violence on the one hand and quietism on the other. Civilized living depends, in this view, on liberal democracy.) Finally, the impressive prescription:

A balance has to be struck, a compromise found that will accommodate the exercise of the right to protest within a framework of public order which enables ordinary citizens, who are not protesting, to go about their business and pleasure without obstruction or inconvenience. The fact that those who at any time are concerned to secure the tranquillity of the streets are likely to be the majority must not lead us to deny the protesters their right to march; the fact that the protesters are desperately sincere and are exercising a fundamental human right must not lead us to overlook the rights of the majority.

The almost hypnotic symmetry of these phrases, energized by the magnetic attraction of the words 'balance' and 'compromise', ensured the celebrity of the judgement.

Yet the apparently familiar invocation contained a novel assumption, the notion of a right to tranquillity. In the age that discovered the 'silent majority', this notion rapidly passed into common sense; yet it was plainly at variance with English tradition. As Eric Barendt has argued, it is unorthodox to talk of the rights of groups or of society as a whole, and hard to see how the content of this alleged right could be specified. In fact, he suggests, 'the view that the majority . . . has a competing moral *right* to order and tranquillity seems wholly misconceived'.[55] The attempt to describe the dynamics of social harmony in a period of mounting conflict accelerated the abandonment of organic in favour of mechanical ideas of balance.

Scarman's subsequent public position has been unique, as a senior judge who has stepped aside from the priestly role so congenial to his colleagues of interpreting the deep truths of the common law, and who has been ready to come out into the arena of social negotiation; he even, in May 1991, led a series of radio debates on the future of the police system. In treading this path he has retained the respect of the police and of their liberal critics. His recommendations have been instrumental in stimulating a large-scale shift in policing practice, and he has been virtually the only public figure committed to monitoring this change. In pulling off these tricks of balance, tact, and reasonableness, Lord Scarman has taken his place in the great tradition of individuals on whose qualities the British way has depended. The tremendous sense of public unease generated by a decade of violent disorders has been partly assuaged by his reassuring presence. If he had not existed, it would certainly have been desirable to invent him.

At the same time, Scarman's very remarkableness underlines the intractability of the problems he was asked to solve. At both the constitutional and the operational levels, the reappraisal demanded by Brixton can go, it appears, only so far. We may, for instance, see straight away that the terms of the 1974 report are either confused or implausible. While there can be definite positive value in the repudiation of 'extremes', there can simply be no way that an effective public demonstration can occur 'without obstruction or inconvenience' to either the business or the pleasure of ordinary citizens. To suggest that these absolutes can in some sense be synthesized is a rhetorical trick which did service for a couple of centuries, but which surely became implausible in the confrontational social matrix carefully identified and described in the first part of Scarman's report on Brixton. Scarman clearly recognized the unprecedented nature of conflict in post-war British society, but maintained that traditional English consensual assumptions must and could be preserved.

Scarman approached the Brixton tumults with a very vivid sense of their larger significance. In his homely, almost banal style—his Grunwick report began with the words 'It was a long hot summer'—he opened with the statement, 'During the week-end of 10–12 April the British people watched with horror and incredulity an instant audio-visual presentation on their television sets of scenes of violence and disorder in their capital city, the like of which had not previously been seen in this century in Britain.' The attack on the police, with stones, bricks, iron bars, and petrol bombs, demonstrated 'the fragile basis of the Queen's peace'.[56] The first substantive part of the inquiry, headed 'Social Conditions', established the general argument that followed: the disturbances were triggered by a deterioration in the relationship between the police and the 'community', sharpened by the 'sense of frustration and deprivation' felt by young unemployed black people. Scarman repeatedly insisted the Brixton was not unique, and that the same underlying social problem existed in many urban areas. 'In analysing communal disturbances such as those in Brixton and elsewhere, to ignore the existence of these factors is to put the nation in peril' (2.34). But his remit had been sharply defined. He was 'not empowered to inquire in detail into [other] disorders'; he was not even empowered to investigate the continuing disorder in Brixton on Monday 13 April. What, one is impelled to ask, could be more English than this rigid, narrow focus? The opportunity for a general inquiry (akin to the Kerner Commission which followed the urban riots in the USA in the mid-1960s)[57] was deliberately side-stepped.

Within this tight focus, Scarman—aided undoubtedly by the acute public concern of which he was well aware, whatever the government's view may have been—successfully tackled the semi-constitutional issue of the police system by means of a careful operational analysis of policing methods, which amounted to the largest part of the report. The centrepiece of this analysis was the exercise in saturation policing which went under the inept code-name 'Swamp 81'. The basic problem identified by the police Commander of the Brixton Division, and accepted by Lord Scarman (after some decorous fencing with statistics) as a genuine concern, was the rapid increase in street crime. This was in the literal sense a public security issue, and the Swamp operation was a clear if rather desperate public security action. The complication was that it was not perceived as a 'law and order'—that is to say, neutral—operation by the ordinary people of Railton or Mayall Road, or, it must be added, by Lambeth Borough Council. This complication had been aggravated, if not caused, by the collapse of attempts to establish a liaison committee between the police and the Council for Community Relations in Lambeth (CCRL), and the repeated intervention of the Special Patrol Group (SPG) to assist in suppressing street crime. On the role of the SPG, Scarman's judgement was moderate: such emergency forces must exist and be available. What he condemned was the police view that it was not necessary or useful to 'consult local opinion' before launching intensive policing operations. Here he touched the core of the issue of operational independence: it was obvious that the liaison committee had been crippled from the start by 'Commander Adams' bleak and, as it appeared to its members, discouraging assertion that *he* was responsible for the public peace and would use the resources *he* believed necessary'.[58]

This was the grievous culmination of the doctrine of police independence, which Scarman restated in a somewhat nineteenth-century spirit: 'The police must exercise independent judgement; but they are also the servants of the community.' But he did not suggest any definite mechanism, other than the police authorities (which do not of course exist in London, except in the distant shape of the Home Secretary), whereby the radically altered meaning of the term 'community' could be articulated. The original symbiosis of justices, watch committees, and police had disappeared along with the close-knit fabric of gentry domination. The subsequent power of police authorities was sharply limited by the police fear of 'politicians and pressure-groups' (4.59), even where they were not such transparent fictions as in London. Scarman could only reiterate that 'there has to be some way in which to secure that the independent judgement of the police can not only operate within the law but with the support of the community' (4.60). He recognized that the main problem, where authorities existed, was that many 'are somewhat uncertain of themselves and do not always exercise the firmness which the statute [the 1964 Police Act] envisages as necessary to the discharge of their awesome responsibility' (5.62); and this diffidence was aggravated by the unwillingness of Chief Constables to trust their authorities—Scarman did not of course put it quite like this: he said that the most urgent need was 'not a change in the formal powers (or duties) of Police Authorities, but that Chief Officers of Police should take Authorities fully into their confidence' (5.64).

This form of exhortation was very characteristic of Scarman's manner of trying to infuse the traditional consensual spirit into the new conflictual society. Brixton had revealed just how far some parts of that society had moved from the time when 'the mob quailed before the simple baton of the police officer' as symbol of the moral force of the nation. Scarman bravely tackled the explosive issue of racism in the police force head-on, whilst putting it in a complex framework of social psychology. His account of the evidence made it clear that the first confrontation, over the black youth wounded in Atlantic Road on Friday evening, took its shape entirely from the fact that in Brixton, amongst people of all ages and colours, 'the worst construction was frequently put upon police action, even when it was lawful, appropriate, and sensible' (3.23). There was an element of chance in the altercation, as all analysts of crowd dynamics have noticed.

Had the crowd dispersed after making their protest, the sad little incident of the injured youth, its detail forgotten or distorted, would have followed many others into that limbo of the half-remembered and the half-imagined from which popular attitudes and beliefs are wont to derive their strength. The legend of police hostility and indifference to black youths would have been marginally strengthened: but no more.(3.24)

Instead, the arrival of a few too many police reinforcements—just how many, Scarman wisely refrained from specifying—triggered a conditioned reflex: 'the crowd of black youths felt, with some reason, that they were being pursued. They turned and fought' (3.25). (The reason, we need not doubt, lay in the demeanour of the police.)

This humane and intelligent analysis instantly opened up daunting public issues which were beyond Lord Scarman's capacity to resolve. The core question was, how was public order to be defined in what he habitually, but vaguely, called a 'plural', or sometimes 'multi-racial' society. On this question he could scarcely go beyond the bafflement of the country as a whole. Commenting that 'police attitudes and methods have not yet sufficiently responded to the problem of policing our multi-racial society', he had to add, 'British society as a whole is no better: we have not yet come to terms with ethnic diversity' (4.70). It was hardly to be expected that Scarman would offer a judgement on the general political development of the country, but it was perfectly reasonable that he should evaluate the viability of the law of public order. His legal analysis was, however, oddly conservative in the light of his wide initial perspective. It is quite striking that at no point, by way either of introduction or conclusion, did he set out a conceptual definition of the disorders. Though he plainly drew a distinction between 'disorder' and 'serious disorder', these terms appeared without explanation in the subheadings of his narrative account: a most English form of analysis. The reader can confidently deduce that the threshold between the two lies at the point when violence begins; but this in itself says very little about the nature or impact of serious disorder. (He himself undermined his own descriptive distinction later by doubting whether 'serious' had any meaning (7.46).)

At the end of his narrative section he faced, with evident reluctance ('I have reached the conclusion that it is necessary to express my opinion'), the question whether the disorders were a riot. His method of deciding this question was to rehearse the antique legal definition of riot (3.97), and to find that by 6.36 p.m. on 10 April an initially non-riotous disorder had become a riot: the turning point was when the crowd turned and stoned the police. This fulfilled the requirement that three or more persons be mutually assisting one another by force in the execution of a common purpose—in this case an attack on the police—in a manner alarming to persons of reasonable firmness. Even a judge with Lord Scarman's unusual sensitivity to modern life, however, remains a judge in the common law tradition. He expressed no doubts about the exactitude with which a medieval legal definition might fit modern social and political conditions. When he moved on, at a later stage, to discuss the submission of the Commissioner of the Metropolitan Police that a new Riot Act was needed, he decided that it was not, for two rather different basic reasons.

The first was that the new offence which the police wanted, that of failure to disperse after a public warning, would be excessively complicated and ambiguous in operation. This was a powerful objection which he worked out in some detail (7.39) by trying to envisage how the public warning would actually operate in the kind of urban setting formed by the junction of Railton, Mayall, and Atlantic Roads, in the noise and confusion that existed; how would people, even if they heard and understood the warning, know where to go, how far to go, and so on? The police might no doubt have responded that in such circumstances most people know pretty well what is expected; so, indeed, on traditional English assumptions, they should. The whole issue about the redefinition of public order in a 'plural society' turns on whether reliance can or should continue to be placed on such public culture, and Scarman ought—in the light of his social analysis—to have faced this issue openly, to encourage some public debate about it. Instead, he sidelined it with a curious argument: 'though I favour a modern restatement of the law relating to public disorder, I see no need for piecemeal reform' (7.40).

His second basic objection was the deeply traditional one that the existing law was adequate. The virtue of section 5 of the 1936 Public Order Act—with section 5A, making incitement to racial hatred an offence, added by the 1970 Race Relations Act—was that it required the prosecution to prove positive acts of criminal behaviour, rather than negative refusal to comply with instructions. Ample powers of arrest, he held, were provided by it and by the common law—albeit 'the extent of this power has given rise to a degree of uncertainty in the case law'. At this crucial juncture he simply listed without comment the string of leading cases running through *Beatty* v. *Gillbanks* to *Duncan* v. *Jones* (7.35).

Altogether, one must conclude that Lord Scarman was surprisingly diffident—in the light at least of his reputation—in confronting the large constitutional dimensions of public order. This was in marked contrast to his confident and progressive attitude to operational matters. Where he was vague on public culture, he was specific on police culture. Without going so far as to say that the behaviour of the police in Brixton was actually shaped by racist attitudes, he identified an organizational culture which had come to accept a level of public non-cooperation—if not outright hostility—that was radically out of line with the consensual assumptions on which the English police system was founded. In this he followed several expert commentators who saw in the post-war evolution of the police a steady drift towards excessive professionalism, reactive 'fire brigade' forms of operation, and general isolation from the community. His picture of Brixton was of a catastrophe waiting to happen, and one that would be repeated in similar areas unless some workable alternative to 'hard policing' could be found.

His recommendations about policing were clear and specific: 'vigorous efforts are required to recruit more black people into the police'; racially prejudiced people should be kept out of the service; the highest priority should be placed on community relations; training should focus on the prevention as well as the handling of disorder, and provide 'an understanding of the cultural backgrounds and attitudes to be found in our ethnically diverse society' (8.30); young police officers should be closely supervised, especially during 'stop and search type operations'. Scarman set out an agenda for a policing task vastly more complicated than anything envisaged when the forces were established, and requiring daunting levels of tact and discretion. 'Differing standards must not be allowed in the application of the law. But the law must be applied sensitively, as well as firmly' (8.42). 'The standards we apply to the police must be higher than the norms of behaviour prevalent in society as a whole' (4.64).

The impact of Lord Scarman's critique of policing has been visible. At least, it has tilted the balance of influence within the police towards those who advocate an adaptive response to social complexity and a more flexible negotiation of public order. In that sense it has checked, at any rate partially, a tendency for the police to assert a strongly conservative version of social order. Warnings of this tendency were already quite familiar by 1981. Even in the placid 1950s, Victorian fears of state over-mightiness persisted; a serious extended anecdote of police practice published in C. H. Rolph's *The Police and the Public* carried the message that 'because the police represent the State and are invested with special powers it is imperative that these powers be vigilantly watched': 'a conscientious officer, in exceeding his authority, may feel quite genuinely that it is, in that useful phrase, "in the public interest" for him to do so ... but his example may be used as a precedent to sustain a practice progressively different in effect'.

With just a little encouragement the police will see themselves as interpreters of morality, arbiters of taste, and judges of merit; controllers of what we shall read, see, hear and be permitted to do. This has not happened in any extreme form in England as yet, but the picture is no fantasy and no joke to anyone who has lived in a police state. And these changes don't happen with any dramatic suddenness. Freedom is eroded little by little, and the only really effective protection is the standard and vigilance of public opinion.[59]

By the late 1970s the name of John Alderson, then Chief Constable of Devon and Cornwall, had become linked with the idea of an alternative—some would say 'liberal', others traditional—mode of policing. Alderson himself began by calling it 'enlightened' policing, and in an early essay took the side of the sociologist Michael Banton against that of Lord Devlin, who had argued that the true role of the police was to fight crime. Rather, Alderson said, the police are 'one of society's major social services', and the British police had been especially successful in overcoming the conflicts inherent in their role. In terms that would endear him to Lord Scarman, Alderson insisted that 'The *balance* is of primary importance', and believed that in spite of 'the enormous problems thrown up for police in a rapidly changing society', 'the notion of consensus still has a high degree of reality in police contexts'.[60] Still, the police 'are truly engaged in the front line of change and social disintegration', and nowhere was this line more delicate than in the sphere of public order.

Alderson's view of public order was not idealized. He was impressed by an unconsciously prophetic statement by Edward Heath at the UN, who said that in the later twentieth century the pattern of warfare would be within rather than between nations.

Public order has been described as the greatest threat to society ... In a way, society is always under threat from public disorder ... civilisation itself has often been revealed as but a thin veneer on primitive passion ... What is new is the increased complexity and consequent vulnerability of society ... It is for these and other reasons that many people are uneasy about the continuing disorder in society, and the growing threat or reality of violence.'[61]

But he still espoused a deeply traditional belief: 'Public security and social peace can best be safeguarded by a people prepared to preserve its own freedom and identity. Order and liberty are not mutually opposed, but inevitably conjoined.' This antique mantra could have uncomfortable implications. In an essay written over ten years later he reiterated the keynote of the earlier title: 'a society really does get the police it deserves'. Police systems were the product of social values, not their cause. Yet it was plain to him that police systems had an inbuilt tendency to encroachment; he clearly recognized the observation made of the French police in the 19th century: 'they admitted only with difficulty that a man who disagreed with them could be honest and sincere. And they were alone in allying this moral certitude with a profound knowledge of the needs of public order.'[62]

This powerful cocktail of expertise had not been without effect in Britain. Driven by the pace of social and technical change, 'we have, over the last twenty-five years, been acquiring a police organisation which could quite easily be converted into an offensive arm' for an authoritarian government. Of course, British traditions militated against this, but the police were developing at a tangent to society: 'whilst British society has become infinitely more diversified and pluralistic, the services on which it depends, including the police, have become more remote and bureaucratic'.[63] The question was, did 'society' really deserve this? What, if anything, could it do about it? The 1981 riots were a fierce danger signal, but it was easier (at least afterwards) to read the signal than to design a response.

Lord Scarman himself publicly surveyed the process of response at intervals over the next decade. In 1985 he examined the extent of compliance with his 1981 recommendations, and found it patchy. He believed (though Alderson did not) that complaints procedures had been improved, even if his recommendation of a system of independent investigation had been rejected by government, and that the Police and Criminal Evidence Act, then passing through Parliament, would solve the problems of consultation and accountability which he had identified. He also believed that policing methods had been substantially improved, in particular by the increased importance of foot patrols, the integration of the Home Beat Officer into the mainstream of operational policing, increased 'opportunities for officers of all ranks to get to know the community they are policing', and a more balanced spread of officers of different ages in inner-city areas. Training had been significantly improved. But he found that the discipline code had not been formally amended to make racially prejudiced conduct an offence, and that the results of the attempt to improve ethnic minority recruitment had been disappointing. These remained immense obstacles to effective policing. Scarman placed much emphasis on the findings of the Policy Studies Institute study commissioned by the Metropolitan Police just before the 1981 riots, which exposed 'as the area of major public concern the safety of people on the streets', and stressed 'the many factors that make policing a diverse society so difficult'. Once more he warned that 'the disorders of 1981 have woken us up to the fragility of public order in a plural society, if that society is blind to its plurality'.[64]

In 1991 he embarked on a larger public inquiry, conducted on BBC radio, into the state of policing, starting from the question: 'Are we sure now that our consultative processes, our doctrine of accountability which is constitutional and our attitude to race and the ethnic minorities are any better than they were then?' (i.e. in 1981). 'If not there will be further disorders and further riots.' This was conceived as an inquiry not simply into public order policing, but into the whole function of the police in society—as a kind of unofficial Royal Commission. Most of its central concerns, however, inevitably reflected the problems identified by the Scarman report ten years before, and above all the problem of securing a genuine democratic input into policing without compromising the operational autonomy of the force (and Scarman was surprisingly vigorous in his insistence that the tendency to use consumerist language—'emphasising too much the salesman customer relationship'—in describing the 'police service' risked blunting awareness of its true nature as 'a citizen force'). The basis of the public co-operation that every police officer knew he needed was that the police should be doing what the public wanted. What the public want is above all protection: 'they want what Sir Richard Mayne called tranquillity, what you and I would call the maintenance of public order'.

This inquiry showed that the underlying problems of police-public relations, which are after all rooted in the tension between the functions of servant and master inherent in the nature of the police, as indeed of state authority generally, were not suddenly going away. Scarman gave the Metropolitan and other forces credit for making great efforts, against the grain, to alter police attitudes, but the inquiry showed a noticeable difference between the rhetoric deployed by the higher ranks and the reality reported by the lower. The most recent model, an experimental system operating in Surrey, called 'total geographic policing' (TGP), represents a deliberate attempt to eliminate the two-tier structure criticized by Scarman, and to increase interaction between police and public. The system seems to be well liked, but even here the line between beneficent preventive visible police presence on the streets ('they just like to see more policemen, they feel more secure, by seeing a uniform round where they live, where they work, where they shop'), and the provocative presence which triggered the 1981 riots, is recognized to be a fine one. The tension between the two functions of police remains unresolved. As one Surrey sergeant put it,

I found that with our system of policing, with officers on the beat, I am able in a non, what I call a non-confrontational situation to talk to people, to have a chat with youngsters on the street without having to get into agendas. I can speak directly to them. I fully endorse and I love the system of actually being on the street. The dilemma is then responding to emergency situations, yes.[65]

The duality of the police is very noticeable in the shape of its internal hierarchy. The structure of authority is clear enough, but the command relationship is significantly different from that in other 'disciplined' services, especially the armed services. It is not a mere etymological accident that the term 'officer' is applied to all ranks: the special customary and statutory powers of the ordinary constable assume a high degree of individual responsibility, a stance radically distinct from the quasi-military formation required during serious public disorder. When large-scale police deployments are made, the function of senior officers becomes correspondingly different from their normal role (well expressed in the use of titles like 'inspector' and 'superintendent' rather than military ranks). Modern emphasis on 'leadership' in police training may be out of place, as one of the BBC's contributors—an ex-soldier—made very clear.

The problem I have is that we talk about leadership, where the first and second line in the police force, they're not leaders of men, they're supervisors ... [and] the thing that has struck me is, there's a distinct lack of supervision. ... I'm left entirely to my own devices, no-one actually turns round and says "this is what we should be doing and how we should be doing it" ... since [I joined] we've had a new chief constable, a new divisional commander, a new sub-divisional commander, a new shift inspector; it's made no difference whatsoever to the way I do my job.[66]

A considerable variation in the patterns of responsibility will have significant implications for the ability of the police to define an approach to public order. Whether or not the lower ranks accept the utility of curbing racism in the force, they seem unlikely to abandon their belief in force itself. One of the respondents in Roger Geary's illuminating survey of police attitudes after the 1984 miners' strike commented

These senior officers, they're all into this low profile, softly, softly, community relations approach ... I think we've been too softly, softly for too long and that's a view shared by many ordinary policemen ... We ought to just once move in hard—that's all it would take and there would be no more problems. These senior officers, well, they're too scared to do that. They're worried about questions being asked in Parliament, about their chances of promotion, about being criticized, about whether they'd have to explain to Scarman why they did this, that or the other ...[67]

Towards the Second Public Order Act

> It provides the context in which our democracy can live and develop without threat, intimidation, disruption and violence.
>
> Giles Shaw, Home Office Minister, 1986

Scarman's impact on the grand constitutional issue of public order may, as has been suggested, have been somewhat less substantial than his influence on police attitudes. In a way he seems deliberately to have stood aside from what was becoming, by 1981, an unprecedented public debate on this issue—and the issue was screwed up to a still higher pitch by the violent confrontations of the 1984 miners' strike and the unparalleled ferocity of the Tottenham riots in 1985. By restricting his attention to the somewhat academic question of whether the Brixton disorders were technically a riot, and dismissing the need for substantive legal reform, he skirted the question whether the post-war period had seen the emergence of novel modes of collective action and a real increase in the propensity for public violence. It was just such questions that had exercised the Society of Conservative Lawyers in their pioneering inquiry of 1970. They identified five major types of 'manifestations of violence and disorder':

1. mass demonstrations and processions with their attendant danger to people and property;
2. passive manifestations in the form of sit-ins and the like, involving the possibility of obstruction;
3. disruption of public meetings with consequent denial of freedom of speech;
4. mass invasion and occupation of houses and other buildings or property without legal right;
5. gang warfare in public places.[68]

This menu obviously bore the imprint of its time—a time when, amongst other things, football hooliganism and flying pickets had not come to be seen as an epidemic problem. This in itself points to some of the difficulties involved in incorporating novel forms of collective action with traditional ones. The report was not alarmist in tone, but pointed out that some new developments might go beyond the old provisions of the law, which 'tended to be scattered, diverse, and in some cases archaic and lacking in clarity'. It found the public order law generally adequate except for 'manifestations of violence with a political content or purpose', and these were plainly what seemed most worrying. (While it asserted that 'we have scarcely experienced in this country gang-warfare in the sense in which it has been seen in some other countries', it was concerned to differentiate such mindless violence from the political kind.) Even peaceful squatting could be viewed as part of 'a more generalised revolt against authority and public order' and therefore intolerable.

This underlining of larger political issues was an important aspect of the report, which naturally (being produced by a political party) proceeded from the sense that public concern was growing, and that appropriate responses to novel problems must be publicly negotiated. More important still, perhaps, was the couching of the basic problem in terms of the need 'to achieve a synthesis of freedom and order'. Over the next decade, the first aspect became exceptionally contentious, while the second slipped quietly into the backwaters of political argument: in place of synthesis there would be balance. The Conservative Lawyers worked on the traditional assumption that their perspective on public order issues would shape that of the mainstream. This unconscious process of 'constructing consensus' was opened up to more intense scrutiny by Stuart Hall and others in their radical reinterpretation of the phenomenon of 'mugging' in the 1970s. Their book *Policing the Crisis*, first published in 1978, started from an attempt to analyse the 'moral panic' which blew up in 1972 over street robbery, and grew into a large book with the pregnant subtitle *Mugging, the State, and Law and Order*.[69] Despite its bulk, and its somewhat diffuse structure, it was reprinted nearly every year over the next decade, and remains the leading example of a Gramscian analysis of the processes by which hegemony is established and maintained. The radicalism of this study—the argument that 'crime waves' are created not by cold statistics but by public sensibility—no doubt limited the extent to which it was accepted, but it represented a severe blow to the traditional rhetoric of synthesis. It would be harder in future to see synthesis as the natural product of English moderation, rather than the tireless manipulation of public symbols by a dense network of agencies from the so-called 'primary definers' outwards.

By the time of Brixton it ought certainly to have been harder, whether or not one accepted Hall's political conclusion—that Britain had reached 'the exhaustion of "consent"'—to preserve the belief that the idea of order was neutral. Lord Scarman's cautious generalities about the 'plural society' indicated the extreme difficulty of specifying the precise content of anything that might be described as consensus in the 1980s. Yet a descent into true multiculturalism would be impossibly dizzying. The attempt to establish what forms of violent disorder were to be absolutely resisted must be made. This attempt can be followed through a remarkable sequence of investigations, by the Home Affairs Select Committee of the House of Commons, the government (in the form of a Green Paper in 1980 and a White Paper in 1985), and the Law Commission.[70] Though published in sequence, these should perhaps be seen as proceeding more or less in parallel, and in counterpoint with the explosive public disorders of 1981, 1984, and 1985. The result of all this was the new Public Order Act of 1986.

In spite of this novel cogitative flurry, there was still 'no attempt to look at the whole of the law of public order from a coherent principled standpoint'.[71] Adherents of the English way may find this reassuring. The inquiries were driven by particular problems, and mostly touched on larger definitional issues in the glancing way familiar in such public discourse. The select committee, for instance, was content to begin from the acceptance that there was no such thing as freedom to demonstrate: 'in English law such freedoms are no more and no less than the right to do anything that is lawful'. Its task was to inquire whether the 1936 Public Order Act went far enough 'to protect the well-being of the people and to keep the peace', since the very substantial increase in the number of processions suggested that the POA was 'now proving inadequate to keep those tendencies in check'.[72] The situation harked back to the 1930s, when there was a 'widespread apprehension' that events might get seriously out of hand, since other countries had witnessed 'a level of public disorder and security which challenged, and in some cases destroyed, normal political processes and lawful authority itself'. This typically anecdotal way of approaching the fundamentals of public peace was linked with the proposition that in the mid-1970s a style of aggressive street politics emerged which caused 'growing concern'; there was 'much public disquiet that expenditure on such a scale should be considered necessary to deal with the activities of what many would see as extremist and self-indulgent groups' (there was, significantly, less public concern about the cost of policing football matches).[73]

The Green Paper likewise began with an attempt to flesh out the view that the amount of disorder was substantially greater than in 'the relatively recent past', and that there was a greater willingness to resort to violence. Obviously the Southall clashes of 1979 loomed largest at that moment, but the increasing frequency of disorder created new issues. Most significant amongst them was the cost, social as well as financial: the idea of 'economic and social disruption', which had long underpinned the system of formal emergency powers, was now introduced into the arena of general public peace. Disorders disturbed the normal pattern of community and individual life, causing major inconvenience, and even—perhaps more ominously— damaging the harmony between 'different sections of the community'.[74] Things were likely to get worse, because the 'immediacy' of contemporary public order problems was enhanced by television. 'The effect which all this has on the attitude of demonstrators . . . should not be underestimated.' At the same time, the Green Paper was cautious in proposing any substantive changes in the law; after considering the idea of introducing a statutory right to demonstrate, it suggested that this would complicate the law and make it more uncertain; but it also accepted that the difficulty with the idea of disruption to the community (as with the idea of 'offensiveness') would be defining the test in a way which could be sufficiently precise and avoid undue interference with democratic rights.[75] Interestingly, though, it held that 'serious public disorder', which Scarman was shortly to describe as a meaningless term, as used in the 1936 Act was 'a criterion that was, as far as possible, both objective and independent of political considerations'.

The expectation that a truly unpolitical consensus could re-emerge lived on: anything else would be too difficult to work out. Change must be governed by tradition. As the 1985 White Paper put it, the uncodified nature of public order law 'reflects the slow processes of historical development'. It was still largely based on common law, with 'the restrictions that Parliament and the courts have felt necessary over the years to impose on the freedom to assemble in public, in the interests of maintaining order'.[76] The power of formal law had visible limits in this sphere. Like the Green Paper before it, the White Paper reminded us that 'the avoidance of disorder depends ultimately on the willingness of us all to observe the law'. Both documents leant squarely on Lord Scarman's observation that British public order policing envisaged 'a society agreed upon essentials'. But of course the whole problem by the 1980s lay in finding these essentials. Invocation of the past no longer did the trick (even if, as Brixton burned, the Home Secretary turned from his television screen to the Hampshire pastoral outside his back windows, and found comfort in the old heart of rural England.[77]) The appeal of Scarman's emphasis on balance, which was headlined in the White Paper ('The Government's Approach: Balancing Freedoms'), was that it provided a mechanism for asserting the countervailing 'rights of the wider community', which the government was in a special position to defend.

In the circumstances, and after an unusually (if not uniquely) careful public preparation, the eventual Public Order Bill and the debate it occasioned were something of an anticlimax. The Parliamentary debate was scarcely more than a rehearsal of familiar pieties on the part of government and opposition. None the less, the fact that this was so has its own significance. The Home Secretary, Douglas Hurd, presented the bill in the traditional manner as a pragmatic adjustment of a pragmatic law (the 1936 Act) which had 'stood the test of time pretty well'; only there was now a 'need to update the framework of public order to ensure that it is strong enough'.[78] The government was responding to the Law Commission's suggestion that public order offences should be clearly restated in modern language. It was also taking cognizance of the response to the White Paper which 'convinced us that we must act to provide the police with more effective powers to protect the public against hooligan behaviour. But', he insisted, 'we have no desire to use the criminal law to enforce a particular social standard.'[79] The government's notion of a social standard was conveyed in quasi-theoretical—but really aesthetic—terms by Hurd in the preface to his speech. 'Public order is the fundamental social good'; 'the right to go about one's lawful occasions in peace is the underlying human right without which all others are nugatory.' The government's ideal was 'quiet streets and a peaceful framework for our individual lives'.

This beguiling picture was further touched up at the end of the debate by Hurd's junior minister, who contended that the bill was 'the most important piece of legislation to be brought before this House for decades. It provides the context in which our democracy can live and develop without threat, intimidation, disruption and violence.'[80] The contention that there was a pressing need 'to prevent the traditional freedoms of assembly and protest from turning into weapons of intimidation and harassment' was familiar from the Green and White Papers, and directly echoed the resonant language of Joseph Chamberlain a century earlier: 'I say that liberty is a mere phantom unless every man is free to pursue his inclinations, to consult his interest within and under the protection of the law.'[81] Chamberlain was then engaged in constructing a Liberal response to the systematic intimidation, culminating in the 'boycott', which was the principal weapon in the Irish land war of the 1880s (and in the process moving from radicalism to conservatism). The 1980s equivalent was even harder to grapple with: an odd compound of aggressive strike picketing, street crime, football battles, lager loutery, hippy convoys, and a faint echo of student activism. The central question was, was all this a threat to democracy?

The opposition view was that it might, still, possibly be part of democracy. But since the Labour front bench shared the same view of the electoral significance of the 'law and order' issue, it trod warily. Gerald Kaufman announced luridly that 'fear of crime has now become a plague, casting a grim shadow across Britain', but suggested that though the bill was stuffed with new offences and penalties, there was 'no evidence that it would have the tiniest effect in preventing disorder'. To say what such evidence might be was a problem for both sides, and Kaufman was on firmer ground in focusing on the potentially far-reaching idea of 'disruption to the life of the community'; this, he thought, would force the police to make big social judgements like 'the right to demonstrate is less important than the right to shop'.[82] Clive Soley pushed this line further with the declaration that 'the use of the word "disruption" is most dangerous to democracy'.[83] Chris Smith touched a sensitive point in suggesting that the bill was simply 'an attempt by the Government to seen to be doing something'. But it was the minority parties which put up the weightiest criticisms. Robert Maclennan of the SDP pointed out that the Home Secretary's introduction had been 'extremely exiguous' and had provided no explanation of the government's 'basic philosophy and objective'; 'he did not say how he felt that the changes he was proposing would increase police effectiveness to control an unacceptable breakdown of public order'. The bill 'contains an element of gesture'. With equal acuity he noted that the government practice was to 'confuse law and order by linking them inextricably'; but he did not go on to develop this perception. He admitted that 'considerable public disquiet' had been caused by 'some substantial breakdowns of public order in recent years', but held that

there is not the same pressing need for an extension of these controls as there was perceived to be in 1936. Merely because fifty years have elapsed is not a good reason, as the Home Secretary seemed to suggest, for enlarging the powers in the way that he proposes.[84]

The Liberal Alex Carlile reasserted the belief that 'the public hold dear, as a matter of tradition and expectation, the freedom to make peaceful and orderly protest against Government and public authority', and fixed on the absence of any legal right to this freedom on which democratic legitimacy rested: the answer was a Bill of Rights.[85]

The fiercest attack on the bill was mounted by Dafydd Elis Thomas of Plaid Cymru: 'This is not a public order Bill; it is about expanding the control of the state over public disorder.' If this introduction of the s-word were not shocking enough, Thomas went on to contend that 'much of that disorder is created directly or indirectly by the activities of the state'. The really central question, he said, was the role of the state in civil society. Was it coercive or participatory? Conservatives had a definite view of society; they saw 'society as out there to be controlled. . . . They do not recognize the essential interaction between the state and civil society at all levels of society and the operation of the state.'[86] Their opponents needed to insist that 'direct democracy is part of our lives'. This view of the state was, of course, meaningless to those Conservatives who believed themselves to be busily engaged in rolling back that ominous abstraction, and who probably (if they agreed with their leader) did not even believe in the existence of that other abstraction, society. The true backwoods, grass-roots perception, was plainly put by Warren Hawksley, who dismissed the 'NCCL version' of the threat to liberty with contempt:

My constituents fear being mugged and attacked, and believe that the police act as a deterrent and are their friends. That is how it should be; that is how the majority of the public believe it is ... People have had enough. They have seen enough on television.[87]

Hawksley was to lose his seat in the following year's general election, but his assessment of majority opinion may have been no less accurate for that.

8

Threatening the Life of the Nation

Those who make an insurrection in order to redress a public grievance, whether it be a real or pretended one . . . are said to levy war against the king, though they have no direct design against his person, for they insolently invade his prerogative by attempting to do that by private authority which he by public justice ought to do, which manifestly tends to downright rebellion.

William Hawkins, *Pleas of the Crown*, 1716

The State of Siege 1920–1969

These opposing sentiments had by that time built up tensions and pressures within the community of such a kind that incidents comparatively small in themselves could readily lead to explosions of violence of a dangerous and serious character.

Cameron Commission Report[1]

In the 1970s the constitution of the United Kingdom and the process of law entered into a new kind of crisis. In some obvious ways, the turmoil of Northern Ireland after 1969, whatever it be labelled—and almost every label from protest through riot to terrorism and civil war has been applied to it at some stage—resembled earlier Irish crises. At least two big 'Ulster crises' had been dealt with, or endured, over the previous century, together with many more outbreaks of serious rioting, systemic political, and sectarian communal violence.[2] The general parameters, and even the precise geographical fault-lines, of such civil conflict seemed to many observers to be transmitted with disconcerting exactness from past ages. Prominent amongst the signs of petrifaction was the eviternity of the state's chief antagonist and tormentor, the Irish Republican Army. But Northern Ireland was not in a time-warp. There had been vital changes, and these actually drove the caustic effects of domestic strife deeper into the political fabric than ever before. The constitutional structure created by the 1920–2 settlement ensured that even the oldest impulses would be forced into new forms and methods. When these forms proved ineffective, the resulting paralysis stretched the 'crisis' out over decades. After twenty years, a crisis becomes something less dramatic but more corrosive.

The reirruption of the Irish Question into British political life was shocking. The shock was of course the greater for the fact that for half a century the persistence of fundamental dissent had been disguised by the semi-detachment of the six counties from the mainland system. This benign neglect had, unfortunately, malign results. It might, of course, be said that malignancy was programmed into the six-county state by its very rationale. The idea of creating a sectarian jurisdiction had always been repugnant to British consensual assumptions. The idea of 'partition'—the emotionally charged and semantically violent term inevitably applied to any kind of special status proposed for the Unionist-dominated north-east—was still more abhorrent to nationalists, so much so that they practically abandoned any chance of negotiating it rationally. Thus they ended up with probably the worst possible partition-line they could have got, and then proceeded to worsen the position of nationalists (that is, Catholics) within that border by refusing to recognize the legitimacy of the northern administrative system.[3]

All this was the more or less inevitable product of the assumptions built into Irish nationalism over the previous half-century, which conflicted diametrically with those of Protestant loyalism. To this extent, the exasperated insistence of many present-day politicians that historical analysis of the partition process is unhelpful because 'we have to deal with things as they are', represents a necessary realism. All the same, the mechanisms by which things came to be this way can tell us a great deal about the limits of the possible. A British disinclination to tamper with the precarious settlement of 1921, or even to subject it to scrutiny, played a major part in permitting the constitutional distortions for which Northern Ireland became notorious. The attitude of resignation expressed by Whitehall officials in the 1930s, when the Fianna Fáil government of Eamon de Valera began systematic protests against discrimination in the six counties, reached back at least as far as the initial separation of the Belfast administration from Dublin, well before the passage of the Government of Ireland Act.[4]

At the core of this, as of the whole home rule question, lay the issue of public order. The threat of ungovernability was the principal means of convincing Asquith and Lloyd George that 'Ulster' must not (because could not) be 'coerced' after 1912. Actual order maintenance was the salient administrative issue in 1920, when Belfast was ravaged by the most ferocious riots since the first home rule crisis in 1886—more murderous in fact than all the nineteenth-century tumults put together. This was riot in the grand manner; street warfare rather than mere disorder or protest. Its form was traditional even if its locale was modern: an attack on the Catholic workers at Harland and Wolff's shipyard by several hundred apprentices and rivet boys, surging out from a mass meeting of 'Protestant and Unionist' workers in the Workman and Clark yard on 21 July. Five thousand Catholics were driven from their work-place, and the pursuit spilled across into the residential areas of east and north Belfast, where Catholic homes and shops were looted and burned day after day for the next week. As in 1886, the police were paralysed by the intensity of the violence—though this time it was not aimed directly at themselves—and merely waited for exhaustion or rain to dampen loyalist ardour. But this time the dampening, when it came, was little more than a transition to prolonged guerrilla conflict, which persisted for the next two years and took the fearsome total of 428 lives.[5]

During the Anglo-Irish Treaty negotiations late in 1921 the 'pogrom', as the Irish republican leaders labelled it—without exaggeration in this case—was still in spate, and Michael Collins did his best to keep it on the table as a cardinal issue in determining the powers of the Belfast parliament. He was stymied not merely by Lloyd George's negotiating skills but by the fact that the violence had itself impelled the creation of a Northern security apparatus a year earlier. The substance of the system which was to endure for fifty years was already in place. At its core was the Protestant citizen militia. In mid-1920 its most recent embodiment, the Ulster Volunteer Force, was resurrected. Like its predecessor it sprang from local initiative, provided this time by Basil Brooke in the border county of Fermanagh. Brooke called his unit the Fermanagh Vigilance Force, and was frank about its primary function: 'I felt that the hot-heads on the Ulstermen's side might take the matter into their own hands if not organized.'[6]

The outbreak of communal warfare persuaded the government that the UVF must be brought under a greater semblance of official control. Despite the hostility of General Macready, who thought that the RIC was no longer capable of making any effective response to the IRA, a new Special Constabulary was enrolled as a police reserve. It was composed of three classes, A, B, and C, of which the first (full-time specials, a rather unattractive career option) and last (the somewhat vaguely framed emergency reserve) soon withered away, leaving the part-time 'B Specials' as the most distinctive prop of the emerging Northern Ireland regime.[7]

The nature of that regime and the precise constitutional status of the territory it kept safe from Dublin rule look like vital issues from the post-1969 viewpoint, but they were not directly addressed by those responsible for setting it up. The only people who had an interest in exploring and defining—with of course the aim of restricting—Northern Ireland's powers, the Irish nationalists, did not get far. Once Collins became joint leader of the Provisional Government in Dublin, he pursued a mixed policy of negotiation and boycott which has generally been judged ill-conceived, and which was certainly not very effective. His death robbed the Free State's posture of both continuity and credibility, the months of increasingly bitter civil war which followed it cementing the Unionist belief in the anarchic violence of the Irish.[8] Behind the smoke of Sinn Féin's internecine combats, Northern Ireland proceeded to define its own powers. The most pungent and enduring symbol of this process was the Civil Authorities (Special Powers) Act (Northern Ireland), passed on 7 April 1922, just a week before the schismatic IRA occupied the Four Courts in Dublin and started the civil war.

The Special Powers Act empowered the Northern Ireland government 'to take all such steps and issue all such orders as may be necessary for preserving the peace and maintaining order'.[9] Though it did not suspend habeas corpus, as some historians have stated,[10] it resurrected the courts of summary jurisdiction composed of two or more resident magistrates to try a wide range of offences created by regulation: the 1934 edition of the *Regulations and Orders* ran to 32 pages. One of its most characteristic provisions was section 2(4): 'If any person does any act of such a nature as to be calculated to be prejudicial to the preservation of peace or maintenance of order in Northern Ireland and not specifically provided for in the regulations, he shall be deemed to be guilty of an offence against the regulations.' Section 5 permitted the two-magistrate courts to order that a person 'if a male, be once privately whipped' in addition to any other sentence imposed for offences against the 1883 Explosive Substances Act, the 1916 Larceny Act, the 1920 Firearms Act, or convicted of arson or malicious damage. Regulations authorized amongst other things the imposition of curfews, closure of licensed premises, restriction of public meetings, requisitioning of land or vehicles, and prohibited possession of unlawful documents, membership of unlawful associations, or collection of information about the police.

Views of the SPA were sharply polarized on political lines. To northern Unionists it was a necessary and reasonable defence against enemies of the state who were all too evidently numerous and active. To Nationalists it was the 'Flogging Bill', a mark of their permanent subordination, oppressive even when—as was mostly the case—it was held in readiness rather than directly applied. No one doubted that it was aimed at one community. A fortnight before it received the royal assent, Michael Collins fiercely denounced it as a means of persecuting Nationalists (by which he meant Catholics, since religion unlike voting preference was publicly determined), and threatened that the Free State would have to retaliate with similar legislation, thus widening the chasm between North and South.[11]

In spite of this, the British government did not make any move to delay or modify the Act. One reason was that it was portrayed by the Northern Ireland government as a lineal descendant of the Restoration of Order Act, necessitated simply by the fact that the Westminster government had promised Sinn Féin not to apply UK legislation to any Irish disorders.[12] Its tenor was, however, different; it was not intended to involve the army in the judicial process, and its powers were more loosely defined. Indeed, it was criticized by one member of the Northern parliament as being too long, since 'one section would have been sufficient: the Home Secretary [*sic*—in fact the Minister for Home Affairs] shall have power to do whatever he likes'.[13] And the Free State, on the brink of civil war, was also moving towards an even more Draconian public safety law, the first of a series of such measures over the next twenty years.[14] The apparent reasonableness of the SPA was buttressed by the fact that it was in the first instance temporary. After a year, however, the twelve-month law was renewed, and so on again annually until 1928, when it became a five-year law. Finally, in 1933, it was made permanent. Thus was instituted what the standard constitutional law text calls 'a radical departure from the procedural safeguards traditionally and justifiably regarded as desirable for the preservation of civil liberties', and the National Council for Civil Liberties labelled 'a permanent machine of dictatorship'.[15]

The hyperbole and paranoia so richly larding criticisms of the SPA are understandable in the context of the general drift of the six-county regime towards permanent confrontation. This was marked most emphatically in the 1920s by the termination of the system of proportional representation created by the Government of Ireland Act. It would indeed be hard to exaggerate the significance of this shift. The inclusion in this vital constitutional statute of so drastic a divergence from British conventions demonstrated an acute awareness that the law would not be acceptable unless it guaranteed protection to minorities in both northern and southern states. It really seemed to mark the beginning of a new epoch, or at least the possibility of such a beginning. The northern state's 'unseemly haste' to abolish proportional representation was a correspondingly bitter and lasting blow to the idea of consensus.[16]

It had its root in the extraordinary absence of systematic discussion concerning the size of the Unionist territory. Only the journalist St Loe Strachey, who was ready to talk about 'North-East Ulster' rather than Ulster *tout court*, seems to have seen the imperative need, from the Unionist standpoint, of securing a politically homogeneous area, even if it meant a 'jigsaw puzzle' of a border.[17] Although, as Nicholas Mansergh has observed, 'it was in Carson's, not Sinn Féin's interest that if there was a boundary, it should rest upon a defensible foundation', the Unionist leader seems to have taken no thought of anything but the six-county area (as being the largest that could be held indefinitely). In traditional military terms, the border he secured was more 'defensible', but such terms were totally irrelevant in the actual circumstances; only Strachey's ethnic homogeneity had any utility. Even a smaller territory would, Mansergh notes, 'still have left the Northern Ireland government with a formidable assignment, but not one of the order of magnitude they assumed'. The Boundary Commission provided another chance to re-engineer the border, and it was deliberately passed up.[18]

The product of this primitive carve-up was a haunting anxiety about public security—the 'siege mentality'[19]—which showed through in discrimination pervading the fabric of the Ulster polity, economy, and society. From the gerrymandering of constituency boundaries, through slanted distribution of jobs and housing, to the symbolic censorship of the 1954 Flags and Emblems Act (allowing the police to ban displays of the Irish tricolour), the system articulated the centrality of the 'constitutional issue'— that is, the opposite views of the legitimacy of the border—to the self-expression of the Protestant Province.[20] It was this which ruled out from the start not merely any notion of 'power-sharing' (a notion with no direct linkage to proportional representation) but any recognition of the full rights of the minority. What those rights might consist of was a question which would eventually become overwhelming, but was of course not raised at the outset. No bill of rights was drafted to underpin PR by relating the franchise to the traditional battery of civil rights. Most of these rights remained as well protected in Northern Ireland as in Britain. (Habeas corpus was not suspended until 1971, and then under British pressure.) The case of the northern minority turned on a much wider conception of rights, in which social and economic rights amplified the older kind, such as religious toleration and equality before the law.

Only after 1945 did such an enlarged framework of civil rights begin to offer the minority an attractive alternative to the internal emigration which had been their first response to partition. Their refusal to accord legitimacy to six-county institutions by participation had substantially worsened their material if not their moral position. Labour agitation in the early 1930s brought their nearest approach to intercommunal solidarity; but as disorder intensified, traditional sectarian divisions reappeared.[21] The Irish Republican Army, which had been uncertainly Marxized in the early 1930s, reverted to a more familiar role, defending Catholic territory. Thus the majority perception of disorder as public crime was reconfirmed.

Always, until the 1960s, the threat or promise of republican violence persisted. The possibility of forcible rescue did not evaporate until the end of the IRA's last 'border campaign'. When it abandoned its attempt to liberate the North by physical force in 1962, the IRA demonstrated that it retained its Fenian belief in open insurrection. But in the interim it had toyed with a very different strategy. Terrorism was the rationale of the brief mainland campaign led by the IRA Chief of Staff Sean Russell in the late 1930s. Mainland operations naturally stepped outside the boundaries of guerrilla action, whose implication of popular support had been exploited by the IRA in the Anglo-Irish war. The drastic anti-terrorist legislation enacted in both London and Dublin in 1939 showed that the IRA had no visible constituency in either island at that time.

It was, however, to be provided with one by the Unionist reaction to the civil rights movement in the 1960s. No more fateful example of the fusion of different senses of order can be found in modern British history. Physically, civil rights demonstrations presented a straightforward public order problem: even in an aggravated form they were much like the situations being faced by police forces in many countries in the late 1960s. Everywhere there were fears of social breakdown. In Northern Ireland, however, official perceptions were shaped by a specific identification of minority rights with a threat to state security. This was not an issue of national security, since the 'nation' to which the Unionists believed themselves to belong did not perceive it as such. The gap that opened up between these perceptions eventually destroyed the Northern Ireland polity. The decisive moment was the 'battle of Burntollet' on 4 January 1969, when the police stood aside to let enraged loyalists attack a large civil rights march from Londonderry to Belfast.[22] The organizers of the march, the radical People's Democracy group, were well aware that such an attack was possible, and some of them may have been counting on it to radicalize their people.[23] All the more reason, one might think, for the authorities to exert control over their 'own' people.

In such circumstances, the decision to allow the loyalist 'marching season'—the annual celebration of the Catholic defeats in 1690—in the summer of 1969 to proceed as usual must appear, in hindsight, astonishing. At the time, however, it was not a decision: rather the Stormont government took the view that 'traditional' marches were none of its business. Its attempt during the spring to reform the 1951 Public Order Act 'so that', as the Prime Minister Terence O'Neill put it, 'disorderly demonstrations, provocative counter-demonstrations, private armies and all the undesirable features of recent months can be properly controlled by law', came too late, and did not face the issue of the historic processions themselves. Being seen as partisan, therefore, it provoked a filibustering opposition which infuriated loyalists.[24] All this merely underlined the fact that the government existed to maintain the ascendancy which these displays ritually asserted. The processions expressed the political order itself, yet their aggressive tone highlit its contentious basis. The outcome was a blaze of street fighting culminating in a mass assault on the Catholic zone of Derry in August. It was the police participation in these assaults which breached the barrier of indifference kept up for so long between Britain and Northern Ireland. Television close-ups of excited policemen amidst street skirmishes, images so genuinely dramatic that they have been re-transmitted year after year since then, drove home one simple point: this was definitely not the British way.

Quasi-war 1969–1988

> THE EARL OF GOWRIE: I have to say that I believe that very few security forces in the world could have dealt with disorder on the scale that we have seen in Northern Ireland in the last 10 years with so little loss of life.
> NOBLE LORDS: Hear, hear!
> LORD PAGET OF NORTHAMPTON: But, my Lords, after 10 years it is still going on.[25]

The fall of the Stormont regime was the inevitable result of this eye-opening. That it did not follow immediately is hardly surprising, since the natural British instinct was to assume that a sensible package of reforms would undo the damage caused by half a century of structural discrimination. These reforms, ranging from policing to 'fair employment', were foisted on Northern Ireland by the kind of irresistible pressure that Griffith, Collins, and Redmond before them, had once imagined Britain was going to apply to preserve the 'essential unity' of Ireland. The reforms destroyed the essential character of Northern Ireland as it had existed since 1920, but had very limited effect in creating a secular, plural society in the British image.[26] Three years of 'intervention', and the twenty years of direct rule which have followed it, have through a sequence of expedients produced a constitutional arrangement for which, as yet, no name has been found.

The British intervention began in August 1969 as the purest form of public-order mission. The British army's task was to separate the warring communities, and relieve the police of their responsibility for holding the line. In order that the police might soon return—or rather turn—to normal British behaviour, they were also relieved of their weapons. For a few months the traditional prescription of 'military aid' appeared to be working: the Catholic community was transparently relieved to be rid of the police, and the Protestants could not loyally protest against their own army. But even a few months was a long time for a military presence to last; Britain was accustomed to measuring such interventions in hours rather than days, let alone weeks or months. There was no difficulty in predicting—as the first military commander in Ulster did—that the minority's unwonted affection for the army would have strict limits.[27] The difficulty lay in finding an alternative force to make and keep the peace.[28]

Maybe a really bold experiment such as the Irish Free State made when, in the midst of civil war, it instituted an unarmed police force, would have had some chance of working at this point. But the moral difficulty of keeping the police unarmed when they were being shot at proved insuperable for the government.[29] The jurist Claire Palley voiced the common sense in seeing it as self-evident that 'in present circumstances it would be impossible to disarm policemen who need weapons for self-defence', and dismissing criticism of this view as 'mealy-mouthed'.[30] The business of shooting at the police grew as the IRA established and enlarged its role as defender of the Catholic community. The army was the first target, but as popular feeling steadily turned against the military presence, the police were in no position to recover control. Securing legitimacy for the RUC has remained a constant prepossession, but it has obstinately stuck in the realms of pious hope.[31] One of the biggest problems was what to do with the old B Specials, who had become the paramount symbol of Protestant dominance. The Hunt Commission on police reform, which succeeded briefly in disarming the RUC, concluded that the Specials must be wound up and replaced by a part-time territorial military force. Thus the UVF went into its third incarnation as the Ulster Defence Regiment (UDR); it was more like a national guard than anything seen in Britain before.[32] This belated concession to General Macready's criticisms of 1920 was accompanied by a clear recognition that the force would continue to be regarded as partisan—more so than the RUC—unless it could recruit across sectarian lines. Initial recruitment to the UDR early in 1970, benefiting from the generally euphoric atmosphere of reform, included a proportion of Catholics as high as one-fifth. The shrinkage of this component thereafter can be read as a measure of the growing conflict: by November 1970 it had fallen to 16 per cent, a year later to 8 per cent. By 1975 it was down to 2 per cent, in political terms a virtual zero.[33]

This steady reappearance of ingrained cultural attitudes counterweighed the statistical decline of disorder and violence from the destructive peak of 1972 and 1973. In the early 1970s the conflict reached an intensity resembling war. Then and since, it has been occasionally referred to as civil war, but by the press rather than by politicians, and in headlines rather than in text where it might be subjected to discussion or evaluation.[34] Once in the 1980s a Prime Minister, Mrs Thatcher, used the word 'war', but quickly insisted that she was employing it merely to describe the deluded outlook of the IRA. War has become too loaded a term, but no viable alternative has been found, apart from the indefinite and overstretched words 'conflict' and 'crisis'. The government has naturally preferred negative descriptions such as 'riot' and 'terrorism'. Riot on the scale which became habitual in the early 1970s implied, of course, an element of public involvement, albeit in unacceptable form; terrorism skirted that awkward point. And though the IRA remained, in its own eyes, a guerrilla army, the geographical limits of its popular constituency drove it to adopt a terrorist strategy as its only means of striking out. Once it did, all that mattered to the government, as the prime minister Edward Heath constantly reiterated, was to 'get on top of the gunmen'.

This terminology is important because it reflects the powers brought into play to preserve or restore order, and the attitudes with which these powers are wielded. The effects of these, reaching from Londonderry in 1972 to Gibraltar in 1988, can be ruinous. The conduct of the 1st Parachute Regiment, when they tore into the crowd in Londonderry on 'Bloody Sunday' in 1972, was a catastrophic and irreversible consequence of political indirection: an unstable fusion of riot control technique with anti-terrorist action.[35] The same was true of the interrogation methods then being used on suspected terrorists, some of which were imported from counter-insurgency campaigns overseas without the modifications that politicians or officials might have thought to make, if they had thought at all, about the actualities of the military intervention, and others of which were inventions exploiting technologies which had not been available in Malaya or Aden. This negligence led Britain to face charges of torture before the European Commission on Human Rights. The accusations were brought by the Republic of Ireland in 1971, and were eventually pronounced upon in 1976.

In the interim, some effort was made to construct a more appropriate framework for the struggle against terrorism. The legal framework had to be recast because of the evident obsoleteness of the old Special Powers Act even before the demise of its parent legislature in 1972. The introduction of internment, the modern term for the suspension of habeas corpus, was a hasty response to a situation closely resembling that of 1920. As Lord Diplock's commission put it, so long as the terrorists 'remain at liberty to operate in Northern Ireland it will not be possible to find witnesses prepared to testify against them in the criminal courts, except those serving in the army or police'.[36] The only way out of the 'dilemma' was the establishment of juryless courts which would convict on the basis of confessions—provided that these were not obtained by torture or by 'inhuman or degrading treatment'. Such tribunals, inevitably christened 'Diplock courts', were created under the Northern Ireland (Emergency Provisions) Act 1973. Since then they have presented the closest approximation to 'due process' thought viable in the circumstances. Criticism of the 1973 Act's implications was muted, though one lawyer held that it had 'strong claims to be considered the most Draconian measure to be put before Parliament since the Emergency Powers Act 1939', and suggested that Diplock's analysis gave 'a possible foretaste of the kind of approach to emergency powers which might be expected in Britain should an acute security situation develop in the years ahead'.[37]

The most acute criticism appeared in the relative obscurity of the *Criminal Law Review*, where W. L. Twining deplored the unnecessary hurry of Diplock's inquiry and the general carelessness with which a major constitutional change had been pushed through. The Diplock inquiry was, in Twining's view, a 'sorry story' which 'reveals the weakness of *ad hoc* response to crisis'. The Diplock courts contravened the principle of 'sterilisation' which Twining held vital to any system of emergency powers: that emergency procedures should be sharply distinguished from ordinary ones, so that public confidence in the ordinary judicial system should not be undermined.[38] This destructive result has indeed been widely observed over the following twenty years, though the issue is excluded from official assessments.[39]

The interrogation techniques triggered a sequence of commissions of inquiry into the balance between the protection of civil rights and the preservation of public security. The Compton Report took a rather easy-going attitude to the first allegations of brutality, concluding that brutality could not happen without cruelty, 'a disposition to inflict suffering', and 'we do not think that happened here'. This complacent approach was quickly overtaken by the reports of the Parker Committee, whose majority accepted that 'urban guerrilla warfare in which completely innocent lives are at risk' necessarily imposed stresses different from those of conventional war. More striking was the report of the minority under the signature of Lord Gardiner, who insisted that if the IRA's 'brutal murders, arson, the use of explosives against innocent men, women and children' had to be regarded as 'virtually a war', it was one in which 'the position of the forces of law and order depends very much on how far they have the sympathy of the local population against the guerrillas'.[40] Secret and illegal methods, developed in 'emergency conditions in colonial-type situations', were alien to British democratic tradition and would undermine the reputation of the legal system, a disaster which Gardiner thought would outweigh even the loss of some lives.

But these were grim computations to have to make. Edward Heath accepted the burden of Gardiner's argument, and ordered the cessation of the notorious 'five techniques' in March 1972. A further committee was set up, under Gardiner himself, to consider 'in the context of civil liberties and human rights, measures to deal with terrorism in Northern Ireland'. Gardiner's report was the most frank, and perhaps the only, public attempt to get to the heart of the issues raised by internment and juryless trial.

Those in favour of detention argue that, when times are relatively normal, the needs of an ordered society may be met by the criminal courts functioning with a high regard for the common law's presumption of innocence and a strict observance of the rules of evidence and the standard of proof. But when normal conditions give way to grave disorder and lawlessness, with extensive terrorism causing widespread loss of life and limb and the wholesale destruction of property, the courts cannot be expected to maintain peace and order in the community if they have to act alone. The very safeguards of the law then become the means by which it may be circumvented.[41]

Gardiner plainly recognized the intractability of this situation, and saw that there were no simple answers. But in line with his reasoning on the Parker Committee, he continued to insist that traditional safeguards were crucial to the legitimacy of the legal process. Detention 'brought the law into contempt'. It created 'an atmosphere of secrecy which undermines sound community life'. Some of his witnesses even argued that it fostered rather than inhibited the growth of terrorist networks. He insisted that even though 'the quasi-judicial system of Commissioners' hearings and reviews operates with a scrupulous regard for the principles of justice', and did not make an excessive number of mistakes, 'it is not perceived as being just by members of the general public'.

Gardiner tackled terrorism itself head-on, and proposed that it should become an offence *per se*. But defining it remained the stumbling-block, and his definition—'the use of violence for political or sectarian ends . . . for the purpose of putting the public or any section of the public into fear'— shared the weaknesses, above all lack of specificity, which had hamstrung earlier attempts to legislate against boycotting and intimidation. This rendered some of Gardiner's larger pronouncements problematic. Thus he held that 'while the liberty of the subject is a human right to be preserved under all possible conditions, it is not, and cannot be, an absolute right', because liberty could be used to oppress others. 'Where freedoms conflict, the state has a duty to protect those in need of protection.' But how could it do this if an intimidated community will not give evidence? Gardiner seemed to think that temporary suspension of legal safeguards might lead to the reimposition of order, though emergency powers could, 'if prolonged, damage the fabric of the community, and they do not provide lasting solutions'.[42] Such solutions could only be political ones, and must include 'further measures to promote social justice between classes and communities'. This conventional piety was reflected in the report's equivocal conclusion about the timing of the abolition of internment.[43]

If Gardiner pulled his punches somewhat, this was due to the complexity of the issues, and the ever-present awareness that the lives of the security forces were on the line. Few people were prepared to take responsibility for changes which might be followed by an increase in the casualty rate. Yet nobody could be sure whether the particular measures in force were controlling or provoking disorder. The secular decline in fatality figures through the 1970s was accompanied by a steady professionalization of the 'terrorist' organizations and the spread of a pervasive system of vigilantism, intimidation, extortion, and black economy, amounting to a culture of 'paramilitarism'—a neologism of the Fascist epoch whose vernacular adoption in Northern Ireland amounted to a popular rejection of the government's labelling.[44] In the end the justifications for anti-terrorist measures have been visceral rather than rational, and of no measure is this more true than the most drastic and far-reaching of all, the 1974 Prevention of Terrorism Act.

The Prevention of Terrorism (Temporary Provisions) Act was born as a rapid reaction to the worst of the IRA's mainland attacks. The line taken by the Labour Home Secretary, Roy Jenkins, in presenting the bill to Parliament as a 'Draconian' law was reminiscent of his predecessor McKenna in 1914. He was demonstrating that something was being done in face of what he called, in American rather than English style, a 'clear and present danger'. Ever since, there has been a subdued debate—conducted in whispers for fear of giving aid and comfort to the enemy or spreading alarm and despondency—about whether it achieves much beyond ensuring that, in Jenkins's words, 'the public should no longer have to endure the affront' of seeing open IRA displays. Its temporary provisions have of course become permanent, under the same Talleyrandian principle (ce n'est que la provisoire qui dure) as its Provisional target. Two years before it was made permanent—subject to annual review rather than renewal—an independent long-term review of it conducted by Lord Colville suggested that

The legislation has cast a blight over the Irish population of Great Britain and is counter-productive in Northern Ireland because amongst other things it alienates the population and discourages the public from any attempt to help in rooting out terrorism. It creates martyrs and tends to cause misplaced sympathy for people who on any rational view have committed terrible crimes.[45]

Colville reported that during his enquiries he had heard the serious suggestion that if all emergency legislation were abolished, the situation would at least be no worse. As far as the PTA itself is concerned, its counter-productive value derives not only from the enlarged powers of arrest and temporary detention (for interrogation) which have been widely employed by the police, but also from its less-utilized but vastly more spectacular power under which individuals can be prohibited from leaving designated parts of the country—that is, confined to Northern Ireland. This exotic provision, inevitably labelled 'internal exile', will ensure the Act's immortality in legal history even if it is some day discarded by the state.[46]

The underlying anxiety of others beside the Irish community in Britain is that such novel powers will never be wholly discarded. One distinguished journalist's comment when the Act was made permanent expresses this: because 'it only takes the emotive assertion that a little loss of liberty saves lives to shut up the critics',

Gradually we have accepted the Thatcher doctrine that some liberty must be sacrificed in the defence of liberty. We have come to accept all sorts of other things in accordance with this insidious calculus—the suspension of trial by jury, and now abridgements of free speech and of the right of accused persons to silence.[47]

Of course this doctrine reaches back much further than Mrs Thatcher; if it has become insidious this is because it has lost its strict connection with a comprehensible notion of emergency as laid down in Rossiter's doctrine of constitutional dictatorship. As so often before, the issue comes down to one of definition.

Some of the terms employed—usually without much sign of deliberation—to describe the Northern Ireland crisis have been touched on earlier. The avoidance of the word 'war' remains especially important in the British context, because of the extreme simplicity of the common law tradition on this point. If it is not war, it must be peace. Yet that evidently does not quite meet the case. The impossibility of finding a term to fit the situation parallels the problem of characterizing the constitutional status of Northern Ireland since 1972. The writer of a study of rebellions against British rule overseas in the 1930s proposed the term 'sub-war' as a basis for creating an appropriate legal and political (and, no less important, mental) framework.[48] Like the term 'sub-state' often applied to Northern Ireland before 1972 this is a relative term, but it could be a contribution to clarity.

The problem is one of political semantics: war is out. 'You do not declare war on rebels.' Lawyers have no difficulty in seeing rebellion as war (as in Hawkins's rugged eighteenth-century view), but politicians find that the word carries a declaration. The obvious alternative is 'rebellion' itself, but this seems to be relished by Irish rebels, and British governments have shown a corresponding aversion to it. 'Insurrection' would offer a less legitimizing option, though even this suggests an intensity of fighting higher than the authorities would like to acknowledge. 'Low-intensity' war or conflict has become a fashionable usage in America but in the process has lost the categorical clarity it had in its original British formulation, and is often taken to be a synonym for limited (that is, not total, but still conventional) war.[49] 'Insurgency' is too academic for the hustings, and still too military for the comfort of the civil power. The adjective 'paramilitary' has the approval of the European Court, though its popularity in the six counties is principally due to its euphemistic utility—it is a way of avoiding saying either 'terrorist' or 'freedom fighter'—rather than its analytical precision. The noun 'paramilitarism' raises too many echoes, not least of 'militarism', to be appropriate; an alternative neologism such as 'parawar' might be more neutral. The Irish Free State's civil war coinage, 'irregularism', would be better both technically and politically, but it has no roots in British political discourse. Maybe, following Allen's signpost into the ghostland of modern administration, the best we can do is to call it quasi-war.

If ever there were an appropriate British situation for a state of emergency, this would look to be it. The contrast with the situation in Ireland is instructive. There a formal state of emergency 'affecting the vital interests of the State' has been declared since 1976. The 1939 Offences Against the State Act, followed by the 1976 Emergency Powers Act, diverged from British tradition in confronting the issues squarely, at least semantically. (As indeed had the first Public Safety Act, which identified the public with the state.) In the style of the Free State's first Minister of Justice during the Civil War, the republic's government was clear that the threat in the 1970s was posed by 'an illegal armed organisation dedicated to the overthrow of the institutions of *this* State'.[50]

In the United Kingdom, however, no such formal emergency has been declared, except during the 1974 Ulster Workers' Council strike which paralysed the province and triggered the (deliberately non-political) Emergency Powers Act. Professor Twining remains practically unique in calling from the start for a formally conceived system.[51] What has happened is rather a constructive than an explicit declaration. When Britain was haled before the European Human Rights Commission, and later the Court, it was faced with the alternative of offering a defence or of derogating from the Convention on Human Rights under Article 15. The derogation may look to have been a foregone conclusion, but it was not unproblematic: it involved a declaration that there was 'a public emergency threatening the life of the nation'. This was quite a severe test, or was intended by the framers of the convention to be so. (Oddly enough, this English phrase was rather more mystical than the original French formulation, which specified 'une situation de crise ou de danger exceptionnel et imminent qui affecte l'ensemble de la population et constitue une menace pour la vie organisée de la communauté composant l'État', terminology in some ways— the word 'État' apart—closer to that of the Emergency Powers Acts.)

In the event, and despite the protests of the Irish government, the Commission and Court were less than exigent in pressing for evidence of such present public danger. The Commission accepted that

The degree of violence, with bombing, shooting and rioting, was on a scale far beyond what could be called minor civil disorder, and it is clear that the violence was in many instances planned in advance, by factions of the community organized and acting on paramilitary lines.[52]

For well over a decade, therefore, Britain was able to operate on the basis of this demi-declaration. But even this characteristic stance began to carry some political dangers through the sheer prolongation of the conflict. One legal specialist has insisted, surely rightly, that 'the concept of emergency is incompatible with a perpetual state of affairs and is necessarily limited in time and space'.[53] And indeed in 1985 Britain notified the Human Rights Committee that it was withdrawing its notice of derogation, since the rights enshrined in the covenant were upheld in its emergency legislation: there was still an emergency, but it could be dealt with under the powers furnished by the Emergency Provisions Act and the Prevention of Terrorism Act.[54] This might seem to raise the question why these Acts, which had been in effect for eleven years, had not previously been thought to provide a satisfactory framework.

The drawback of derogation was that it opened up the issue of the extent and severity of the threat to public security. As the PTA's most notorious provision made plain, the emergency was definitely confined to one part of the state, but it was not politically desirable to raise the question of the exact relationship of that part to 'the nation'.[55] There was no threat that the state itself would be overthrown, though there was a direct attack on the political allegiance of one group of its members, and of course a partial fracture of its overall legitimacy in so far as that rests on its capacity to maintain public order.[56] There can be no doubt that, as in the earlier Troubles, the authorities have found it convenient to avoid addressing the status of the conflict itself, and to work within the implication that it is an aggravated public order problem, one that is only occasionally aggravated beyond the unaided capacity of the civil power to control. The vast political embarrassment caused by the admission that there were 'no-go areas' early in the 1970s led to the biggest military operation of the whole period; since then, the winding-up of internment and the 'political status' of terrorist detainees have been followed by the policies of 'criminalization' (the obverse of political status) and 'Ulsterization' (the odd term for the visible enlargement of the police role in order-maintenance).[57]

The emphasis on civil supremacy, which has been upheld against military arguments that its cosmetic value is negated by its technical inefficiency, is of course not merely convenient for government. Nor is its value purely cosmetic: in the battle for hearts and minds, as all counter-insurgency experts agree, the projection of basic values is vital. The whole of the British experience militates against clarification, 'going over the precipice'. Traditionally this was the way of avoiding extremes, and especially of avoiding tyrannical military government. The present situation, however, suggests the possibility that there are other dangers, less spectacular (and archaic) but more insidious (and modern) than the man on horseback. Some are indicated by semantic slippage such as the unwonted abandonment of archaism in rechristening the 'forces of the Crown' the 'security forces'. Others have a more directly destructive side: the term 'baton rounds' for rubber (later PVC) bullets, measures the distance travelled from the 'simple baton' before which Victorian mobs quailed, and opens the way to a use of force which can only be described as skirmishing rather than 'riot control'.[58]

The official orthodoxy—'the chief constable and the general officer commanding consider that baton rounds are the most effective means of controlling riots consistent with the principle of minimum force'—has been characteristically gnomic. Effectiveness is a term intended to preclude public debate. Even when ministers, like Lord Gowrie quoted here, have ventured a further judgement about this 'very unpleasant weapon indeed', it has been of this kind: 'the presence and the knowledge about this weapon has reduced the need for the police to use other kinds of arms which could be more lethal'. But this was precisely to avoid the arguments which had been made in Parliament on that occasion that careful use of more lethal weapons might cause less injury, and that quite different alternatives, such as water cannon, were available.[59]

There may, in the end, be worse things than a formal state of emergency. After a decade of undeclared emergency, Britain was confronted with a sequence of unpalatable—and, because of the situation, inexplicable—events. In the absence of any coherent official explanation, these came to be lumped together in the public view as the 'shoot-to-kill policy'.[60] On 11 November 1982, for instance, three IRA men were killed in a car near Lurgan; an astonishing 109 bullets were fired by the 'security forces' (in this case the RUC). There was no evidence that the targets had fired back. For a system that had consistently placed such emphasis on the doctrine of minimum force this was an extraordinary fact, which was very far from self-explanatory. Or rather, the obvious explanations were highly unflattering to the forces involved. But official progress towards a public account of such events was halting. This and two other fatal encounters were investigated by a senior police officer from Manchester, John Stalker, whose own account of the resistance he met within the RUC, and the odd coincidence by which he was suspended from duty at the most sensitive stage of his inquiry, was published in the form of an autobiography after he left the force.[61] His report itself, completed by Chief Constable Sampson, was never made public. The decision not to publish it was announced by the Attorney-General in January 1988 as taking account of 'all relevant circumstances, including matters concerning the public interest'. The shock of this announcement unhinged the opposition spokesman's grasp on syntax: 'I find it incredible beyond belief', Kevin MacNamara expostulated, 'that the Government have come to this conclusion'. His belief that this was a 'grave blow' to efforts to restore confidence in the administration of justice even drove him to break the convention which his party had long endorsed, and 'ask what the grounds of national security are'. But the legacy of 'bipartisanship' insulated the Attorney from such attempts at interrogation: 'in conformity with the policy of long standing of successive governments I am not prepared to comment on national security'.[62]

The absence of comment is not hard to understand. It arises out of the contradictions of undeclared war. The Stalker affair demonstrated the incompatibility of the 'normal' standards, which Stalker thought should apply to any police force, with the exceptional position of the RUC. The most telling feature of the affair was the fact that nobody thought to tell him at the outset that he could not expect to apply normal standards in a situation where the authorities had tacitly conceded that the intelligence service must make its own rules. Maybe few senior police officers would have failed to acknowledge the implicit limits of an inquiry in the field of national security, but one was enough. Likewise, few judges might have hit on Lord Justice Gibson's ill-starred way of commending the police for bringing the three IRA men 'to justice; in this case, to the final court of justice' at Lurgan. Yet an atrocious aberration like this was more likely to happen than not in the course of a protracted abnormality.

One thing of which the authorities can be sure is the virtual impossibility of guaranteeing exactness in the use of force. The everyday fiction that troops posted—say—in rooftop firing positions can stop, question, and if necessary arrest people on the street according to normal police procedure, will inevitably break down periodically.[63] The most spectacular breach of what lawyers call 'proportionality' followed a few weeks later, when an IRA Active Service Unit was wiped out by the SAS in Gibraltar on 6 March 1988. This was an operation which fell fractionally short of brilliant success: the targets were exactly identified, and they might have been on the point of carrying out an attack, but they were not. To have made absolutely sure of this would have required an intelligence system more sophisticated than the authorities had any right to expect. It is, in other words, in the nature of this emergency that such events are likely to happen. These operations are chancy. Mistakes may be minimized, but even a single one will have a tremendous political impact, and once done can never be undone.

Secrecy and Censorship

> I do not accept the unshakeable view of the Administration that no
> issue of security is ever to be justiciable in Britain, that legal represen-
> tation must always be denied if the Administration chants the magic
> words 'national security'.
>
> Harry Street[64]

The idea of open government is most unlikely to make progress amidst a
civil war in which the safety—that is, the lives—of the security services,
the safety of the people, and the safety of the state seem inextricably
fused. Yet some disentangling would in principle be possible, were clarity,
rather than a blanket of secrecy, seen to be 'in the public interest' (or were
secrecy to be regarded *prima facie* as more likely to be a shield for
incompetence than a sign of effectiveness). Such a version of the national
good seems to be in fairly steady decline in twentieth-century Britain.
Michael Foot's outrage at Tony Benn's suggestion that the time had at
last come for open government cannot be wholly explained by personal
aversion. It may be an exaggeration to speak, as is common nowadays, of
a British governmental 'obsession' with secrecy, but a marked predisposition
towards it has been evident for a long time.[65] As a result of this process,
we can be sure that public security is more important than ever, but we
become less and less sure what it is. Nor do we know how to find out
what it is, because the responsibility for determining it rests with government,
which cannot make public its reasons.

All this was made clear—as far as the nature of the issue permitted—by
the inquiry into Section 2 of the Official Secrets Act conducted by Lord
Franks in 1972. The nearest that the modern British state has come to
constructing a definition of national security is to be found in chapter 9 of
Franks's report, entitled 'The Security of the Nation and the Safety of the
People'. There is no definition as such, perhaps unsurprisingly since the
notion is accepted as a common-sense one by many if not most people.
(Even academics write books about national security without offering any
definition of it.[66]) Instead there is a linked and sometimes overlapping
series of propositions about 'what most reasonable people would accept'.
The tropes in the argument at the start of the chapter are characteristic:

National security is widely accepted as the prime justification for employing criminal
sanctions to protect official information. But this is too vague a concept by itself to
be of much help in identifying the major categories of official information requiring
special protection . . . [These categories] all go to the fundamentals of government.
They are all matters of major importance. They are all matters which affect the

nation as a whole. A safe and independent life for a nation and its people requires effective defence against the threat of attack from outside. It requires the maintenance of the nation's relations with the rest of the world, and of its essential economic base. It requires the preservation of law and order, and the ability to cope with emergencies threatening the essentials of life.[67]

The initial distinction drawn between nation and people is slightly problematic. Franks speaks both of 'the nation as a whole' and of 'a nation and its people'. Is 'nation' here being used as a euphemism for 'state', or is something more being implied? A little later he speaks of 'the country's resources', and of 'other countries' as well as 'other nations'; sometimes 'the country suffers', and at others it is 'the life of the nation' (echoing that idiosyncratic translation of the Human Rights convention); only when he reaches the technical section on classification of information does he use the word 'state'—with a capital S.[68] Perhaps the conclusion that must be drawn from this is that, notwithstanding the almost animist language employed here and there about the nation, the differences between the terms are not expected to matter too much. The only possible view about who is to determine the content of the national way of life that is to be defended, is that which would be taken by the judge in the case of Clive Ponting: the government of the day.

(The same seems to be true of the explanation furnished some years later by the Home Secretary of 'subversive activities', which he said were 'generally regarded as those which threaten the safety or well-being of the state'. Since the notion of well-being would, as one critic has pointed out, be irrelevant to a narrow executive reading of the word 'state',[69] it must have been elided with larger, more ambiguous concepts like 'society' or 'community'. The implications of this elision are large: the Home Secretary's 'implicit notion of public order characterizes disruption of government policy as a threat to order'; 'industrial and political freedom consistent with that notion of public order is limited to non-disruptive opposition', so that 'public order is synonymous with the interests of those holding power, not the whole society'.[70])

What was seen to matter was the basis on which information is classified as secret, and here clarification was needed if the law was to operate in a more satisfactory way, as Franks wished. Franks was obliged to go some way to spell out the essential reasons for secrecy; for instance, 'the value of reports [from representatives overseas about our relations with other governments] is limited if they cannot be completely frank'. This argument can of course be applied to almost any kind of report; it leaves unanswered the question of who should be entitled to such confidentiality. Franks plainly thought there was a sensible answer to such a question, and that it could be determined by the gravity of the likely damage or harm caused by openness. So far, so good, but who is to measure the harm? On this point, Franks accepted the official argument that only ministers could do it.

In relation to these basic functions of government, the question of injury to the nation is essentially political, in the broadest sense of the term, not judicial. It is essentially a Government responsibility to assess the importance of information. . . . The Government is accountable to Parliament and the electorate for its discharge of these basic functions.[71]

The problem with this is: how can this antique doctrine of accountability, which was obviously based on the premiss that Parliament and the electorate would know what had happened, function when nothing can be revealed about what the government has done? Under the OSA there is no way of establishing whether the government has exercised its political function 'in the broadest sense' or in the (at least equally possible) narrower party sense.

Under the OSA, some would suggest, the doctrine of ministerial accountability has been rendered nugatory.[72] It is not clear whether Franks and his committee still believed in it (which, one jurist suggested, would have been 'ingenuous in the extreme'[73]), or whether they repeated the old mantra because it had at least the great public virtue of resolving potentially awkward inconsistencies. The potential awkwardness of this issue burst out in the case of Clive Ponting, an official who believed that a minister had indeed interpreted the public interest as being identical to that of his party, and had misled Parliament about decisions taken in relation to operations during the Falklands War. When prosecuted under the OSA for giving information to an MP, Ponting's defence was that which the Home Office had expressly rejected in its submission to the Franks committee—that disclosure was in the public interest. Franks had agreed with the civil servants that this argument would lead to the courts becoming involved in political decisions. In the Ponting case, the judge also agreed that the court was not competent to determine the national interest. This came as no surprise to legal observers; what did come as a surprise to everyone was the jury's dissent.

Clive Ponting's acquittal might have become the focus of a major public debate about the nature of state secrecy. A century earlier it certainly would have; but in the 1980s the government moved to repair the damage with remarkably little hindrance. Public indifference to the whole question of open government and 'freedom of information' had something to do with this; but the ongoing IRA campaign had more. In 1988 two vital steps further along the path of restriction were taken. On 19 October the Home Secretary, Douglas Hurd, issued a notice banning material relating to listed Northern Ireland organizations from the broadcast media. This prohibited the broadcasting of the actual voices of members of 'listed organizations', though the text of their speeches and writings could still be printed, and even spoken in the voices of others dubbed over theirs. The faint absurdity of this aspect of the ban may have deflected some public attention from its substance, though of course it did not divert journalists from the main thrust of their furious counter-attack: this was a curtailment of the freedom of speech which was a fundamental element of the constitution.[74] Without free reporting, as the Deputy Director-General of the BBC pointed out, the democratic requirement of an educated public opinion becomes meaningless.[75]

Against this, there was fierce support for the ban from those who accepted the underlying contention that terrorism lives on 'the oxygen of publicity', and those who felt like the bereaved mother quoted by Mrs Thatcher: '"Where is the freedom of the press?" I hear them cry. Where is my son's freedom?' Journalists who tried to refute this emotional *non sequitur* were aware that they were walking on eggs: Peter Jenkins asked, 'How does abridgement of one freedom compensate for the loss of another? Did the Prime Minister mean to suggest to the bereaved mother that her lost son would be alive today had it not been for television?' The argument that the ban would protect the sensibilities of victims' relatives, he suggested, 'has nothing to do with effectively combating terrorism'.[76] At least, the government saw no need to demonstrate the link.

The broadcasting ban and the abridgement of an accused person's right to silence must, Jenkins held, be set before the backdrop of the near-farcical attempt to secure a worldwide ban on the publication of a secret-serviceman's autobiography. The Wright fiasco ('the disproportionate lengths to which the Government was prepared to go ... and the quite shocking arguments put forward in the courts'), and the 'Zircon affair', in which the Speaker of the Commons was effectively enlisted as an agent of the executive by being given a secret national security briefing on Privy Council terms, demonstrated that reasons of state had achieved a wholly novel weight in the constitutional balance.[77] The final act in 1988 was the publication in December of the long-awaited bill to reform Section 2 of the OSA. This was presented with practised reasonableness by Douglas Hurd as a liberalization of the original law, less restrictive even than the Franks

Committee's recommendations. But this was a liberalization designed to make it enforceable where its predecessor had failed.

Whether this was consonant with the British way was a matter of political if not of public debate. The contrary view was put not only by hostile jurists, and by former Conservative Prime Ministers (Edward Heath denounced the Act's 'failure to weigh the rights of the individual against possible abuses of state powers'[78]), but also and more acutely by a classical liberal, Lord Bonham-Carter, who saw the 'formal release' of wide swathes of information once within the scope of the OSA as a 'largely theoretical achievement', since those kinds of information had never in practice been controlled.

In these large areas the writ of the 1911 Act never ran. Even in those parts covering security and defence, after Ponting a prosecution was a risky and unpredictable business. So it could be argued that this country found itself without an Official Secrets Act, and hence the necessity of the one that we have before us, which I would argue is in some respects wider in its scope and more easily enforced than the one it succeeds.[79]

Most instructive of all was Roy Jenkins's revelation that as Home Secretary he had abandoned his own attempt to reform the OSA: a 'war of resistance' by powerful departments where 'secrecy had become a way of life' had driven him to the conclusion that 'any measure which emerged might actually make things worse and not better'. This conclusion may not compel us into pessimism, but it surely invites us down that path.

9

Losing the Trick

> To decide the question of what the police ought to be in a free nation is a problem which will require for its solution the exercise of the wisest heads.
>
> Josephine Butler

Treason, sedition, subversion; disaffection, riot, rebellion; with such words we circle the core of public order, normality, the dominant sense of collective identity. Consensus, the lodestar of the British way, is not a static 'fact' but rather the dynamic outcome of multiple ambitions and loyalties. It is a truism that in the nation-state, which is the characteristic embodiment of modern social identity—whether imagined as ethnic or civic—there exists a common way of life. However it may be constructed in the first place, its survival is continuously negotiated in Renan's 'plébiscite de toutes les journées'. In this negotiation, the truism itself, the necessary myth, plays a vital part. The day-to-day outcome is always likely to be conservative. The way of life makes its own sense. Maintenance of ambiguity, for instance, seems to be one of the ways in which the English have connived in shielding their state from scrutiny. Even those who arraign the state usually do so without defining it.[1] This is easier to see than to explain. Is this a deliberate governmental device, or a diffused cultural construct, internalized by the majority as an innate 'national characteristic'—in short a hegemonic mechanism?

The deployment of the concept of public order presents several clear examples of the hegemonic process, and has generally been marked by an uncanny absence of overt contention. Leading exponents of this Gramscian view see the definition of public security as a struggle in which the winners are always—by definition—'the authorities'; obviously the aim of such writers is to reconstruct the traditional idea of class war in a more sophisticated form. But even without straining the concept of hegemony, it has helped to indicate the mechanisms through which stability is maintained.

Stuart Hall's search for the 'primary definers' who shape the agenda and terms of public debate has special relevance for the definition of public order. The question which has to be faced in contemplating the state of public culture at the end of the 1980s is whether the process of definition is still functioning effectively; or has the British trick stopped working?

The official reaction to the sudden and unexpected intensification of disorder in the 1980s has taken both explicit and covert forms. The 1986 Public Order Act represents an attempt to counter the degradation of domestic peace by making more explicit than ever before the basic mechanics of tolerance and self-restraint on which the 'British way' has been assumed to depend. Whereas the 1936 Act was mainly confined to quite narrow means of dealing with a specific political mode of collective violence, the 1986 Act had a pedagogical strain: it told people they would have to try harder to preserve or rebuild the convention of orderliness and reasonableness. The underlying ideology was made still more explicit after enactment, with the Home Secretary's unusual public discourse on the idea of 'active citizenship'.

> The need to foster responsible citizenship is obvious. Freedom can only flourish within a community where shared values, common loyalties and mutual obligations provide a framework of order and self-discipline. Otherwise, liberty can quickly degenerate into narrow self-interest and licence.[2]

That these homilies on civic virtue were thought necessary is interesting; that they might be thought useful says quite a bit about the etiolation of 'organic' society amidst both modern secularism and postmodern multiculturalism—the latter bringing a sectarian divergence which was bound to subject the relaxed liberal notion of pluralism to tremendous stress.

Hurd's analysis was somewhat less banal than its opening suggested. At its heart was an attempt to translate the organic prescriptions of Edmund Burke into multicultural society. 'For most of us, family, neighbourhood and nation command the strongest loyalties, these three being the dominant themes in a harmony of allegiances which will be different for each individual.' The government was, Hurd contended, 'energetically seeking to thrust power outwards—away from the corporatist battalions to the little platoons'. But this exploitation of Burke ducked the question whether the 'harmony of allegiances' might not be shattered when religion joined the dominant themes (producing, in Burke's time, volcanic disorders such as the Gordon riots). And in emphasizing the role of 'the fashion ... for denigrating authority and tradition' in the 'fraying' of the old 'sense of social cohesion', he sounded a note of rude Toryism which—if true—surely rendered his whole project anachronistic. Social 'fashions' are less manipulable than this season's shoulderline or next year's boot spoilers. Yet he went on the following year to declare that the government would mount an offensive against the 'stupid drinking' which produced 'lager lout' disorders. The Chief Constable of Surrey took the same line: stronger family and church ties, and teachers able to mete out physical punishment, would quell the rising violence.[3]

The role of government in reshaping larger social conventions was of course central to the advocacy of 'active citizenship'. Conservative orthodoxy stressed the limits of state economic intervention, and, by a parallel (if not wholly consistent) logic, the limits of police power to impose order. 'The idea of active citizenship is a necessary complement to that of the enterprise culture', the Home Secretary explained, though he side-stepped the question how far the relation between free market and ordered society could be pressed. The contemporary manifestation of active citizenship is Neighbourhood Watch. Spreading from the first scheme in Cheshire to 74,000 other places by the time Hurd was writing, seven years later, these schemes were much less dramatic and demanding than their vigilante label might have suggested. Herein lay their attraction, for, as he admitted—though with a deprecatory air—'academics still argue about their precise effect in reducing crime'. The real value of the initiative was less statistical than moral, like much of contemporary 'feel-good' politics. Public security is first and foremost a state of mind.

The growth of the Neighbourhood Watch scheme was reassuring not only to the public but also to the police. For nothing has been more expressive of the troubles of the 1980s than the destruction of the special public status of the police on which the society (at least via its interpreters) had prided itself. This trump card in the British trick was lost by the schizoid police reaction to intensified disorder. The positive side of this response should not be discounted: it has been promoted assiduously and with apparent conviction by the police force, at any rate the majority of its higher ranks. Whether or not the contentious term 'community policing' is used, the stress on the acceptability of the public face of the police 'service' has been a coherent response to Lord Scarman's encouragement—even if Scarman himself insists that 'force' must remain the only correct description of an organization whose fundamental purpose is to enforce the law.[4] But this has not been enough to arrest the 'spiral of mutual mistrust between police and people'. Roger Graef, maker of the film *Talking Blues*, suggested that this followed a breakdown of the 'collective myths' on which policing by consent had rested. The prime factor in this breakdown was the habitu-ation to violent confrontation since the 1981 riots, and above all since the miners' strike. This was the negative aspect of the police response.

Reversing the state's defeat at the hands of the miners ten years before valorized a confrontational outlook in which the policed could become the enemy. 'The police were sent far from home, in quasi-military convoys, to work against people they did not know', Graef wrote in mid-1989. 'I believe it played havoc with their sense of purpose in ways still not understood.'[5] One of his respondents underlined the corrosive effects of direct assertion of police power:

it was slightly awesome but after a while it became easy. You enjoy the power it gives to inflict the collective will of the job on to a large crowd of people. It's much easier than walking the street by yourself, when you've got to make decisions. You are part of a vast crowd and if the whole thing is wrong or illegal, it's not you who's going to be picked up for it. That sort of violence becomes addictive.[6]

The view from the top was substantially the same; one of Robert Reiner's Chief Constables mused that

people got used day after day for almost a year to scenes of police officers in riot gear armed with truncheons facing the people. They saw police officers being injured, they saw police officers inflicting injuries, and it's commonplace now. As a result my fear is that the whole perception of police–public relations has changed in people's minds.[7]

The dominant public image of the police had acquired at least a tinge of the military.

The adjective 'military', whether modified as 'semi' or 'quasi', or even 'para', is an emotive as much as a descriptive one, especially in its derivative 'militarism'. The perceived 'militarization' of the police inevitably forms a point of acute contention between the force and its critics. The official view is that no such process has occurred.[8] Instead there has been 'a reluctant, incremental reaction to a developing situation'. The creation of special forces and the elaboration of riot techniques and technology are an unavoidable response to what Sir Kenneth Newman called 'the higher threshold of violence shown by rioters', or what Reiner describes as 'a qualitative sharpening of disorder'.[9] (One Chief Constable's remark fixes the 'totally different atmosphere' as well as any: 'taking the micro-situation of a PC going to a pub disturbance. I could recall when even a diminutive chap like me could be called and people would freeze and everything would stop. Now the likelihood is that they would all turn on the police and assault him.'[10])

This perspective is undoubtedly valid in one important way. It is not so much a question of who provoked whom, around which argument has been endless and ultimately sterile, as of the larger resonances of the term 'militarization'. The sensitive point of the terminology is the implication of an overweighting of military as against civilian attitudes. That is the plain burden of the charge that the 'policing revolution' has become the spearhead of a 'strong state', a deliberate creation—or reversion to type—in face of radical challenges.[11] This charge is surely overstated. Militarism does not happen invisibly: military and civil values are too sharply distinct to be mistaken. It is clear that the police have not been militarized in this strong sense.

There is, though, a weaker but none the less profoundly consequential sense in which militarization can occur incrementally and pragmatically— the very modes privileged in British political culture. And indeed Britain has witnessed such a process more than once, albeit at a remove: in Ireland and overseas, British police forces typically responded to sustained political violence by adopting measures such as concentration in central barracks, replacement of beat work by motorized patrolling, use of armoured vehicles and more powerful weapons. All these measures were unequivocally military, but they were regarded as purely technical matters which would not modify the inner ethos of the police forces. Or at least the risk of such contamination was seen as a risk worth taking in order to keep the police 'in the field' and preserve the mantle of the civil power: the lesser of two evils. Each time this plausible case was disputed within the police system— usually more strongly than by the civil government—both on the moral ground that it breached the traditions at the heart of British policing, and on the utilitarian ground that it would be ineffective at best, at worst disastrous. Nobody put this conviction that militarization was an admission of failure more tersely than Sir Charles Wickham, then Inspector-General of the RUC, commenting on the policing of Palestine after 1945: 'an armoured car performs no useful police duty'.[12]

So we may accept that it is possible to 'drift into a law and order society', as Stuart Hall contends, and that there are cumulative effects from the use of military technology and even from some forms of organization.[13] The deliberately menacing undertone of John Alderson's phrase 'tooling up' may be repudiated by later Chief Constables, but these do not deny that very untraditional tools are now in police hands. The rationale is 'professional', not military. New kinds of units have been created, again, on the argument that they are better than the alternative of a 'third force': 'because it's deployed in line with public police thinking'.[14] The fact that demands for the creation of a third force, a true 'riot squad' like the French CRS, have tended to come from the left, may appear strange at first sight.[15] To judge from the uncharacteristically sketchy argument on the issue in P. A. J. Waddington's demi-official study of 'armed and public order policing', the police would prefer to head off any discussion of things which are so intensely 'political'.[16] This is understandable, but it misses the point that undiscussed changes may prove even less desirable.

The concentrations of police deployed to achieve the required control of pickets during the miners' strike, and the tactical units ('serials') developed in response to more violent rioting, inevitably have an impact on operational culture.

Public order structure is almost the very opposite of the normal watch and ward structure. In normal policing, the constable is on his own, he is told to think for himself and act on his initiative, to be an individual. In the public order structure it is the very opposite. He is part and parcel of a group, a platoon or a company. He is told *not* to act on his own but to wait for orders, *not* to use his initiative.[17]

Robert Chesshyre, who made a participant study of a Metropolitan division towards the end of the decade traced the consequences of the fact that lone bobbies could no longer face hostile crowds, or indeed any group of people. 'You don't survive as a PC unless you can be part of a team', he was told; 'You like to know that when you call for assistance you have 20 or 30 friends backing you up.' Such security has a price. Group identity, Graef notes, has pushed many policemen into an impossible dilemma: loyalty ('cover-ups') or 'trust in the essential ideals of the service' ('grassing'). As a result, as a disillusioned resignee told Chesshyre,

The core of the Metropolitan Police is slowly being torn out. They'll be left with officers concerned solely with enforcement. They'll be the people you recruit, and so it will go on and on.[18]

This pessimism is not wholly extravagant.

The British police have always been acutely conscious of the role of image and symbol in their public face. Shifting images are likely to have substantial effects. The most arresting symbol of the pressure generated by recent disorders is the nine-acre riot training centre established by the Metropolitan Police on Hounslow Heath. 'Riot City'—its title a bleak echo of Copland's urban tone-poem—consumes 3,000 empty milk bottles each month to feed its stream of petrol bombs. Such statistics, however fearsome, are maybe less important than the atmosphere of this 'macho location, where it would be easy [Chesshyre thought] to become infected with the notion that the world is a hostile place'. Here the conflicting outcomes of 'professionalism' are etched in the novel visual images whose shock value has been readily apparent to journalists. The significance of such images is never straightforward. The reluctance of the police to abandon the antiquated Prussian helmet which had (paradoxically) become the symbol of the force's unmilitary role, bears testimony to the perceived utility of image. Modern helmets arouse an irrational public dislike—though objectively they follow the same pattern of evolution from Victorian values as that which has equipped, say, construction workers with hard hats in place of cloth caps. Only an organization which placed a low value on the comfort and safety of its employees could have persisted so long with the original.

An installation like Riot City by its nature evaluates police experience of success and failure in street conflicts, and may well frame them in terms of 'victory' and 'defeat'. Such terms are scree on a slope. Observers have been struck by the potency of the 1985 Tottenham riots, especially, in generating a collective urge to reversal and revenge which is normally encouraged as part of the *esprit de corps* of military units. Whether such group spirit is containable in a police force is an exceptionally sensitive question; it was, in fact, exactly the question raised by the creation of the 'Black and Tan' police in Ireland in 1920. Then, camaraderie became the standard Parliamentary explanation for police reprisals.[19] These went a long way beyond a present-day policeman's admission that 'it's difficult when you see your colleagues being assaulted not to react with excessive force', but the distance is not so great as one might like to think.

In a situation where the exacerbation of such instincts is seen as unavoidable, a tremendous weight devolves on the command structure of the force. (In 1921 the army, no admirer of the Black and Tans, accepted that those Auxiliary Companies which were well officered were quite effective—albeit as *gendarmes*, not as police.) 'A busload of coppers is hard to handle once violence has broken out', Chesshyre quotes one inspector as saying. 'Their instinct is to get stuck in.'[20] The worst public dangers of militarization arise from the fact that the police system of command and discipline was not designed to handle armed forces in situations of intense or large-scale violence. Recent changes in command structure for public order purposes have only underlined the incompatibility of police and military logic, as Waddington's sympathetic discussion shows.[21] It is clear that British police placed in what are now called 'public order situations' have often found their commanders inadequate. 'If the day ever comes, I hope I have an inspector who has something up top, who knows what he's doing. If you don't it can be a shambles, a mockery.'[22]

Do the police in fact have no alternative but to respond to violence by 'professionalization'? If this is the case, the public seems to have little inclination to accept it. Survey evidence indicates consistent preference for what people think of as 'traditional' police behaviour, and aversion to the 'rudeness and excessive force' which they now expect to encounter.[23] It was a grim indication that a leading serious daily newspaper, giving a guarded welcome to Sir Peter Imbert's 'Plus Programme' (described with arch cosmopolitanism by the *Guardian* as 'the Met's version of perestroika') in 1989, should have suggested that if it failed

the resulting lack of co-operation in maintaining law and order will not only facilitate the spread of crime. It will also degrade the quality of life, making Britain less like a free society, in which people choose to obey the law, and more like an occupied country.[24]

The police have never ceased to lay formal stress on the need for public support, defined by the Metropolitan Police as 'a state of affairs in which most people find themselves in sympathy with the policing methods of the day'.[25] Yet the obvious corollary, that there should be effective public consultation about policing methods, has never commended itself to them. Such a public debate would appear to be especially relevant in the matter of public order, if most people are to be persuaded that the responses seen as unavoidable by the police are indeed so. If this were achieved, the order-maintenance capacity of the police must be substantially increased.

In the context of public order, 'professionalism' is a euphemism, if not exactly for militarism, then certainly for the posture of segregation from the public which is the most obvious defect of military government. It is the product of a tendency to specialization which has been consistently abetted by the Home Office and the civil government generally. (Recall the faith reposed in 'specialists such as experienced police officers used to handling crowds';[26] Harold Lasswell, in his seminal work on modern militarism, in fact identified the enlarging sphere of the 'specialists on violence' as the key element in the emerging 'garrison state'.[27]) The observations of the Fulton Commission on civil service reform may be borne in mind: the word 'professional' implied two main attributes. 'One is being skilled in one's job—skill which comes from training and sustained experience. The other is having the fundamental knowledge of and deep familiarity with a subject that enables a man [*sic*] to move with ease among its concepts. Both spring from and reinforce a constant striving for higher standards.' Thus professionalism is a neutral standard whose content must be supplied by definition of the 'job'. In the case of policing, the

definition implied—though not, of course, specified—by the actual usage
of 'professional' since the 1970s derives in part from the play made with
the term in army recruitment advertising. 'The Professionals' are not quite
the same kind of people as the Met's Plus Programme would suggest might
be found in the local 'cop shop'.

This role tension, and the stress it imposes on individuals moving quickly
from one role to the other, has been noticed by most writers on contemporary
policing. It showed vividly in the BBC TV documentary *The Queen's
Peace*, made shortly after the Broadwater Farm riots. (Sir Peter Imbert
later said publicly that officers now 'have a duty to be chameleon-like,
even "schizophrenic" '.[28]) Equally noticeable has been the common reaction
of ordinary policemen, disillusionment: 'the public has a better police force
than it deserves'. What underlies this situation has not been so widely
recognized. The idealized conception of public order generated in the late
nineteenth century now imposes impossible demands on the police. It was
a formative myth for police culture, and a transformative myth for public
culture generally. Its abandonment looks so perilous that few people, and
least of all politicians, are ready to face up to it.[29]

There are several reasons why public consultation is unappealing, amongst
them the general tendency of any executive who can avoid accountability
to do so. As one lawyer and local politician acutely put it, 'Government
has the feeling that to involve the public is to court trouble.' The feeling
derives in part from the problem of finding a viable mechanism for operating
this mainstay of democratic rhetoric. 'To involve the public'—as distinct
from sections like the press or even the educated middle class—is to civil
servants 'a meaningless expression'.[30] In the sphere of policing, however,
the notion of the public has been always been more manageable. As the
Met candidly says, 'Police officers have to listen to everybody. But there
will come a time when they must decide that some voices count more than
others.'[31] As a matter of historical practice, bodies existed to give form to
public opinion in this sphere, perhaps uniquely in the modern state. Yet
the functions of these bodies, the Police Authorities, have been attenuated
by the consciously 'professional' autonomy of Chief Constables. In the
only case where an Authority has been created *de novo*, in Northern
Ireland when the RUC Inspector-General became a Chief Constable—a
very plain recognition of the need for public support—the reach of 'operational' autonomy has been greater than anywhere else.

The 'qualitative sharpening of disorder' has set the seal on this steady
attenuation. As operational matters have become more military in form,
associated attitudes have become more pervasive. The ACPO Tactical

Options Manual was a major step on this path, as much through its ambience as through its specific content.[32] The latter might well have been accepted as necessary, but the secrecy shrouding the manual was not. Why was secrecy considered necessary by the COPs?[33] One Chief Constable reacted thus to Robert Reiner's question whether, since there had been misunderstandings, it would not have been better to introduce the manual with some public consultation:

No! It's got nothing to do with police authorities at all. It's an operational matter. The difficulty of informing anybody about what's in the Manual, the moment you start making it public, you reduce its effectiveness. I mean Army Joe is hardly going to discuss his tactics before he goes to war! Really, we would be crazy to come open.[34]

The idea that public knowledge will reduce rather than enhance the effectiveness of police action is as radical a reversal of traditional policing logic as could well be imagined.

The underlying rationale of such an approach is that the police can no longer afford to trust the public, or to rely on 'common sense'. Reiner's pioneering inquiry shows that while many, perhaps most Chief Constables hang on to a hope that things will come right, they are baffled by the present situation. As one put it, 'there's not a lot the police can do about it unless society changes'. (This is in relation to using plastic bullets: 'The reality is you've got to respond. You've got a vicious circle.') It is a complex historical development which has put Chief Constables in the position of being the only people who are required to 'respond', unaided, unadvised, and responsible only to 'the law' (not, as the Court of Appeal recently reiterated, to any actual court, except presumably for manifestly criminal irregularity.)[35] But does 'society' have to wait and see if it 'changes', or can it do anything about it? The British way, of course, militates against direct discussion of anything as fundamental as public order. The Court of Appeal put this fact with unusual clarity:

From time to time a need for more exact definitions arises. The present need arises from a difference of view between the Secretary of State and a police authority over what is necessary to maintain public order, a phenomenon which has been observed only in recent times. There has probably never been a comparable occasion for investigating a prerogative of keeping the peace within the realm.[36]

This novel phenomenon may possibly recur. But it is likely that redefinition of fundamental issues will only occur in the context of a larger constitutional debate.

Such a debate may now be beginning. The government's revival of 'active citizenship' was ill judged in one respect at least, in that it focused attention on a word which was slightly exotic to a conservative tradition. Britons, English and other, had habitually been taught to aspire to the status of 'good subjects', not citizens. The interplay between these labels had provided a theme for radical writers, but had hardly entered into the mainstream of public discourse until the *Independent* newspaper launched its series of articles on constitutional reform under the title 'Citizens or Subjects?' in the summer of 1991. This was an attempt to breathe life into the apparently stillborn Charter 88 movement, which culminated in an enthusiastic (but small) 'Constitutional Convention' in November.[37] The keystone of this movement is the belief that the unwritten constitution no longer functions as the best defence of civil liberties, and that a Bill of Rights is required to ensure that civil disorder does not become the endemic mode of post-industrial society. Lord Scarman himself has long been an advocate of inscription.[38]

The tenacity of the traditional belief, powerfully illustrated in the hostility of the Labour Party to reform, may prove to be unshakeable. Roy Hattersley reacted to Charter 88 by condemning the idea of a written constitution on the ground that it 'diminishes the importance of positive freedom'. The only rights which would command sufficient general assent to be included would be couched in excessively general and negative terms. This pessimism led him to label the movement 'the charter of despair'. Predictably, his solution to such despair was to replace 'Thatcherism' by a Labour government. This may well be the preferred public solution too. Certainly there is no sign of public enthusiasm for inscription generally, or for such crucial planks of open government as 'freedom of information'. And opinion surveys suggest that as few as 56 per cent of people want a Bill of Rights to guarantee freedom of assembly.[39]

Traditional drift will leave unanswered some big questions which have gone on growing, no less during Labour administrations than Conservative. The biggest is whether the stresses of modern political violence have exhausted the flexibility which has always been the chief virtue of the unwritten constitution. The spirit of tolerance cannot be specified. The modern emphasis on 'balance' is inherently more mechanical than traditional ideas of social harmony; it seems that here partial definition brings distortion. The common law tradition could deal with traditional war, but is stranded on the reefs of 'low intensity' rebellion and terrorism, just as the policing tradition has been disintegrated by 'slow rioting'. A protracted crisis raises new problems, for which the solutions so far arranged are not simply unsatisfactory but possibly dangerous: quite as dangerous, maybe, as are riots and terrorism to the assumptions which have underpinned the tradition. Imprecision and ambiguity may turn from virtues into vices if they shield the development of covert counter-terror.

While it may be that the expectation of due process—symbolized above all by jury trial—is so deeply rooted that even a 'temporary' abrogation of twenty (or fifty, or a hundred?) years will not eradicate it, the same is unlikely to be true of a conception of public order which was never so definite or so amenable to institutional formation. The right of public meeting, for example, was once believed to exist, and to be intrinsic to the British way. It is now clearly understood never to have existed. Yet we have gained a new right: the right to order. That is a big shift of awareness, whose implications are only beginning to be worked out. Writers on policing may express the hope that the public 'demand for order' does not come to require such rigorous law enforcement that the traditional discretion of the police is lost; yet the Chief Constable who interprets 'bringing the law into disrepute' as a breach of public order has already gone a long step down this road.[40] The public interest may never have been determined by the public as such, but people somehow believed it was. That belief can hardly be widespread now. Somewhere between Brixton and Bogside, Grunwick and Gibraltar, sometime in the last decade, the British way seems to have petered out. It looks as if we must now do it somebody else's way.

Abbreviations

ACPO	Association of Chief Police Officers
BL	British Library
BUF	British Union of Fascists
C.	Cabinet minute
CAB	Cabinet papers
CC	Chief Constable
CO	Colonial Office
COP	Chief Officer of Police
CP	series reference of Cabinet paper
CRS	Compagnies républicaines de Sécurité
DO	Dominions Office
DORA	Defence of the Realm Acts, 1914 and 1915
DORR	Defence of the Realm Regulations
EP 2	Emergency Powers committee, second report
GT	series reference of Cabinet paper
HC	House of Commons paper
HC Deb.	House of Commons Debates (Hansard)
HL Deb.	House of Lords Debates
IWM	Imperial War Museum
MEPO	Metropolitan Police papers
NLI	National Library of Ireland
PP	Parliamentary Papers
PRO HO	Public Record Office, Home Office papers
PRO FO	Public Record Office, Foreign Office papers
PRONI	Public Record Office of Northern Ireland
RIC	Royal Irish Constabulary
WO	War Office

Notes

Chapter 1

1. L. Radzinowicz and R. Hood, *A History of the English Criminal Law and its Administration from 1750*, v. *The Emergence of Penal Policy* (Stevens, London, 1986), 113–33. T. A. Critchley, *The Conquest of Violence: Order and Liberty in Britain* (Constable, London, 1970), *passim*. V. A. C. Gatrell 'The Decline of Theft and Violence in Victorian and Edwardian England,' in V. A. C. Gatrell, B. Lenman, and G. Parker (eds.), *Crime and Law: The Social History of Crime in Western Europe since 1500* (Europa, London, 1980).

2. W. L. Burn, *The Age of Equipoise* (Allen & Unwin, London, 1964), 58. This general shift is confirmed in local studies such as D. Philips, 'Riots and Public Order in the Black Country, 1835–1860', in R. Quinault and J. Stevenson (eds.), *Popular Protest and Public Order. Six Studies in British History 1790–1920* (Allen & Unwin, London, 1974), 141–73.

3. J. Saville, *1848: The British State and the Chartist Movement* (Cambridge University Press, Cambridge, 1987), 102–25.

4. The Great Exhibition of 1851, he added, was 'the Pageant of domestic peace'. G. M. Young, *Portrait of an Age: Victorian England* [orig. edn. 1936], annotated G. Kitson Clark (Oxford University Press, Oxford 1977), 89.

5. For the origins and early agenda of professional policing see S. H. Palmer, *Police and Protest in England and Ireland 1780–1850* (Cambridge University Press, Cambridge, 1988). Also D. Philips, ' "A New Engine of Power and Authority": The Institutionalization of Law Enforcement in England, 1780–1830', in Gatrell *et al.* (eds.) *Crime and the Law*; D. Jones, *Crime, Protest, Community and Police in Nineteenth-century Britain* (Routledge, London, 1982).

6. S. Hall, C. Crichter, T. Jefferson, J. Clarke, and B. Roberts, *Policing the Crisis: Mugging, the State, and Law and Order* (Macmillan, London, 1978), 53 ff.

7. F. M. L. Thompson, *The Rise of Respectable Society: A Social History of Victorian Britain 1830–1900* (Fontana, London, 1988), 331–2. E. P. Thompson, 'The Secret State', *Writing by Candlelight* (Merlin, London, 1980), Cf. also M. Brogden's emphasis on the salience of 'moving on' in the repertoire of police activity: 'The mandate of these officers was to keep the Liverpool streets clean, as a kind of uniformed garbage-men.' *On the Mersey*

Beat: Policing Liverpool Between the Wars (Oxford University Press, Oxford, 1991), 1.

8. A. Silver, 'The Demand for Order in Civil Society: A Review of Some Themes in the History of Urban Crime, Police, and Riot', in D. J. Bordua (ed.), *The Police: Six Sociological Essays* (Wiley, New York, 1967), 21.

9. A similar process has been remarked for an earlier period: 'the very capacity of high medieval English government, puny though it may seem by modern standards, may have lowered the social threshold for the perception of unacceptable violence and disorder'. R. W. Kaeuper, *War, Justice and Public Order: England and France in the Later Middle Ages* (Oxford University Press, Oxford, 1988), 175.

10. G. Pearson, *Hooligan: A History of Respectable Fears* (Macmillan, London, 1983).

11. Sir Thomas Elyot, *The Boke Named the Governour*, ed. and introd. S. E. Lehmberg (Dent, London, 1962), 2. W. H. Greenleaf, *Order, Empiricism and Politics: Two Traditions of English Political Thought 1500–1700* (Oxford, Oxford University Press, 1964).

12. E. Burke, *Thoughts and Details on Scarcity* (F. & C. Rivington, London, 1800). The current orthodoxy is that the salient unit of community in early modern England was the county (e.g. A. Fletcher, *A County Community in Peace and War: Sussex, 1600–1660* (Longman, London, 1975); but the concept has been all but demolished by A. Macfarlane, 'History, Anthropology and the Study of Communities', *Social History* 5 (1977), 631–52.

13. Elyot, *The Boke*, 3.

14. P. Laslett, *The World We Have Lost* (3rd edn., Methuen, London, 1983), 4.

15. R. N. Berki, *Security and Society: Reflections on Law, Order and Politics* (Dent, London, 1986), 98–9.

16. K. Wrightson, 'Two Concepts of Order', in A. Fletcher and J. Stevenson (eds.), *Order and Disorder in Early Modern England* (Cambridge University Press, Cambridge, 1985), 22.

17. C. K. Allen, *Law and Orders: An Inquiry into the Nature and Scope of Delegated Legislation and Executive Powers in England* (Stevens, London, 1956).

18. A. Macintyre, *After Virtue* (Duckworth, London, 1981), 181.

19. Though there have been studies of medieval 'public order', such as J. Bellamy, *Crime and Public Order in England in the Later Middle Ages* (Routledge, London, 1973) and Kaeuper, *War, Justice and Public Order*, the term seems to be a modern extrapolation (Kaeuper, personal communication).

20. This was reflected in neglect of the concept by both historians and social scientists; perhaps the first critical historical essay is G. E. Aylmer, 'The Peculiarities of the English State', *Journal of Historical Sociology* 3: 2 (1990).

21. Berki, *Security and Society*, ch. 1, provides a thoughtful analysis of the 'Paradoxes of Security'.

22. T. Starkey, *A Dialogue between Cardinal Pole and Thomas Lupset* (ed. T. F. Mayer, Camden Fourth Series vol. 37, Royal Historical Society, London, 1989), 2, 8; M. E. James, 'The Concept of Order and the Northern Rising 1569', *Past and Present* 60 (1973).

23. P. Williams, *The Tudor Regime* (Clarendon Press, Oxford, 1979), 391.

24. J. G. A. Pocock, *The Ancient Constitution and the Feudal Law* (Cambridge University Press, Cambridge, 1957), 32, 55.

25. Ibid., 33.

26. Ibid. 51; K. Dyson, 'The Word State in the British Intellectual Tradition', in *The State Tradition in Western Europe: A Study of an Idea and an Institution* (Martin Robertson, Oxford, 1980).

27. F. L. Neumann, *The Rule of Law: Political Theory and the Legal System in Modern Society* (Berg, Leamington Spa, 1985); E. M. Barendt, *Freedom of Speech* (Oxford University Press, Oxford, 1985).

28. Wrightson, 'Two Concepts of Order', 25.

29. E. P. Thompson, *Whigs and Hunters: The Origin of the Black Act* (Allen Lane, London, 1975); 'The Peculiarities of the English', in *The Poverty of Theory* (Merlin, London, 1978).

30. D. Hay, 'Property, Authority and the Criminal Law', in D. Hay, P. Linebaugh, and E. P. Thompson (eds.), *Albion's Fatal Tree* (Allen Lane, London, 1975); J. H. Langbein, 'Albion's Fatal Flaws', *Past and Present* 98 (1983), 96–120; J. Innes and J. Styles, 'The Crime Wave: Recent Writing on Crime and Criminal Justice in Eighteenth-century England', *Journal of British Studies* 25 (1986), 380–435.

31. Fletcher and Stevenson (eds.), *Order and Disorder*, 15.

32. Langbein, 'Albion's Fatal Flaws', 118. Cf. the view of Taine's disciple Émile Boutmy, who found the accretion of laws and the absence of principles to be an outcome of the English incapacity to generalize. *The English People: A Study of their Political Psychology* (Putnam, London, 1904), 19, 164 ff.

33. E. Colson, *Tradition and Contract. The Problem of Order* (Aldine, Chicago, 1974); C. Maxwell, *Country and Town in Ireland under the Georges* (W. Tempest, Dundalk, 1949), 182. H. Foster, 'Shooting the Elephant: Historians and the Problem of Frontier Lawlessness', in R. Eales and D. Sullivan (eds.), *The Political Context of Law: Proceedings of the Seventh British Legal History Conference* (Hambledon Press, London, 1987), 135–44, provides a sharp indication of the problems involved in the analysis of legal culture.

34. T. Hobbes, *Leviathan, or the Matter, Forme and Power of a Commonwealth Ecclesiasticall and Civil*, ed. M. Oakeshott (Blackwell, Oxford, n.d.), 85.

35. E. J. Hobsbawm, *Primitive Rebels: Studies in Archaic Forms of Social Movement in the 19th and 20th Centuries* (Manchester University Press, Manchester, 1959), 119. M. Supperstone (ed.), *Brownlie's Law of Public Order and National Security* (2nd edn., Butterworth, London, 1981), 2. C. K. Allen, *The Queen's Peace* (Stevens, London, 1953); D. G. T. Williams,

Keeping the Peace: The Police and Public Order (Hutchinson, London, 1967). Neither of these last sees a need to define peace except in the breach.

36. *Manchester Mercury* and PRO HO 43 11, quoted in J. Bohstedt, *Riots and Community Politics in England and Wales 1790–1810* (Harvard University Press, Cambridge, Mass. 1983), 115, 139. It may be noted, though, that Maurice Cranston translated Rousseau's 'On vit tranquille' as 'There is peace'.

37. Vigorously criticized in C. Herrup, 'Crime, Law and Society', *Comparative Studies in Society and History* 27: 1 (1985), 159–70; A. Macfarlane and S. Harrison, *The Justice and the Mare's Ale: Law and Disorder in Seventeenth-century England* (Blackwell, Oxford, 1981), 18–19; A. Macfarlane, 'Violence. Peasants and Bandits', in *The Culture of Capitalism* (Blackwell, Oxford, 1987), 53–76. J. Brewer and J. Styles, *An Ungovernable People: The English and Their Law in the Seventeenth and Eighteenth Centuries* (Hutchinson, London, 1980). L. Stone, 'Interpersonal Violence in English Society 1300–1980', *Past and Present* 101, (Nov. 1983), 22–33; but see J. S. Cockburn, 'Patterns of Violence in English Society: Homicide in Kent 1560–1985', *Past and Present* 130 (1991), 70–106.

38. R. Chamberlin, *The Idea of England* (Thames & Hudson, New York, 1986), 81–94.

39. G. Gorer, *Exploring English Character* (Cresset, London, 1955), 13–14.

40. Especially his speculations (App. 1, 305–12) about the reciprocal relationship between the image of the police and the national self-image.

41. Kaeuper, *War, Justice and Public Order, passim*; lawyers' accounts can still be more sentimental: e.g. J. K. Weber, 'The King's Peace: A Comparative Study', *Journal of Legal History* 10 (1989), 135–60.

42. Bellamy, *Crime and Public Order*, 200.

43. C. Herrup, *The Common Peace: Participation and the Criminal Law in Seventeenth-century England* (Cambridge University Press, Cambridge, 1987), 200.

44. R. D. Storch, ' "Please to Remember the Fifth of November": Conflict, Solidarity and Public Order in Southern England, 1815–1900', in R. D. Storch (ed.), *Popular Culture and Custom in Nineteenth-century England* (Croom Helm, London, 1982). There is a lucid view of 'the cultural background of the police idea' in E. Bittner, *The Functions of the Police in Modern Society* (National Institute of Mental Health, Chevy Chase, Md., Nov. 1970).

45. Bohstedt, *Riots and Community Politics*, 4 takes as a functional definition an incident involving a crowd of over 50 people 'on the assumption that crowds of that size acted upon "public", that is social motives'.

46. J. F. Stephen, *A History of the Criminal Law of England* (Macmillan, London, 1883), i. 203, on the 'singular effect' of the Riot Act; W. E. Nippel, ' "Reading the Riot Act": The Discourse of Law Enforcement in 18th Century

England', *History and Anthropology* 1: 2 (1985), 401–26, esp. 405; J. Stevenson, 'Social Control and the Prevention of Riots in England, 1789–1829', in A. P. Donajgrodski (ed.), *Social Control in Nineteenth-century Britain* (Croom Helm, London, 1977), 35.

47. Hobsbawm, *Primitive Rebels*, 111.

48. C. Tilly, 'The Web of Contention in Eighteenth-Century Cities', in L. A. Tilly and C. Tilly (eds.), *Class Conflict and Collective Action* (Sage, London, 1981), 39.

49. Q. Skinner, *The Foundations of Modern Political Thought*, i (Cambridge University Press, Cambridge, 1978), 181.

50. Laslett, *The World We Have Lost*, 195.

51. H. O. Arnold-Forster, *The Citizen Reader* (Cassell, London, 1900), 153.

52. J. H. Plumb, 'Riot', in *In the Light of History* (Allen Lane, London, 1972), 182.

53. F. Munger, 'Contentious Gatherings in Lancashire . . . 1750–1830', and L. A. Tilly, 'Conclusion', in L. A. and C. Tilly, (eds.), *Class Conflict and Collective Action*.

54. Home Office memo, 'Riots in the Metropolis', n.d., PRO HO 42 37, quoted in Stevenson, 'Social Control', 30.

55. E. Cruickshanks and H. Erskine-Hill, 'The Waltham Black Act and Jacobitism', *Journal of British Studies* 24: 3 (1985), 358–65.

56. Philips, 'Riots and Public Order', 141, 169, found fear of 'a breaking down of the order of civil society' and a sense that public disorder was 'a serious social threat' until the 1850s.

57. N. Gash, *Aristocracy and People: Britain 1815–1865* (Arnold, London, 1979), 98–9.

58. F. O. Darvall, *Popular Disturbances and Public Order in Regency England* (Oxford University Press, London, 1934).

59. E. J. Hobsbawm and G. Rude, *Captain Swing* (Penguin Books, Harmondsworth, 1973), 219–20.

60. Peel to Maj.-Gen. Sir Henry Bouverie, 29 Aug. 1830. PRO HO 40 26.

61. Peel to Bouverie, BL Add. MSS 40401 fo. 253, quoted in N. Gash, *Mr Secretary Peel* (Longman, London, 1961), 620; also PRO HO 41 8 29–65, ibid. 648.

62. PRO HO 41 8 18, 30 Oct. 1830, ibid. 620–1.

63. L. Radzinowicz, 'New Departures in Maintaining Public Order in the Face of the Chartist Disturbances', *Cambridge Law Journal* (Apr. 1960), 51.

64. L. Radzinowicz, *A History of the English Criminal Law*, iv (Stevens, London, 1968), 239.

65. R. Fyson, 'The Crisis of 1842: Chartism, the Colliers' Strike and the Outbreak in the Potteries', in J. Epstein and D. Thompson (eds.), *The Chartist Experience: Studies in Working-Class Radicalism and Culture, 1830–60* (Macmillan, London, 1982), 208.

66. Ibid. 215, 209. Cf. F. C. Mather, 'The General Strike of 1842', in J. Stevenson and R. Quinault (eds.) *Popular Protest and Public Order: Six Studies in British History, 1790–1920* (Allen & Unwin, London, 1974).

67. R. D. Storch, 'Policing Rural Southern England before the Police: Opinion and Practice, 1830–1856', in D. Hay and F. Snyder (eds.), *Policing and Prosecution in Britain 1750–1850* (Oxford University Press, Oxford, 1989), 235.

68. Graham to Queen, 16 Aug. 1842, C. S. Parker, *Life and Letters of Sir James Graham 1792–1861*, i (John Murray, London, 1907), 320.

69. Philips, 'A New Engine'; Storch, 'Policing Rural England', 236 ff., argues that the 'rhetorical' version of public order frequently voiced during the Quarter Sessions debates on the Constabulary Commission proposals in 1839 was a creation of the eighteenth century. But it was resilient. Josephine Butler was still asserting the old idea in the 1870s: 'Personal security is purchased at too high a cost if it be obtained at the price of personal liberty' (*Government by Police*, Dyer Brothers, London, 1879, 7). Boutmy, *The English People*, 270, noted wonderingly that 'it was not until 1857 that the public safety was secured by the hand of the state'.

70. He was unable to find anybody who had actually been garotted; N. J. Hall, *Trollope: A Biography* (Oxford University Press, Oxford, 1991), 353.

71. Representative consensus studies are Critchley, *Conquest of Violence*; C. Reith, *The Police Idea* (Oxford University Press, London, 1938) and *The British Police and the Democratic Ideal* (Oxford University Press, London, 1942); D. Ascoli, *The Queen's Peace: The Origins and Development of the Metropolitan Police 1829–1979* (Hamish Hamilton, London, 1979). The conflictual approach was led by R. D. Storch, 'The Plague of the Blue Locusts: Police Reform and Popular Resistance in Northern England, 1840–57', *International Review of Social History* 20: 1 (1975), 61–90. The issue is analysed in D. J. V. Jones, 'The New Police, Crime, and People in England and Wales, 1829–1888', *Transactions of the Royal Historical Society* 33 (1983), 151–68.

72. The most trenchant critique is F. M. L. Thompson, 'Social Control in Victorian Britain', *Economic History Review* 2nd ser. 34: 2 (1981); see also S. Cohen and A. Scull (eds.), *Social Control and the State* (Martin Robertson, Oxford, 1983), esp. M. Ignatieff, 'State, Civil Society and Total Institutions', 75–105.

73. W. R. Miller, *Cops and Bobbies: Police Authority in New York and London, 1830–1870* (Chicago University Press, Chicago, 1977), 13.

74. e.g. D. J. V. Jones, *Crime, Protest, Community and Police in Nineteenth-century Britain* (Routledge, London, 1982); C. Steedman, *Policing the Victorian Community: The Formation of English Provincial Police Forces, 1856–80* (Routledge, London, 1984).

75. Anon., *The Special Constable: His Duties and Privileges* (Arthur Pearson, London, 1914), 11.

76. Bloomfield to Palmerston, 14 Aug. 1857, PRO FO 64 332, quoted in B. Porter, *Origins of the Vigilant State* (Weidenfeld, London, 1987), 2; S. H. Palmer, *Police and Protest*, 36; Philips, 'A New Engine', 183, 188–9.

77. Philips, 'Riots and Public Order', 142.

78. L. Lustgarten, *The Governance of Police* (Sweet & Maxwell, London, 1986), ch. 3.

79. Steedman, *Policing the Victorian Community*, 19.

80. 'The Police and the Thieves', *Quarterly Review* 99 (1856), 170, quoted in P. T. Smith, *Policing Victorian London: Political Policing, Public Order, and the London Metropolitan Police* (Greenwood, London, 1985), 45.

81. J. W. Gerard, *London and New York* (1851), quoted in Miller, *Cops and Bobbies*, 34, 81 n. 19.

82. *Vide* the exiguous file at PRO MEPO 2 60.

83. 'The Police of London', *Quarterly Review* 129 (1870), 48.

84. J. R. Western, *The English Militia in the Eighteenth Century* (Routledge, London, 1965); A. J. Hayter, *The Army and the Crowd in Mid-Georgian England* (Macmillan, London, 1978).

85. C. Townshend, 'Martial Law: Legal and Administrative Problems of Civil Emergency in Britain and the Empire 1800–1940', *Historical Journal* 25 (1982), 171.

86. L. Keller, 'Public Order in Victorian London: The Interaction Between the Metropolitan Police, the Government, the Urban Crowd, and the Law', Ph.D. thesis, Cambridge University, 1976, 1.

87. Radzinowicz, *History of English Criminal Law*, iv. 151.

88. Radzinowicz, 'New Departures', 74–8.

89. H. Weisser, 'Chartism in 1848: Reflections on a Non-Revolution', *Albion* 13 (Spring 1981), 13, 24.

90. Ibid. 15; cf. John Frost's letter To the Working Men of Monmouthshire, 27 Apr. 1848: 'PEACE, LAW AND ORDER is the motto of the Chartists', quoting Blackstone in defence of the right of public meeting. D. J. V. Jones, *The Last Rising*, 76.

91. Saville, 1848, 112, 113.

92. Ibid. 96.

93. Stubbs, *Constitutional History of England*, i. 39; J. Campbell, *Stubbs and the English State* (The Stenton Lecture, 1987, Reading University, Reading, 1989) revives Stubbs's claim to be taken seriously about the English *Sonderweg*.

94. Stubbs, *Lectures on Early English History* (Longmans, London, 1906), 326, quoted in J. W. Burrow, *A Liberal Descent: Victorian Historians and the English Past* (Cambridge University Press, Cambridge, 1981), 136.

95. A. P. Thornton, *The Habit of Authority: Paternalism in British History* (Allen & Unwin, London, 1964), 180.

96. *Australia and New Zealand* (London, 1873), quoted in Hall, *Trollope*, 166.

97. M. J. Wiener, *English Culture and the Decline of the Industrial Spirit*,

1850–1980 (Cambridge University Press, Cambridge, 1981). J. B. Priestley confronted the same puzzle, writing of a host who 'though a capable man of business is at heart, I suspect, a country gentleman': 'There are a lot of men like him in this country; members of the educated, technical middle-class, excellent at their jobs, but who long to be rid of them, and only keep working until their children are educated and off their hands, after which they retire happily in the country . . . They are all pleasant sensible fellows, and I cannot yet decide whether they are ruining us or keeping us sane'. *English Journey* (Harper and Brothers, London, 1934), 207.

98. Young, *Portrait of an Age*, 94.

99. J. Crump, 'The Identity of English Music: the Reception of Elgar 1898–1935', in R. Colls and P. Dodd (eds.), *Englishness: Politics and Culture 1880–1920* (Croom Helm, London, 1986), 164–90.

100. A. Howkins, 'The Discovery of Rural England', in Colls and Dodd (eds.), *Englishness*, 62–88. A. Rogers, 'People in the Countryside', in G. E. Mingay (ed.), *The Rural Idyll* (Routledge, London, 1989), 103.

101. Hobsbawm and Rudé, *Captain Swing*, 218.

102. De Ros to Sir Duncan McGregor, 23 Jan. 1848. NLI MS 7617 fo. 4.

103. Ford Madox Hueffer, *The Heart of the Country* (Alston Rivers, L), 6. R. A. Stradling, review of Colls and Dodd, and of Wiener, *Textual Practice* 2 (1988), 431.

104. Steedman, *Policing the Victorian Community*, 2; on the 1839 Act see Palmer, *Police and Protest*, 425–7.

105. Herrup, *The Common Peace*, 55.

106. J. C. D. Clark, *Revolution and Rebellion: State and Society in England in the Seventeenth and Eighteenth Centuries* (Cambridge University Press, Cambridge, 1986), 34. This is a classically English work in that it offers no definition of revolution, rebellion, or state.

107. This is of course to avoid the vexed question of whether there were ever any 'peasants' in the strict sense: see A. Macfarlane, 'Peasants', in *The Culture of Capitalism*, 1–24. Macfarlane's general attack on the application of modernization theory to England, premised on a kind of English *Sonderweg* starting in the twelfth century if not earlier, does not address itself to perceptions of change, with which this book is principally concerned.

108. T. Nairn, *The Break-up of Britain* (2nd edn., Verso, London, 1981), 42–5.

Chapter 2

1. F. C. Mather, *Public Order in the Age of the Chartists* (Manchester University Press, Manchester, 1959), 33.

2. R. B. McDowell, *The Irish Administration 1801–1914* (Routledge, London, 1964).

3. Following the pioneering research and persuasive interpretation of George

Cornewall Lewis, *Local Disturbances in Ireland* (B. Fellowes, London, 1836).

4. C. Townshend, *Political Violence in Ireland: Government and Resistance since 1848* (Clarendon Press, Oxford, 1983), 6 ff. and ch. 1, *passim*.

5. *The Times*, 13 May 1871, quoted in Townshend, *Political Violence in Ireland*, 50.

6. HC Deb. 3rd ser. vol. 204 col. 1194.

7. Sir J. R. Seeley, *The Expansion of England* (Macmillan, London, 1883), 5, 206.

8. F. Harrison, *Martial Law: Six Letters to the 'Daily News'* (The Jamaica Committee, London, 1867); G. Dutton, *The Hero as Murderer: The Life of Edward John Eyre 1815–1901* (London, 1967), 23.

9. B. Semmel, *The Governor Eyre Controversy* (MacGibbon & Kee, London, 1962).

10. Though the mystical entity continued to tantalize believers in national efficiency such as Alfred Milner.

11. Sir J. F. Stephen, *A History of the Criminal Law of England*, iii (Macmillan, London, 1883), 332, quoted by his colleague and mutual dedicatee Sir John Strachey, *India: Its Administration and Progress* (3rd edn., Macmillan, London, 1903), 96.

12. Ibid. 97; Strachey added that this was still 'equally true more than twenty years later'.

13. Radzinowicz and Hood, *English Criminal Law*, v. 723.

14. L. Radzinowicz, *Sir James Fitzjames Stephen 1829–1894 and His Contribution to the Development of Criminal Law* (Selden Society, London, 1957), 18.

15. Ibid. 21.

16. 'Shooting Niagara: And After?', *Macmillan's Magazine* 16 (1867), 324–5.

17. J. F. Stephen, *Liberty, Equality, Fraternity*, ed. R. J. White (Cambridge University Press, Cambridge, 1967), 62.

18. Ibid. 87–8.

19. A. P. Thornton, *The Habit of Authority*, 153–5.

20. Hunter, *Life of Mayo*, ii. 169, quoted in E. Stokes, *The English Utilitarians and India* (Oxford, Oxford University Press, 1959), 302.

21. Stephen, *Liberty, Equality, Fraternity*, 112–15.

22. F. Harrison, 'The Religion of Inhumanity', *Fortnightly Review* (June 1873), 689–91.

23. Sir J. F. Stephen, 'Foundations of the Government of India', *The Nineteenth Century* 80 (Oct. 1883), 558.

24. The classic attack on this process, Herbert Spencer's *The Man Versus the State* (London, 1884) did not offer a definition of the state, equating it with coercion and the tyranny of the majority.

25. Burrow, *A Liberal Descent*, 79.

26. W. Bagehot, *The English Constitution* (Oxford University Press, London, 1867), 287.

27. D. Spring, 'Walter Bagehot and Deference', *American Historical Review* 81 (1976), 524–31.

28. D. Kavanagh, 'The Deferential English: A Comparative Critique', *Government and Opposition* 6: 3 (1971), 346.

29. Ibid. 347.

30. Bagehot, *English Constitution*, 268.

31. Ibid. 143–4. See the weight accorded to the word 'business' by George Eliot's Caleb Garth, and Boutmy's observation (*English People*, 9) of 'the volume of meaning conveyed by the word "business" as compared with our word "affaires"'.

32. S. T. Coleridge, *On the Constitution of Church and State* (Pickering, London, 1839), 54; H. C. G. Matthew, *The Liberal Imperialists* (Oxford University Press, London, 1973), 140.

33. Thomas Duncombe, HC Deb. 3rd ser. vol. 75, col. 899, quoted in D. Vincent, 'Communication, Community and the State', in C. Emsley and J. Walvin (eds.), *Artisans, Peasants and Proletarians 1760–1860* (Croom Helm, London, 1985), 182.

34. D. Vincent, 'The Origins of Public Secrecy in Britain', *Transactions of the Royal Historical Society* 6th ser., 1 (London, 1991), 229.

35. Vincent, 'Communication, Community and the State', 182.

36. Ibid. 181.

37. Thornton, *The Habit of Authority*, 14.

38. Ibid. 254.

39. Ibid. 236.

40. Ibid. 241.

41. Ibid. 280.

42. Ibid. 281.

43. H. G. Wells, *The Future in America: A Search After Realities* (Harper, New York, 1906), 153, 167.

44. Thornton, *The Habit of Authority*, 320.

45. H. Eckstein, 'The Sources of Leadership and Democracy in Britain', in S. H. Beer and A. B. Ulam (eds.), *Patterns of Government: The Major Political Systems of Europe* (2nd edn., Random House, New York, 1962), 101.

46. On all of the OED's meanings, Eckstein's assertion is merely tautologous.

Chapter 3

1. D. C. Richter, *Riotous Victorians* (Ohio University Press, Athens, Oh., 1981), 163.

2. S. Clark, *Social Origins of the Irish Land War* (Princeton University Press, Princeton, NS, 1979) provides the most systematic assessment of its

significance. A. Warren, 'Forster, the Liberals and New Directions in Irish Policy 1880–1882', *Parliamentary History* 6 (1987), 96–126, analyses the crisis of order.

3. Harcourt to Gladstone, 9 July 1882. Bodleian Library, Harcourt papers 8.

4. Townshend, *Political Violence in Ireland*, 173–4.

5. Ibid. 158–66; K. R. M. Short, *The Dynamite War: Irish-American Bombers in Victorian Britain* (Gill & Macmillan, Dublin, 1979) provides a solid factual account.

6. Even R. N. Berki makes heavy weather of political crime in his generally lucid (if discursive) *Security and Society*.

7. P. Norton (ed.), *Law and Order in British Politics* (Gower, Aldershot, 1984), 7 ff.

8. Porter, *Origins of the Vigilant State*, 18.

9. Richter, *Riotous Victorians*, 139.

10. *Spectator*, 19 Nov. 1887 , 1561; quoted in R. M. Kamm, 'The Home Office, Public Order, and Civil Liberties, 1880–1914', Ph.D. thesis, Cambridge University 1981, 18.

11. Harcourt to Chairman, Metropolitan Board of Works, Aug. 1883. HO 45 12731, quoted in Richter, *Riotous Victorians*, 93.

12. Matthews to Monro, [2?]3 May 1890. MEPO 2 248.

13. Kamm, 'The Home Office', 88, 101.

14. Porter, *Origins of the Vigilant State*, 96 ff. See also N. Vance, *The Sinews of the Spirit* (Cambridge University Press, Cambridge, 1985).

15. *R. v. Burns and others* [1886], quoted in B. L. Ingraham, *Political Crime in Europe: A Comparative Study of France, Germany, and England* (California University Press, Berkeley, Calif., 1979), 209.

16. Ingraham, *Political Crime*, 209.

17. HC Deb. 4th ser vol. 80 (15 Mar. 1900) col. 975 D. G. T. Williams, 'Protest and Public Order', *Cambridge Law Journal* 28: 1 (1970), 99.

18. W. S. Jevons, *The State in Relation to Labour* (Macmillan, London, 1882), ch. 5.

19. R. Geary, *Policing Industrial Disputes: 1893 to 1985* (Cambridge University Press, Cambridge, 1985), 6–24.

20. C. Townshend, '"One man whom you can hang if necessary": The discreet charm of Nevil Macready', in J. Hattendorf and M. Murfitt (eds.), *The Limits of Military Power* (Macmillan, London, 1990).

21. J. Morgan, *Conflict and Order: The Police and Labour Disputes in England and Wales 1900–1939* (Clarendon Press, Oxford, 1987), 46.

22. Maj. G. Anson, CC Staffs., memo 7 Apr. 1911. MEPO 3 200.

23. *Episodes and Reflections, being some Records from the Life of Major-General Sir Wyndham Childs* (London, 1930), 84.

24. Macready to Churchill, 15 Nov. 1910. HO 144 1551 199768 sec. 69.

25. Macready to Churchill, 26 Nov. 1910. HO 144 1551 199768 sec. 139.

26. *Colliery Strike Disturbances in South Wales: Correspondence and Report*, Cd. 5568, 49.

27. Macready to Churchill, 30 Dec. 1910. HO 144 1552 199768 sec. 197.

28. *Daily Mail*, 21 Aug. 1911, quoted in Kamm, 'The Home Office', 231.

29. G. R. Searle, *The Quest for National Efficiency: A Study in British Politics and Political Thought, 1899–1914* (Blackwell, Oxford, 1971).

30. Report of the Departmental Committee Appointed to Inquire into the Disturbances at Featherstone, C. 7234; Report of the Inter-Departmental Committee on Riots, Appointed by the Home Secretary, May 1894, C. 7650.

31. Report of the Select Committee on Employment of Military in Cases of Disturbances, PP 1908 VII. 365.

32. 'The Powers possessed by the Executive in times of emergency and war', 1908. Notes by Col. J. E. Edmonds, 1909. Liddell Hart Centre, King's College, London. Edmonds MSS IV/4.

33. Memo by Sir C. Ilbert, 6 Aug. 1896. In General Staff memo. CAB 16 31 EP2.

34. Edmonds notes, Edmonds MSS IV/4.

35. Ibid. 37.

36. Memo, 10 Nov. 1897, Edmonds notes, Edmonds MSS IV/4.

37. Ibid. 38–9.

38. Ibid. 22.

39. C. Townshend, 'Martial Law: Legal and Administrative Problems of Civil Emergency in Britain and the Empire, 1800–1940', *Historical Journal* 25 (1982).

40. A. V. Dicey, *Introduction to the Study of the Law of the Constitution* (Macmillan, London, 1885; 10th edn., 1959), 290.

41. A. V. Dicey, 'The Prevalence of Lawlessness in England' (written 20 July 1883), *The Nation*, 2 Aug. 1883, 95.

42. Sir H. Thring, *A Summary of the Law of Riot and Insurrection* (HMSO, London, 1881).

43. C. L. Rossiter, *Constitutional Dictatorship: Crisis Government in the Modern Democracies* (Princeton University Press, Princeton, NJ, 1948), 146.

44. C. Townshend, *Britain's Civil Wars: Counterinsurgency in the Twentieth Century* (Faber, London, 1986), 13–15.

45. F. Pollock, 'What is Martial Law?', *Law Quarterly Review* 18 (1902).

46. C. Dodd, 'The Case of Marais', *Law Quarterly Review* 18 (1902).

47. Opinion of the Law Officers of the Crown, 17 July 1913. CAB 16 31 EP2.

48. Director of Military Training to Chief of General Staff, 11 Oct. 1908. WO 32 5270.

49. Quoted in 'Prevention of Civil Disturbance in London in Time of War'. WO 32 5270.

50. Memo by CC Lanarkshire, 6 Feb. 1909. WO 32 5270.

51. Commissioner to GOC London District, 18 July 1910. HO 144 1650 fo. 179987. But cf. his later view that it was 'useless to keep in peace' such a

register, because 'men would not register ... although they would be ready to come forward in time of emergency'. 30 Jan. 1913, WO 32 5270.

52. Eckstein, 'The Sources of Leadership', 82

53. B. Harrison, 'The Act of Militancy: Violence and the Suffragettes, 1904–1914', in *Peaceable Kingdom: Stability and Change in Modern Britain* (Clarendon Press, Oxford, 1982), 26–81.

54. Jevons, *The State in Relation to Labour*, 135.

55. Townshend, *Political Violence in Ireland*, ch. 5.

56. The historiography of the showdown is large and still growing. Apart from the two well-known book-length accounts by Ryan and Fergusson, there are important analyses in Jalland, *The Liberals and Ireland* (Harvester, Brighton, 1980) and R. Holmes, *The Little Field-Marshal: Sir John French* (Cape, London, 1981). The consensus trend towards relabelling the 'mutiny' an 'incident' is followed in E. Muenger, *The British Military Dilemma in Ireland: Occupation Politics, 1886–1914* (Gill & Macmillan, Dublin, 1991); whilst it may be technically more accurate, the anodyne word 'incident' manifestly fails to signal the larger significance of the crisis.

57. The decisive contribution is the collection of documents assembled by I. Beckett (ed.), *The British Army and the Curragh Incident* (Army Records Society, Bodley Head, London, 1986), amplified by I. Beckett, 'Some Further Correspondence relating to the Curragh Incident of March 1914', *Journal of the Society for Army Historical Research* 69: 278 (1991) where the full venom of the Goughs' contempt for any officer from French, Paget ('these skunks ... knaves, traitors and cowards'), and Fergusson ('miserably weak', 'sheer lack of nerve') downwards ('How Romer and Hickie could have gone beats me but I will never trust either the yard again') practically scorches the page.

58. Notes for addresses given to artillery officers of the 5th Division by Brig.-Gen. J. E. W. Headlam, 21 Mar. 1914 (holograph). Beckett, 'Some Further Correspondence', 103.

59. B. Porter, 'The Origins of Britain's Political Police' (Warwick Working Papers in Social History no. 3, 1985), 26.

60. Gladstone to Harcourt, 5 Apr. 1883. Bodleian Library, MS Harcourt dep. 9 fo. 31. See also 'Return showing number of Police specially employed for protection of Her Majesty's Ministers and Public Buildings', 17 Mar. 1883, and correspondence. MS Harcourt dep. 101 fos. 11–15.

61. Porter, 'Origins of Britain's Political Police', 27.

62. Parliamentary Debates (Commons), 28 Mar. 1889, quoted in T. Bunyan, *The History and Practice of the Political Police in Britain* (Julian Friedmann, London, 1976), 6.

63. The best study of the OSA is D. G. T. Williams, *Not in the Public Interest: The Problem of Security in Democracy* (Hutchinson, London, 1965). The 1911 Act has disappeared from history in a curious way: it rates only a passing

reference in P. Rowland's large-scale study, *The Last Liberal Governments*, ii (Barrie & Jenkins, London, 1971), 26, with the comment that it 'paled into insignificance' alongside the National Insurance Bill.

64. Report of the Departmental Committee on Section 2 of the Official Secrets Act 1911, 1972 (Cmnd. 5104), i. 123.

65. K. G. Robertson, *Public Secrets: A Study in the Development of Government Secrecy* (Macmillan, London, 1982), 59.

66. Ibid. 68.

Chapter 4

1. H. N. Brailsford, *Property or Peace* (Gollancz, London, 1934), 60.

2. L. Rogers, 'The War and the English Constitution', *The Forum*, July 1915, 27; H. M. Bowman, 'Martial Law and the English Constitution', *Michigan Law Review* 15: 2 (1916), 96; S. W. Clarke, 'The Rule of DORA', *Journal of Comparative Legislation and International Law* 3rd ser., 1 (1919), 36–7; *Law Magazine and Review*, Feb. 1915, quoted in Rogers, 'The War and the English Constitution', 36.

3. Ingraham, *Political Crime in Europe*, 295.

4. A. J. B. Marwick, *The Deluge: British Society and the First World War* (2nd edn., Macmillan, London, 1973), 36–7.

5. J. M. Bourne, *Britain and the Great War 1914–1918* (Arnold, London, 1989), 191–2; S. Wallace, *War and the Image of Germany: British Academics 1914–1918* (J. Donald, Edinburgh, 1988); T. Wilson, *The Myriad Faces of War: Britain and the Great War 1914–1918* (Cambridge University Press, Cambridge, 1986), at p. 154 (out of 853). Cf. the extensive treatment in F. W. Hirst, *The Consequences of the War to Great Britain* (Oxford University Press, London, 1934), 103–42.

6. Important examples are Lloyd George's own *The War Memoirs of David Lloyd George*; D. French, *British Economic and Strategic Planning 1905–1915* (Allen & Unwin, London, 1982), esp. 162–4; K. Middlemas, *Politics in Industrial Society: The Experience of the British System since 1911* (Deutsch, London, 1979); K. Robbins, *The Eclipse of a Great Power: Modern Britain 1870–1975* (Longman, London, 1983), 129. There is a good treatment of industrial applications of DORA in B. Weinberger, *Keeping the Peace? Policing Strikes in Britain, 1906–1926* (Berg, Oxford, 1990), ch. 6.

7. S. Hynes, *A War Imagined: The First World War and English Culture* (Macmillan, London, 1990), 78 ff. His less than helpful index, though, contains no reference to DORA or to censorship. This is also true, and equally surprising, of Stuart Wallace, *War and the Image of Germany*.

8. Clarke, 'The Rule of DORA', 36.

9. Bowman, 'Martial Law and the English Constitution', 94.

10. HC Deb. 5th ser. vol. 88 (23 Nov. 1914), cols. 915 ff.

11. 5 Geo. V. c. 36.

12. *Attorney-General* v. *De Keyser's Royal Hotel Ltd* [1920] AC 509; D. R. Lowry, 'Terrorism and Human Rights: Counter-insurgency and Necessity at Common Law', *Notre Dame Lawyer* 53: 49 (1977), 60.

13. HL Deb. 5th ser. vol. 18 (27 Nov. 1914), cols. 206, 216.

14. Ibid., col. 208.

15. Ibid., col. 209.

16. Ibid., col. 220.

17. Bowman, 'Martial Law and the English Constitution', 101.

18. HL Deb. 5th ser. vol. 18 (11 Mar. 1915), cols. 683 ff.

19. Bowman, 'Martial Law and the English Constitution', 114.

20. HC Deb. 5th ser. vol. 70 (24 Feb. 1915), col. 289.

21. Bowman, 'Martial Law and the English Constitution', 95.

22. Bourne, *Britain and the Great War*, 192.

23. Rossiter, *Constitutional Dictatorship*, ch. 9.

24. T. Baty and J. H. Morgan, *War: Its Conduct and Legal Results* (John Murray, London, 1915), 111; Rossiter, *Constitutional Dictatorship*, 165. Even defenders of the constitution like L. S. Amery, *Thoughts on the Constitution* (Oxford University Press, London, 1947), later recognized the 'serious' erosion of second-reading debates which had occurred, but without being able to propose a remedy.

25. Rossiter, *Constitutional Dictatorship*, 158.

26. Ibid. 163.

27. Ibid. 154.

28. Ibid. 162.

29. Clarke, 'The Rule of DORA', 39.

30. Bowman, 'Martial Law and the English Constitution', 97.

31. CID Ad Hoc Subcom., minutes, 30 June 1914. EP 2, CAB 16 31.

32. G. R. Rubin, 'The Royal Prerogative or a Statutory Code? The War Office and Contingency Legal Planning, 1885–1914', in R. Eales and D. Sullivan (eds.), *The Political Context of Law* (Hambledon Press, London, 1987), 155.

33. M. Bentley, *The Climax of Liberal Politics: British Liberalism in Theory and Practice 1868–1918* (Arnold, London, 1987), 122.

34. HC Deb. 5th ser. vol. 68 (23 Nov. 1914), cols. 918–19.

35. S. J. Hurwitz, *State Intervention in Great Britain* (Columbia University Press, New York, 1949). Weinberger, *Keeping the Peace?*, 128 ff.

36. Lowry, 'Terrorism and Human Rights', 58. Cf. also G. J. Alexander, 'The Illusory Protection of Human Rights by National Courts during Periods of Emergency', *Human Rights Law Journal* 5: 1 (1984), 29–31.

37. Lowry, 'Terrorism and Human Rights', 55. Hirst, *Consequences of the War*, thought Shaw's opinion sufficiently important to print in full.

38. C. Campbell, 'Emergency Law in Ireland, 1918–25' (Ph.D. thesis, Queen's University of Belfast 1989), 129.

39. Allen, *Law and Orders*, 45 n. 30.
40. Ibid.
41. Rogers, 'The War and the English Constitution', 30.
42. Campbell, 'Emergency Law in Ireland', 134.
43. Williams, *Not in the Public Interest*, 34.
44. Ibid. 31
45. Ibid. 34.
46. 'Scheme for the Suppression of Civil Disturbance in London'. HO 144 1650; WO 32 5270, para. 3.
47. Home Office to War Office (draft), May 1915. HO 144 1650.
48. Ibid.; in fact King's Regulations had misstated part of the relevant law until 1912, giving rise to the 'unsound idea that the Magistrate should direct military operations'; only after 1921 did para. 1246 read 'When thus requested it will be the duty of the officer to take such military steps as in his opinion the situation demands.' Notes by Sir Charles Biron, 17 Nov. 1932. MEPO 2 3132.
49. Ibid.: 'the question whether military action (that is, charging the crowd, firing, etc.) should be taken would depend on the proceedings of the mob . . . and not on information previously collected'.
50. Telegram, Chief Sec. to PM, 28 Apr. 1916. Bodleian Library, Asquith papers 42 fo. 34.
51. Note by Sir M. Nathan, 26 Apr. 1916. Bodleian Library, Nathan papers 476 fo. 295.
52. Holograph note, Att.-Gen. to Under-Sec., Ireland 29 Apr. Nathan papers 476 fo. 677; memo by Att.-Gen. Ireland, 20 May 1916; Asquith papers 42 fos. 148–9.
53. Memo by PM, 19 May 1916. House of Lords Record Office, Bonar Law papers 63/C/5.
54. Maxwell to Long, 17 and 18 July 1916, in memo by Sec. of State for the Colonies, 21 July 1916. Bonar Law papers 63/C/29. Maxwell had issued a spate of proclamations, for instance ordering the surrender of all arms and ammunition, requiring police authorization for all political and sporting meetings, processions, and parades, and imposing a system of identity checks for travel between Ireland and Britain, on his own authority, with no mention either of martial law or DORA.
55. Report on the State of Ireland since the Rebellion, 24 June 1916. CAB 37 150 18.
56. C. Townshend, 'Military Force and Civil Authority in the United Kingdom, 1914–1921', *Journal of British Studies* 28 (1989), 283.
57. Ibid. 284–5.
58. Memo by Chief Sec., 9 Oct. 1916. Bonar Law papers 63/C/47.
59. Lord Lieutenant to Chief Sec., 4 Nov. 1919. Bodleian Library, Strathcarron papers. Holmes, *The Little Field Marshal*, 350. Cf. E. O'Halpin, *The Decline*

of the Union: British Government in Ireland, 1892–1920 (Dublin, 1987), 156–213, on the failure of French's proconsular government.

60. Memo by Lord Lieutenant, 17 Feb. 1917. Asquith papers 45; memo by Secretary of State for the Colonies, 31 Dec. 1918. GT 6574, CAB 24 72/1.
61. Townshend, 'Martial law', 182.
62. Memo by Chief Secretary for Ireland, 24 July 1920. CP 1682, CAB 24 109.
63. Cabinet 51(20), App. 4. CAB 23 22.
64. Jones to Lloyd George, 24 July 1920. T. Jones, *Whitehall Diary*, ed. K. Middlemas, iii (Oxford University Press, London, 1971), 31.
65. Diary of Mark Sturgis, 10 Dec. 1920. PRO 30 59/3.
66. Anderson to Macready, 11 Jan. 1921. Anderson papers, CO 904 188.
67. GOC-in-C Ireland to GOC 5th Division, 11 Dec. 1920. IWM, Jeudwine papers.
68. Townshend, 'Military Force and Civil Authority', 289.

Chapter 5

1. S. Humphries, *Hooligans or Rebels? An Oral History of Working-Class Youth 1889–1937* (Blackwell, Oxford, 1981), 187.
2. Townshend, 'Martial Law', 187–94; *Britain's Civil Wars, passim*; 'The Defence of Palestine: Insurrection and Public Security, 1936–1939', *English Historical Review* 103 (1988), 917–49.
3. See Sir J. Simon's observation, p. 63 above.
4. A. Babington, *Military Intervention in Britain: From the Gordon Riots to the Gibraltar Incident* (Routledge, London, 1990), 147.
5. Memorandum on the Riot Act, Aug. 1919. PRO HO 45 10990/111765.
6. Ibid.
7. Minute by Sir E. Troup, 27 Jan. 1914, on file on Cornish Clay Pit strike, Sept. 1913. HO 45 10710, quoted in Morgan, *Conflict and Order*, 183.
8. 'The Duties of a Clerk to Justices in Case of Riot', *The Justice of the Peace* 84, 15 May 1920.
9. Their confidence seems borne out by Stephen Humphries's lucid study of inter-war resistance, which shows a kind of internal emigration on the part of the disadvantaged. Most important were the strict limits to the violence of the street gangs. *Hooligans or Rebels?*, 189–93.
10. K. Jeffery and P. Hennessy, *States of Emergency: British Governments and Strikebreaking since 1919* (Routledge, London, 1983), 31.
11. Adj.-Gen. to Deputy CIGS, 13 Oct. 1919. WO 35 5611.
12. GOC-in-C GB, Report on military measures taken during the recent railway strike, 17 Oct. 1919. WO 32 5467; K. Jeffery, 'The British Army and Internal Security 1919–1939', *Historical Journal* 24: 2 (1981), 379.
13. R. H. Desmarais, 'The Supply and Transport Committee, 1919–26: A Study of the British Government's Method of Handling Emergencies Stemming

from Industrial Disputes', Ph.D. thesis, University of Wisconsin 1970, 45.
14. Col. 20 (22), CAB 23 29.
15. Home Office memorandum, GT 8394. CAB 24 90. Jeffery and Hennessy, *States of Emergency*, 19–20.
16. Jeffery and Hennessy, *States of Emergency*, 279.
17. Ibid. 16.
18. Middlemas, *Politics in Industrial Society*, 150.
19. Jeffery and Hennessy, *States of Emergency*, 27.
20. STC minutes and memoranda, 15 Jan. 1920, CAB 27 73; CAB 27 74. Jeffery, 'The British Army', 383, speaks at this point of the 'near-hysteria' of the politicians.
21. Diary, 22 Jan. 1920. Wilson papers, IWM. Jeffery, 'The British Army', 383.
22. Jeffery and Hennessy, *States of Emergency*, 53.
23. *The Times*, 26 Oct. 1920.
24. Taylor, *English History 1914–1945*, 144.
25. K. O. Morgan, *Consensus and Disunity: The Lloyd George Coalition Government 1918–1922* (Clarendon Press, Oxford, 1979), 57.
26. Rossiter, *Constitutional Dictatorship*, 173.
27. Ibid. 174.
28. Memorandum by Home Secretary (E. Shortt), 23 Mar. 1921. CP 2767. CAB 24 121.
29. Memorandum by Dr H. A. L. Fisher, 'Preservation of Public Order: powers for dealing with seditious speeches and writings', 1 Jan. 1921. CP 3007. CAB 24 125.
30. Responsibilities of the Secretary of State and Local Authorities for Maintenance of Order', 27 Oct. 1926. HO 45 24878.
31. Ibid.
32. Sir E. Troup, 'Police Administration, Local and National', *Police Journal* 1 (1928), 9.
33. Desmarais, 'The Supply and Transport Committee', 118.
34. Notes on Defence Force 1921; minute by Dep. Asst. Director TA, 13 Sept. 1925. WO 32 2674.
35. War Office to home GOCs, 3 May, 11 June 1921. WO 32 5314. Jeffery, 'The British Army', 386–7.
36. Memorandum, 15 Sept. 1921, CP 3308. CAB 24 128; Jeffery and Hennessy, *States of Emergency*, 67.
37. Morgan, *Conflict and Order*, 193–4.
38. It is however worth noting that, at a Home Office conference to discuss the draft code of Emergency Regulations on 6 December 1935, it was he who pointed out that the proposed power to require persons to exercise functions or recover the costs of providing functions 'might be regarded as perilously close to industrial conscription, which was prohibited' (by the EPA 1920). HO 45 25456.

39. Report by CGI, 13 Feb. 1923. MEPO 2 1958; HO 45 11275.

40. Jeffery and Hennessy, *States of Emergency*, 78–9.

41. Desmarais, 'The Supply and Transport Committee', 188.

42. K. Martin, *The British Public and the General Strike* (Leonard and Virginia Woolf, London, 1926), 12.

43. Morgan, *Conflict and Order*, 206, 204.

44. Desmarais provides a sensible, if hostile, critique of the *British Gazette*; he also notes of the middle-class mobilization, that 2,345 out of 3,600 Oxford undergraduates joined the emergency forces.

45. Report on the general strike as it affected troops in the London District, WO 32 3456.

46. Memo by Lt.-Gen. H. S. Jeudwine, Director-General, TA, 8 May 1926. WO 32 2674.

47. Ibid., Minute.

48. Adj.-Gen. to CIGS, 12 Feb. 1927. WO 32 3456.

49. Principles of Employment of Troops in Aid of the Civil Power, minute by Col. Dobbie, 28 Jan. 1927, WO 32 3456; WO 33 1159.

50. Ibid. 129–30.

51. Minutes by Adj.-Gen. and Under-Sec., 5 Dec. 1926 and 13 May 1927. WO 32 3456.

52. Williams, *Not in the Public Interest*, 37.

53. 'Codification of the Criminal Law: Treason, Sedition and Allied Offences', The Law Commission Working Paper no. 72, London, 1977, 56 (para. 89).

54. Attempts at objective assessment of the revolutionary threat have been few. For the argument that the Communist Party hampered the revolutionary capacity of the labour movement see W. Kendall, *The Revolutionary Movement in Britain 1900–1921: The Origins of British Communism* (Weidenfeld, London, 1969). Cf. also Desmarais, 'The Supply and Transport Committee', 20.

55. Jones, *Whitehall Diary*, ii. 45 (for 10 May 1926).

56. Earl Baldwin of Bewdley, *On England* (Penguin Books, Harmondsworth, 1937), 11. This was the fourth full edition and eighth impression of the collection.

57. 'Peace in Industry', ibid.

58. 'Political Education', ibid., 155–6.

59. 'Peace in Industry, II', ibid., 52.

60. Middlemas, *Politics in Industrial Society*, 145.

61. Draft Bill For the more effective Preservation of Public Order, and memoranda, CP 2767, 2767A, 3007. CAB 24 121, 125.

62. T. Young assisted by M. Kettle, *Incitement to Disaffection* (Cobden Trust, London, 1976), 62–4.

63. I. Jennings, *The Sedition Bill Explained* (New Statesman and Nation, London, 1934), 10–11.

64. HC Deb. 5th ser. vol. 288 (16 Apr. 1934), cols. 744–6.

65. Ibid., cols. 774–5.

66. Jennings, *Sedition Bill*, 24–5.

67. For a modern critique, see H. Street, *Freedom, the Individual and the Law*, Penguin Books, Harmondsworth, 1963, 203.

68. Incitement to Disaffection file, WO 32 3948.

69. Adj.-Gen. to Sec. of State, 7 July 1925; minute by Adj.-Gen., 9 Oct. 1929. WO 32 3948.

70. Internal Security Instructions (1933) Army. WO 33 1202.

71. HC Deb. 5th ser. vol. 288, col. 742.

72. Ibid., col. 774.

73. HC Deb. 5th ser. col. 838.

74. HC Deb. 5th ser. vol. 293, 30 Oct. 1934. Young and Kettle, *Incitement to Disaffection*, 66–7.

75. J. B. Priestley, Preface to Jennings, *Sedition Bill*, 6.

76. Ibid., 7.

77. *Manchester Guardian*, 31 May 1934. G. D. Anderson, *Fascists, Communists, and the National Government: Civil Liberties in Great Britain, 1931–1937* (Missouri University Press, Columbia, Mo., 1983), 84–93, shows the range of public criticism.

78. R. Kidd, *British Liberty in Danger* (Lawrence & Wishart, London, 1940), 67.

79. Anderson, *Fascists, Communists*, 97, sensibly points out that printers thereafter 'avoided anything that might be considered seditious if it fell into the hands of servicemen'. Such indirect censorship might be trivial in quantity, but it can plainly form part of a larger network of mental restrictions.

80. Kidd, 24.

81. Supperstone, *Brownlie's Law of Public Order*, 112; Barendt, *Freedom of Speech*, 208.

82. HC Deb. 5th ser. vol. 293, 30 Oct. 1934.

83. Morgan, *Conflict and Order*, 227.

84. Ibid. 218.

85. Commissioner to Deputy Commissioner, 30 Apr. 1932, 'Hostile Demonstrations', MEPO 2 3033.

86. Duties and Powers of the Commissioner of Police of the Metropolis in relation to meetings and processions in streets or public places, MEPO 3035.

87. Commissioner to Assistant Commissioner, 14 Nov. 1933, MEPO 3035.

88. Williams, *Not in the Public Interest*, 128.

89. Cabinet, 18 July 1934. CAB 23 79.

90. 'Wearing of "Political Uniforms"', Memo by Home Secretary. CP 144(34), CAB 24 249.

91. 'Preservation of Public Order', Memo (marked 'To Be Kept Under Lock and Key') by Home Secretary, July 1934. CP 189(34), CAB 24 250.

92. Cabinet Committee on Preservation of Public Order, Report by Sir J. Simon, 26 Oct. 1936. CP 282(36), CAB 24 265; Cabinet, 14 Oct. 1936. C.57(36)2, CAB 23 85.
93. HC Deb. 5th ser. vol. 317 (16 Nov. 1936), cols. 1350–6.
94. HC Deb. 5th ser. vol. 318 (23 Nov. 1936), col. 143.
95. HC Deb. 5th ser. vol. 317 col. 1426; vol. 318 col. 54.
96. HC Deb. 5th ser. vol. 318 col. 168.
97. Ibid., col. 164.
98. Ibid., col. 178.
99. Ibid., cols. 1674, 1689.
100. Ibid., col. 1770.

Chapter 6

1. 'Civil Liberties in Great Britain in Wartime', *Bill of Rights Review* 2 (1942), 243.
2. HC Deb. 5th ser. vol. 351, col. 64.
3. Ibid., col. 66.
4. Ibid., col. 69.
5. Ibid., cols. 72, 76.
6. Ibid., col. 100.
7. U. Bialer, *The Shadow of the Bomber: The Fear of Air Attack and British Politics 1932–1939* (Royal Historical Society, London, 1980), concentrates (like its official sources) on the prospects of physical damage; but it notes (129–30) that when the Joint Planning Committee produced its characteristically oblique suggestion that 'the Germans may believe that if our people and particularly our women and children were subject to these horrors' they would demand surrender, it also thought that the Germans 'might well succeed' in this.
8. N. Stammers, *Civil Liberties in Britain During the Second World War: A Political Study* (Croom Helm, London, 1983), 8.
9. Cf. P. Addison, *The Road to 1945: British Politics and the Second World War* (Cape, London, 1975), ch. 1, *passim*.
10. More recently the linkage of 'subversion' with any disruptive opposition has been observed. R. J. Spjut, 'Defining Subversion', *British Journal of Law and Society* 6 (1979). See also the survey in E. Grace and C. Leys, 'The Concept of Subversion and its Implications', in C. E. S. Franks (ed.), *Dissent and the State* (Oxford University Press, Toronto, 1989), 62–85.
11. Law Commission, Working Paper no. 72 (London, 1977), paras. 21, 14.
12. Brownlie, *International Law*, 236.
13. S. A. de Smith, *Constitutional and Administrative Law*, 5th edn. by H. Street and R. Brazier (Penguin Books, Harmondsworth, 1985), 470.

14. Brownlie, *International Law*, 239.
15. D. W. Brogan, *The English People: Impressions and Observations*, Hamish Hamilton, London, 1943, 27.
16. Laski, 'Civil Liberties'.
17. A. W. B. Simpson, *In the Highest Degree Odious: Detention without Trial in Wartime Britain* (Clarendon Press, Oxford, 1992), pp. 106–8.
18. WP (G) (40) 131, CAB 67 6.
19. Simpson, *In the Highest Degree Odious*, ch. 16, provides a full legal analysis of the internment orders.
20. Memo by Commissioner, 12 June 1940. MEPO 2 6260. Stammers, *Civil Liberties*, 98.
21. Ibid. 99.
22. Kidd, *British Liberty*, 195–6.
23. HC Deb. 5th ser. vol. 363 (16 July 1940), col. 65.
24. Ibid., col. 66.
25. Ibid., col. 72.
26. Ibid., col. 74.
27. J. Harvey (ed.), *The Diplomatic Diaries of Oliver Harvey 1937–1940* (Macmillan, London, 1970), 332 (for 24 Dec. 1939).
28. HC Deb. 5th ser. vol. 363 (16 July 1940), col. 103.
29. Ibid., col. 729.
30. Aneurin Bevan, ibid., col. 120.
31. Ibid., col. 850.
32. Laski, 'Civil Liberties', 245–6.
33. D. G. T. Williams, 'The Donoughmore Report in Retrospect', *Public Administration* 60: 2 (1982), 273–91.
34. For a trenchant analysis of Reg. 18B see Allen, *Law and Orders*, App. 1.
35. *Liversidge* v. *Anderson* [1942] AC 206.
36. R. F. V. Heuston, '*Liversidge* v. *Anderson* in Retrospect', *Law Quarterly Review* 86 (1970), 86.
37. E. C. S. Wade and G. G. Phillips, *Constitutional Law* (7th edn., Longmans, London, 1965), 723.
38. C. K. Allen, 'Regulation 18B and Reasonable Cause', *Law Quarterly Review* 58 (1942), 232–3.
39. Ibid. 233.
40. Ibid. 240.
41. Ibid. 241.
42. Rossiter, *Constitutional Dictatorship*, 196–7, 200.
43. C. P. Cotter, 'Emergency Detention in Wartime: The British Experience', *Stanford Law Review* 6 (Mar. 1954), 253–4.
44. His pessimism abated somewhat in subsequent editions, when 'gives' was replaced by 'purported to give', and the arguments he rejected were described

as 'sophistries not likely to be revived in time of peace', *Law and Orders* (3rd edn., 1965), 370–1.

45. Rossiter, *Constitutional Dictatorship*, 184.
46. Ibid. 199–200.
47. Cotter, 'Emergency Detention', 285.
48. Heuston, '*Liversidge* v. *Anderson* in Retrospect', 47, 66; the information is described in the second volume of the autobiography of D. N. Pritt, *From Right to Left*, Lawrence & Wishart, London, 1965), 232–3.
49. Simpson, *In the Highest Degree Odious*, 667–71.

Chapter 7

1. I. N. Stevens and D. C. M. Yardley, *The Protection of Liberty* (Blackwell, Oxford, 1982), 48.
2. R. Clutterbuck, *Britain in Agony: The Growth of Political Violence* (Faber, London, 1978).
3. There is a perceptive survey of the notions of 'Britain in crisis' in ch. 2 of Colin Leys, *Politics in Britain* (Heinemann, London, 1983). The radical orthodoxy was brilliantly established by P. Anderson, 'Origins of the Present Crisis', *New Left Review* 23 (1964), 26–53, and in J. Habermas, 'What Does Crisis Mean Today? Legitimation Problems in Late Capitalism', *Social Research* 40: 4 (1973), 643–67.
4. Pearson, *Hooligan*.
5. *Public Order: A Report by a Committee of the Society of Conservative Lawyers* (Conservative Political Centre, London, 1970), 4.
6. B. Crick and W. A. Robson (eds.), *Protest and Discontent* (Penguin Books, Harmondsworth, 1970).
7. 'Cambridge University Volunteers in the General Strike', Baldwin MSS 22 fos. 88–9, quoted in Jeffery and Hennessy, *States of Emergency*, 114.
8. G. J. Morton, *Just the Job: Some Experiences of a Colonial Policeman* (Hodder & Stoughton, London, 1957),
9. S. Hall, C. Crichter, T. Jefferson, J. Clarke, and B. Roberts, *Policing the Crisis: Mugging, the State, and Law and Order* (Macmillan, London, 1978), 183–4. There is a rich elaboration in ch. 4 of S. Chibnall, *Law and Order News: An Analysis of Crime Reporting in the British Press* (Tavistock Publications, London, 1977).
10. H. Wilson and H. Glickman, *The Problem of Internal Security in Great Britain 1948–53* (Doubleday, Garden City, NY, 1954), 6.
11. Ibid. 3.
12. Ibid. 12.
13. Ibid. 35.
14. Ibid. 80.
15. Ibid. 74.

16. Allen, *Law and Orders*, 64.
17. HL Deb. vol. 189 (17 Nov. 1954), cols. 1579 ff.; Allen, *Law and Orders*, 68.
18. Ibid. 70.
19. K. O. Morgan, *Labour in Power 1945–1951* (Oxford University Press, Oxford, 1985), 136.
20. Pearson, *Hooligan*, 13.
21. Unnamed COP, Robert Reiner, *Chief Constables* (Oxford University Press, Oxford, 1991), 332.
22. Notes from Conference, Nov. 1922. HO 45 24878.
23. D. H. Bayley, 'The Police and Political Development in Europe', in C. Tilly (ed.), *The Formation of National States in Western Europe* (Princeton University Press, Princeton, NJ, 1975), 334.
24. R. Graef, *Independent*, 12 May 1989.
25. F. Gregory, 'The British Police System—with Special Reference to Public Order Problems', in J. Roach and J. Thomanek (eds.), *The Police and Public Order in Europe* (Croom Helm, London, 1985), 38.
26. J. D. Brewer, A. Guelke, I. Hume, E. Moxon-Browne, and R. Wilford, *The Police, Public Order and the State* (Macmillan, London, 1988), 8.
27. Lustgarten, *The Governance of Police*, 74.
28. Ibid. 32.
29. G. Marshall, *Police and Government: The Status and Accountability of the English Constable* (Methuen, London, 1965), 33.
30. M. Cain, 'Towards a Political Sociology of the British Police: A Review of 1979 and 1980', in R. Donelan (ed.), *The Maintenance of Order in Society* (Canadian Police College, Ottawa, 1982); D. Kavanagh, *British Politics: Continuities and Change* (Oxford University Press, Oxford 1990), 285.
31. Lustgarten, *The Governance of Police*, 46.
32. HO 45 23974/1, 4 Oct. 1902.
33. CC Derby to HO, 8 May 1922; R. G. Tarran to Herbert Morrison, 18 Apr. 1942. HO 45 23974/1.
34. Discussions between Watch Committee and Police, Gateshead, Feb. 1946. HO 45 23974.
35. *Report of the Committee on Police Conditions of Service*, Cmnd. 7831, 1949; I. Oliver, *Police, Government and Accountability* (Macmillan, London, 1987), 19.
36. A. Judge, editorial, *Police*, Sept. 1976, quoted in Oliver, *Police, Government and Accountability*, 56.
37. Reiner, *Chief Constables*, 352.
38. E. P. Thompson, 'On the New Issue of Postage Stamps', *New Society*, Nov. 1979; *Writing by Candlelight*, 200.
39. Allen, *Law and Orders*, 351.
40. Brewer *et al.*, *The Police and Public Order*, 19.
41. T. A. Critchley, *A History of Police in England and Wales* (Constable,

London, 1978), 185, 195. The procedures and status of ACPO are carefully examined in Reiner, *Chief Constables*, ch. 12 and App. C.

42. G. Northam, *Shooting in the Dark: Riot Police in Britain* (Faber, London, 1988), 41.

43. Lustgarten, *The Governance of Police*, 110–11.

44. A. Roberts, 'The Police at Midnight', *New Statesman*, 22 Sept. 1961, 376.

45. Clutterbuck, *Britain in Agony*, 152, 151.

46. B. Sewill, former special adviser to the Chancellor of the Exchequer, in R. Harris and B. Sewill, *British Economic Policy, 1970–74: Two Views* (Institute of Economic Affairs, London, 1975), 50, quoted in Jeffery and Hennessy, *States of Emergency*, 235.

47. Babington, *Military Intervention in Britain*, 178. The description 'purposeless' seems slightly odd from Babington's own perspective, since he views the demonstrations against US policy in Vietnam as being planned 'by a group of professed Trotskyites' who presumably had a very deliberate purpose.

48. A. Judge, 'Why the Police Must be Given More Powers', *The Times*, 17 Aug. 1978.

49. P. Evans, 'The Crisis Facing our Police Forces', *The Times*, 3 Dec. 1979.

50. Stevens and Yardley, *The Protection of Liberty*, 55–60 provided a careful legal analysis of the disturbances.

51. L. Mackie, 'Blasts of the Past', *Guardian*, 5 Apr. 1980.

52. R. Chesshyre and G. Brock, 'The Revolt of Britain's Lost Tribe', *Observer*, 6 Apr. 1980.

53. Clutterbuck, *Britain in Agony*, 221.

54. Reiner, *Chief Constables*, 120.

55. Barendt, *Freedom of Speech*, 193–4.

56. Lord Scarman, *Report to the Secretary of State for the Home Department on the Brixton Disorders of 10–12 April 1981*, Cmnd. 8427, Nov. 1981, para. 1.2.

57. National Advisory Commission on Civil Disorders, *Report* (1968); however, it may be argued that more attention was paid to Scarman's narrower recommendations than to Kerner's larger ones: M. Lipsky and D. J. Olson, *Commission Politics: the Processing of Racial Crisis in America* (Transaction Books, New Brunswick, NJ, 1977).

58. Cmnd. 8427, paras. 4.11–4.43.

59. J. Chandos, 'Constabulary Duty', in *The Police and the Public: An Enquiry Presented by C. H. Rolph* (Heinemann, London, 1962), 22–4.

60. J. C. Alderson, 'The Principles and Practice of the British Police', in J. C. Alderson and P. J. Stead (eds.), *The Police We Deserve* (Wolfe, London, 1973), 44–6.

61. Ibid. 50–1.

62. J. C. Alderson, 'Police and the Social Order', in Roach and Thomanek (eds.),

Police and Public Order, 15–16.

63. Ibid. 26.

64. Lord Scarman, 'Brixton and After', in Roach and Thomanek (eds.), *Police and Public Order*, 8–13.

65. 'The Scarman Report', programme 1, BBC Radio 4, May 1991.

66. Ibid., programme 2.

67. Interview with unidentified Inspector, in Geary, *Policing Industrial Disputes*, 125.

68. *Public Order: A Report by a Committee of the Society of Conservative Lawyers* (Conservative Political Centre, London, 1970), 4.

69. S. Hall and T. Jefferson (eds.), *Resistance Through Rituals* (Hutchinson, London, 1976); *Policing the Crisis, passim*.

70. Fifth Report from the Home Affairs Committee, 'The Law Relating to Public Order', HC 756 I, PP XLVIII (1979–80); *Review of the Public Order Act 1936 and related legislation*, Cmnd. 7891 (1980); Law Commission, Working Paper no. 82, *Offences Against Public Order* (1982), and Report no. 123, *Offences Relating to Public Order* (1983); *Review of Public Order Law*, Cmnd. 9510 (1985).

71. D. Bonner and R. Stone, 'The Public Order Act 1986: Steps in the Wrong Direction?', *Public Law* 1987, 203.

72. HC 756, p. v.

73. Ibid., p. vii.

74. Cmnd. 7891, p. 2.

75. Ibid., pp. 8–12.

76. Cmnd. 9510, p. 5.

77. W. Whitelaw, interview on *Class Rule*, BBC2, 17 Dec. 1991.

78. HC Deb. 6th ser. vol. 89 (13 Jan. 1986), col. 799.

79. Ibid. cols. 792–4.

80. Ibid., col. 862.

81. J. L. Hammond, *Gladstone and the Irish Nation* (Longman, London, 1938), 251.

82. HC Deb. 6th ser. vol. 89 (13 Jan. 1986), cols. 801, 811.

83. Ibid., col. 855.

84. Ibid., cols. 823–6.

85. Ibid., col. 851.

86. Ibid., cols. 842–3.

87. Ibid., cols. 827–8.

Chapter 8

1. *Disturbances in Northern Ireland*, Cmd. 532 (Belfast 1969), para. 6.

2. A. T. Q. Stewart, *The Narrow Ground: Aspects of Ulster 1609–1969* (Faber, London, 1977), provides a luminous commentary.

3. C. O'Halloran, *Partition and the Limits of Irish Nationalism* (Gill & Macmillan, Dublin, 1987), 97 ff. esp. chs. 4 and 5.

4. 'It is of course obvious that Northern Ireland is, and must be, a Protestant "state" otherwise it would not have come into being and would certainly not continue to exist.' Home Office notes, 27 Mar. 1938. DO 35 893. C. Townshend, 'Northern Ireland', in R. J. Vincent (ed.), *Foreign Policy and Human Rights* (Cambridge University Press, Cambridge, 1985), 124.

5. RIC Reports, CO 904 112. H. Patterson, *Class Conflict and Sectarianism: The Protestant Working Class and the Belfast Labour Movement 1868–1920* (Blackstaff, Belfast, 1980), 115–16. M. Farrell, *Northern Ireland: The Orange State* (Pluto, London, 1976), chs. 1–2.

6. Brooke to Sir Ernest Clark, Sept. 1920. PRONI D.1022, quoted in M. Farrell, *Arming the Protestants: The Formation of the Ulster Special Constabulary and Royal Ulster Constabulary, 1920–7* (Pluto, London, 1983), 16.

7. The most careful, albeit critical account is Farrell, *Arming the Protestants*; Sir Arthur Hezlet, *The B Specials: A History of the Ulster Special Constabulary* (Stacey, London, 1972), provides a sympathetic version.

8. M. Laffan, *The Partition of Ireland 1911–1925* (Dublin Historical Association, 1983), 95–8.

9. 12 & 13 Geo. V. c. 5, s. 1.

10. e.g. J. M. Curran, *The Birth of the Irish Free State 1921–1923* (Alabama University Press, Alabama, 1980), 177.

11. Collins to Churchill, 21 Mar. 1922. CP 3884, CAB 24 134.

12. C. Palley, 'The Evolution, Disintegration and Possible Reconstruction of the Northern Ireland Constitution', *Anglo-American Law Review* 1: 3 (1972), 400.

13. D. Harkness, *Northern Ireland since 1920* (Gill & Macmillan, Dublin, 1983), 30. For the question whether the SPA was *ultra vires* the Northern Ireland parliament, see Palley, 'The Evolution of the Northern Ireland Constitution', 401–2.

14. From the Public Safety [Emergency Powers] Act of 1 Aug. 1923 to the Offences Against the State Act 1939.

15. NCCL, *Report of a Commission of Inquiry Appointed to Examine the Purpose and Effect of the Civil Authorities (Special Powers) Acts (Northern Ireland) 1922 and 1933* (London, 1936), 38–40. H. Calvert, *Constitutional Law in Northern Ireland: A Study in Regional Government* (Stevens, London, 1968), 381, justly observes of its 'objectionable' features that this adjective is taken to mean 'failure to conform to an ideal which has not always been pursued with unbending zeal even by the United Kingdom parliament'.

16. N. Mansergh, *The Unresolved Question: The Anglo-Irish Settlement and its Undoing 1912–72* (Yale University Press, New Haven, Conn., 1991), 253.

17. Strachey to Carson, 12 Feb. 1920. Carson papers, PRONI D 1507/1/1920/6; Mansergh, *The Unresolved Question*, 252.

18. G. J. Hand (ed.), *Report of the Irish Boundary Commission* (Irish Universities Press, Shannon, 1969); 'MacNeill and the Boundary Commission', in F. X. Martin and F. J. Byrne (eds.), *The Scholar Revolutionary: Eoin MacNeill 1867–1945 and the Making of a New Ireland* (Irish Universities Press, Shannon, 1973).

19. F. S. L. Lyons, *Culture and Anarchy in Ireland* (Clarendon Press, Oxford, 1979).

20. The British 1936 Public Order Act did not of course apply in Northern Ireland; when it was partially incorporated via the Public Order Act (NI) 1951, the concern with quasi-military organizations was omitted and the Act merely enlarged the powers of the Home Affairs minister and police to ban meetings and make arrests without warrant. Palley, 'The Evolution of the Northern Ireland Constitution', 404.

21. Farrell, *Northern Ireland*, ch. 6.

22. B. Egan and V. McCormack, *Burntollet* (LRS Publishers, no place of pub., 1969).

23. *Disturbances in Northern Ireland: Report of the Commission appointed by the Governor of Northern Ireland*, Sept. 1969. Cmd. 532.

24. Williams, 'Protest and Public Order', 97.

25. HL Deb. 5th ser. vol. 424 (20 Oct. 1981), col. 690.

26. There is an early, optimistic account of the reform package in Palley, 'The Evolution of the Northern Ireland Constitution', 406 ff. For a recent assessment, see D. J. Smith, *Inequality in Northern Ireland* (Oxford University Press, Oxford, 1991).

27. D. Hamill, *Pig in the Middle: The Army in Northern Ireland 1969–1984* (Methuen, London, 1985), 'Phase One'.

28. D. G. Boyce, ' "Normal Policing": Public Order in Northern Ireland since Partition', *Eire–Ireland* 14 (1979).

29. The documentary evidence does not permit an exact account of how the Provisional Government overcame this difficulty. See C. Brady, *Guardians of the Peace* (Gill & Macmillan, Dublin 1974), 40 ff.

30. Palley, 'The Evolution of the Northern Ireland Constitution', 416 n. 229.

31. Surveying the early police reforms, Palley asserted that 'these changes have removed entirely the basis for criticism formerly levied against those responsible for the administration of justice' ('The Evolution of the Northern Ireland Constitution', 418). In theory they did.

32. Ulster Defence Regiment Act 1969, 18 Eliz. II c. 69.

33. SDLP submission to Secretary of State's conference, 1980. L. O'Dowd, B. Rolston, and M. Tomlinson, *Northern Ireland: Between Civil Rights and Civil War* (CSE Books, London, 1980), 185.

34. Eamonn McCann's outstanding *War and an Irish Town* (Penguin Books,

Harmondsworth, 1974) is no doubt seen by the authorities as a subversive tract. It is possibly more striking to find the conflict listed as the 'Northern Ireland Civil War of 1969– ' in G. C. Kohn's *Dictionary of Wars* (Facts on File, New York and Oxford, 1986), 318.

35. Hamill, *Pig in the Middle*, 86–94. *Report of the Tribunal appointed to inquire into the events on Sunday 30th January 1972, which led to loss of life in connection with the procession in Londonderry that day*, HC 220, Apr. 1972.

36. *Report of the Commission to consider legal procedures to deal with terrorist activities in Northern Ireland*, 1972 Cmnd. 5185, para. 27.

37. W. L. Twining, 'Emergency Powers and Criminal Process: The Diplock Report', *Criminal Law Review* 1973, 407.

38. Ibid. 417, 409.

39. In *Emergency Powers: A Fresh Start* (Fabian Tract 416, Mar. 1972) Twining set out eight principles which should govern the approach to emergency powers. Subsequent criticism of the Diplock conclusions is detailed in S. C. Greer and A. White, *Abolishing the Diplock Courts: The Case for Restoring Jury Trial to Scheduled Offences in Northern Ireland* (Cobden Trust, London, 1986). The official view is in Sir George Baker's *Review of the Operation of the Northern Ireland (Emergency Provisions) Act 1978*, Cmnd. 9222 (Apr. 1984).

40. *Report of the Committee of Privy Counsellors appointed to consider authorized procedures for the interrogation of persons suspected of terrorism*, 1972 Cmnd. 4901, Minority Report, paras. 12, 15.

41. *Report of a Committee to consider, in the context of civil liberties and human rights, measures to deal with terrorism in Northern Ireland*, 1975 Cmnd. 5847, para. 140.

42. Ibid., paras. 15, 17, 19, 21.

43. Ibid., para. 148.

44. There is a patchy literature on aspects of paramilitary activity (an example is A. Aughey and C. McIlheney, 'Law before Violence? The Protestant Paramilitaries in Ulster Politics', *Eire–Ireland* 19 (1984), 55–74), but surprisingly little analysis of the term's popular usage, or its relation to the less esoteric concept of vigilantism. See Charles Townshend, 'The Culture of Paramilitarism in Ireland', in M. Crenshaw (ed.), *Terrorism in Context* (Penn State University Press, University Park, Pa., forthcoming). The excellent S. Bruce, *The Red Hand: Protestant Paramilitaries in Northern Ireland* (Oxford University Press, 1992) appeared too late to be incorporated here.

45. *Review of the Operation of the Prevention of Terrorism (Temporary Provisions) Act 1984*, 1987 Cm. 264.

46. H. Street, 'The Prevention of Terrorism (Emergency Provisions) Act 1974', *Criminal Law Review* 1975, 192–9.

47. P. Jenkins, 'Liberties eroded in an emotive cause', *Independent*, 7 Dec. 1988, 23.

48. H. J. Simson, *British Rule, and Rebellion* (Blackwood, London, 1938).

49. Much has now been written about what was first called 'low intensity warfare', and later 'conflict' (LIC)—see, e.g., US Department of Defense, *Proceedings of the Low-Intensity Warfare Conference*, 14–15 Jan. 1986— but little if any of this writing has the conviction of Frank Kitson's brilliant and disturbing *Low Intensity Operations* (Faber, London, 1971). There is an intelligent overview of the American usage in M. Klare and P. Kornbluh (eds.), *Low-Intensity Warfare: Counterinsurgency, Proinsurgency and Antiterrorism in the Eighties* (Pantheon, New York, 1988).

50. Dáil Éireann Debates vol. 292, quoted in T. C. Salmon, 'The Civil Power and Aiding the Civil Power: the Case of Ireland', in Roach and Thomaneck (eds.), *The Police and Public Order*, 80.

51. Twining, 'Emergency Powers', 408 n. 6, insisted that 'all emergency powers should be clearly and precisely formulated by statute so that the security authorities are not left to operate under vague and general common law powers', but he withdrew his earlier idea of a permanent Security Act, because 'in the present political climate, it is unlikely that such legislation would comply with the principles set out [in his article]'.

52. *Ireland* v. *United Kingdom*, Report of the European Commission (1976) 19 YB-ECHR, 584, 586.

53. S. R. Chowdhury, *Rule of Law in a State of Emergency: The Paris Minimum Standards of Human Rights Norms in a State of Emergency* (St Martin's Press, New York, 1989), 27.

54. Ibid. 26.

55. Unionists have protested vehemently against their marginalization in this way; see A. Aughey, *Under Siege: Ulster Unionism and the Anglo-Irish Agreement* (C. Hurst, London, 1989).

56. The Detention of Terrorists Order 1972 justified internment by the need for 'protection of the public'; the 1973 Emergency Provisions Act created 'offences against public security', but offered no elucidation of the term.

57. Hamill, *Pig in the Middle*, 159 ff.

58. As in the operations to which police witnesses testified in the inquest on Norah McCabe; A. Jennings, 'Bullets Above the Law', in *Justice Under Fire* (Pluto Press, London, 1988), 137.

59. HL Deb. 5th ser. vol. 424 (20 Oct. 1981), cols. 689–90.

60. This is not strictly a coherent term, since it has always been orthodox military practice, when fire is resorted to, to fire 'with effect'. What is meant is not *merely* shooting to kill, but doing so without legal justification; or, in extreme form a 'strategy of assassinating known or suspected Republican activists through their deliberate engagement by the security forces in armed confrontation'. A. Jennings, 'Shoot to Kill: The Final Courts of Justice', in *Justice Under Fire*, 104.

61. J. Stalker, *Stalker* (Harrap, London, 1988); also P. Taylor, *Stalker: The Search for the Truth* (Faber, London, 1987); T. Hadden, 'The law in their

Hands', *Times Literary Supplement*, 4–10 Mar. 1988, 237.

62. HC Deb. vol. 126 (25 Jan. 1988), cols. 22–5.

63. See, e.g., C. P. Walker, 'Shooting to Kill: Some of the Issues in *Farrell* v. *Secretary of State for Defence*', *Modern Law Review* 43 (1980), 591–4; R. J. Spjut, 'The "Official" Use of Deadly Force by the Security Forces Against Suspected Terrorists: Some Lessons from Northern Ireland', *Public Law* Spring 1986, 39–66.

64. *Criminal Law Review* 1975, 196.

65. T. Benn, *Conflicts of Interest: Diaries 1977–80*, 34 (Hutchinson, 1990). On the obsessive side, see K. D. Ewing and C. Gearty, *Freedom under Thatcher: Civil Liberties in Modern Britain* (Oxford University Press, Oxford, 1990), 129 and *passim*.

66. As R. E. Eichenberg, *Public Opinion and National Security in Western Europe* (Macmillan, London, 1989); cf. T. Pangle, 'The Moral Basis of National Security: Four Historical Perspectives', in K. Knorr (ed.), *Historical Dimensions of National Security Problems* (National Security Education Program, Kansas University Press, 1976). The most acute critique is B. Buzan, *People, States, and Fear: An Agenda for International Security Studies in the Post-Cold War Era* (Routledge & Kegan Paul, London, 1973).

67. 1972 Cmnd. 5104, para. 116.

68. Again, 'we are concerned here with the major secrets of the State ... secret in the sense of the word commonly used by ordinary people'. Ibid., para. 151.

69. Spjut, 'Defining Subversion', 256.

70. Ibid. 260–1.

71. Cmnd. 5104, para. 145(d).

72. Robertson, *Public Secrets*, 86–7. A systematic critique of the 'convention' is S. E. Finer, 'The Individual Responsibility of Ministers', *Public Administration* 34 (1956), 377–96.

73. W. Birtles, 'Big Brother Knows Best: The Franks Report on Section Two of the Official Secrets Act', *Public Law* 1973, 110.

74. H. Young, 'A Freedom to Deny Public Understanding', *Guardian*, 17 Nov. 1988.

75. J. Birt, 'Gagging the Messenger', *Independent*, 21 Nov. 1988.

76. 'A Government too Careless of Freedom', *Independent*, 17 Nov. 1988.

77. A. W. Bradley, 'Parliamentary Privilege, Zircon and National Security', *Public Law* 1987, 488–95, accepts the view of the minority of the Committee of Privileges that the Speaker ought not to receive national security briefings on executive terms, repeating Speaker Lenthall's admonition to King Charles I that he had 'neither eyes to see, nor tongue to speak' save as the House directed him. But of course the Commons, like state security itself, is not what it was in the seventeenth century.

78. E. Heath, 'A State of Secrecy', *New Statesman and Society*, 10 Mar. 1989.

79. Ewing and Gearty, *Freedom under Thatcher*, 207.

Chapter 9

1. A good example is the vigorous and thoroughgoing critique by P. Hillyard and J. Percy-Smith, *The Coercive State* (Fontana, London, 1988), which pays no heed to the rather extensive debate in the social sciences about the notion of coercion, and deploys 'coercive' as a synonym for 'overcentralized' or (in old-fashioned terms) 'overmighty', likewise 'state' as a pejorative term for 'government'. (Indeed it goes so far in this as to talk of the 'local state', a truly eccentric usage.) The chapter challengingly entitled 'The State versus the People' is really about central versus local government, and inner versus outer cabinets.

2. D. Hurd, 'Freedom will flourish where citizens accept responsibility', *Independent*, 13 Sep. 1989.

3. 'Disorder is blamed on indiscipline', *Independent*, 17 Jan. 1989. Cf. the more honest perplexity of one of Robert Reiner's respondents: 'people's attitudes towards being well behaved have somehow changed. There are less inhibitions among people to express themselves in a vigorous and violent way. There is a restlessness about', *Chief Constables*, 169.

4. D. Rose, 'Forces of change', *Guardian*, 21 Feb. 1990.

5. Graef, 'A spiral of mutual mistrust', *Independent*, 12 May 1989.

6. Ibid.

7. Reiner, *Chief Constables*, 183.

8. Although Sir Peter Imbert was induced to admit to the BBC's *File on 4* in September 1987 that a 'move towards paramilitarism . . . had occurred', this was an exceptional statement. See Northam, *Shooting in the Dark*, 172 and *passim*.

9. Metropolitan Police Force, *Public Order Review: Civil Disturbances 1981– 1985* (London, 1986), Introduction, para. 5. Reiner, *Chief Constables*, 166.

10. Reiner, *Chief Constables*, 167.

11. C. Ackroyd, K. Margolis, J. Rosenhead, and T. Shallice, *The Technology of Political Control* (Penguin Books, Harmondsworth, 1975); S. Mainwaring-White, *The Policing Revolution: Police Technology, Democracy and Liberty in Britain* (Harvester, Brighton, 1983); P. Scraton (ed.), *Law, Order and the Authoritarian State* (Open University Press, Milton Keynes, 1987).

12. Report on Palestine Police by Sir Charles Wickham, 2 Dec. 1946. CO 537 2269. It is worth noting that Wickham, like most Inspectors-General before World War II, was a former army officer. See Townshend, *Britain's Civil Wars, passim*, for accounts of the process of militarization in Ireland and elsewhere.

13. For Hall's phrase, see his polemical Cobden Trust Human Rights Day Lecture for 1979, *Drifting into a Law and Order Society* (Cobden Trust, London, 1980). See also Hillyard and Percy-Smith, *The Coercive State*, 236–49, who provide a somewhat loosely-stitched but plausible set of

military elements, notably the 'show of force' in public order policing; also Northam, 'The Paramilitary Drift', in *Shooting in the Dark*, 29–43.

14. Reiner, *Chief Constables*, 179.
15. See, e.g., T. Morris, 'The Case for a Riot Squad', *New Society*, 29 Nov. 1985.
16. P. A. J. Waddington, *The Strong Arm of the Law: Armed and Public Order Policing* (Clarendon Press, Oxford, 1991), written under the auspices of the Police Foundation, mentions the CRS only once to point out their fearsome reputation (p. 124), and goes on to argue that such units would either stand idle most of the time or be given functions which would blur their distinct role. However, this does not seem to have occurred with the CRS. Otherwise, foreign exemplars are deployed as bogies (pp. 136, 154).
17. Former Commissioner, Royal Hong Kong Police, quoted in Northam, *Shooting in the Dark*, 138.
18. R. Chessyre, 'This is no riot', *Sunday Times Magazine*, 15 Oct. 1989, 36; also Graef, 'A spiral of mutual distrust'.
19. C. Townshend, *The British Campaign in Ireland 1919–1921*, Oxford University Press, Oxford, 1975, 116–22.
20. Chesshyre, 'This is no riot', 33.
21. Waddington, *The Strong Arm of the Law*, 142–7.
22. Ibid. 34.
23. Graef, 'A spiral of mutual distrust'; T. Kirby, 'Chief constable may switch officers to "popular policing"', *Independent*, 31 May 1990.
24. Editorial: 'The Police and Public Confidence', *Independent*, 27 Nov. 1989.
25. Metropolitan Police Force, *Public Order Review*, para. 2.1.
26. See p. 82.
27. H. D. Lasswell, 'The Garrison State and the Specialists on Violence', *American Journal of Sociology* 46 (1941), 455–68.
28. Northam, *Shooting in the Dark*, 171.
29. See the almost unique article by P. Waddington, 'Are Our Politicians Chasing an Illusion?', *Police* 15: 3 (Nov. 1982), 24–6.
30. J. Jacob, 'Some Reflections on Governmental Secrecy', *Public Law* 1974, 43–4.
31. Metropolitan Police Force, *Public Order Review*, para. 2.4.
32. There is a lucid critique in Northam, *Shooting in the Dark*, 65 ff.
33. This issue is carefully discussed by Northam, *Shooting in the Dark*, 60–1, who demonstrates senior police dissent from the policy of secrecy, but no action to reverse it.
34. Reiner, *Chief Constables*, 174.
35. *R. v. Secretary of State for the Home Department, ex p. Northumbria Police Authority*, discussed in Reiner, *Chief Constables*, 25–8.
36. Nourse LJ, quoted in Reiner, *Chief Constables*, 28.
37. M. Warner, 'How Cecil Parkinson helped me see the light', *Independent*,

28 Oct. 1991.

38. Lord Scarman, 'Human Rights in an Unwritten Constitution', *Denning Law Journal* 129 (1987), 129–35. For a concise expression of his argument see his reply to Max Beloff, 'How a Bill of Rights would protect the vulnerable', *Independent*, Letters, 10 Oct. 1991.

39. P. Dunleavy and S. Weir, survey report, *Independent*, 2 Oct. 1991. By contrast, 88% wanted a guarantee of 'NHS hospital treatment within a reasonable time'. The right to silence was supported by 40%.

40. See p. 148; for the warning, C. Vick, 'An Introduction to Aspects of Public Order and Policing', in J. R. Thackrah (ed.), *Contemporary Policing: An Examination of Society in the 1980s* (Sphere, London, 1985).

Bibliography

ACKROYD, C., MARGOLIS, K., ROSENHEAD, J., and SHALLICE, T., *The Technology of Political Control*, Penguin Books, Harmondsworth, 1975.

AINSLEY, H., 'Keeping the Peace in Southern England in the Thirteenth Century', *Southern History* 6 (1984).

ALDERSON, J. C., *Policing Freedom*, Macdonald & Evans, Plymouth, 1979.

—— *Law and Disorder*, Hamish Hamilton, London, 1984.

—— 'Police and Public Order', *Public Administration* 63: 4 (1985).

ALDERSON, J. C. and STEAD, P. J. (eds.), *The Police We Deserve*, Wolfe, London, 1973.

ALEXANDER, G. J., 'The Illusory Protection of Human Rights by National Courts during Periods of Emergency', *Human Rights Law Journal*, 5: 1 (1984).

ALLEN, C. K., 'Regulation 18B and Reasonable Cause', *Law Quarterly Review* 58 (1942).

—— *The Queen's Peace*, Stevens, London, 1953.

—— *Law and Orders: An Inquiry into the Nature and Scope of Delegated Legislation and Executive Powers in England*, Stevens, London, 1956.

AL-RAZEE, A., *Constitutional Glimpses of Martial Law: In India, Pakistan, and Bangladesh*, University Press, Dhaka, 1988.

AMERY, L., *Thoughts on the Constitution*, Oxford University Press, London, 1947.

ANDERSON, D. M. and KILLINGRAY, D. (eds.), *Policing the Empire: Government, Authority and Control c.1830–1940*, Manchester University Press, Manchester, 1991.

ANDERSON, G. D., *Fascists, Communists, and the National Government: Civil Liberties in Great Britain 1931–1937*, Missouri University Press, Columbia, Mo., 1983.

ANDERSON, P., 'Origins of the Present Crisis', *New Left Review* 23 (1964).

ARNOLD-FORSTER, H. O., *The Citizen Reader*, Cassell, London, 1900.

ARTHURS, H. W., *'Without the Law': Administrative Justice and Legal Pluralism in Mid-Nineteenth-Century England*, University of Toronto Press, Toronto, 1985.

ASCOLI, D., *The Queen's Peace: The Origins and Development of the Metropolitan Police 1829–1979*, Hamish Hamilton, London, 1979.

AUGHEY, A. and McILHENEY, C., 'Law Before Violence? The Protestant Paramilitaries in Ulster Politics', *Eire–Ireland* 19 (1984).

AYLMER, G. E., 'The Peculiarities of the English State', *Journal of Historical Sociology* 3: 2 (1990).

BABINGTON, A., *Military Intervention in Britain: From the Gordon Riots to the Gibraltar Incident*, Routledge, London, 1990.

BAGEHOT, W., *The English Constitution*, Oxford University Press, London, 1867.

BAILEY, V. (ed.), *Policing and Punishment in Nineteenth-Century Britain*, Croom Helm, London, 1981.

BALAZS, J., 'A Note on the Interpretation of Security', *Development and Peace* 6 (1985).

BALDWIN, S. (Earl Baldwin of Bewdley), *On England*, Penguin Books, Harmondsworth, 1937.

BARENDT, E. M., *Freedom of Speech*, Oxford University Press, Oxford, 1985.

BARTHELEMY, J., 'Le Droit public en temps de guerre', *Revue du Droit Public* 32 (1915).

BATY, T. and MORGAN, H. J., *War: Its Conduct and Legal Results*, John Murray, London, 1915.

BAXTER, J. and KOFFMAN, L. (eds.), *Police, the Constitution, and the Community*, Professional Books, London, 1985.

BECKETT, I. (ed.), *The British Army and the Curragh Incident*, Army Records Society, Bodley Head, London, 1986.

—— 'A Note on Government Surveillance and Intelligence during the Curragh Incident, March 1914', *Intelligence and National Security* 1: 3 (1986), 435–40.

—— 'Some Further Correspondence Relating to the Curragh Incident of March 1914', *Journal of the Society for Army Historical Research* 69: 278 (1991).

BELLAMY, J., *Crime and Public Order in England in the Later Middle Ages*, Routledge, London, 1973.

BENDITT, T. M., 'The Public Interest', *Philosophy and Public Affairs* 2: 3 (1973).

BENEWICK, R., *Political Violence and Public Order*, Penguin Books, Harmondsworth, 1969.

BENYON J., 'Going Through the Motions: The Political Agenda, the 1981 Riots, and the Scarman Inquiry', *Parliamentary Affairs* 38 (1985).

—— and SOLOMOS, J., 'The Simmering Cities: Urban Unrest during the Thatcher Years', *Parliamentary Affairs* 41 (1988).

BERKI, R. N., *Reflections on Law and Order*, Hull Papers in Politics No. 35 (Hull University Department of Politics, 1983).

—— *Security and Society: Reflections on Law, Order and Politics*, Dent, London, 1986.

BEVAN, V., 'Protest and Public Order', *Public Law* 1979.

—— 'Is Anybody There?', *Public Law* 1980.

BIRTLES, W., 'Big Brother Knows Best: The Franks Report on Section 2 of the Official Secrets Act', *Public Law* 1973.

BITTNER, E., *The Functions of the Police in Modern Society*, National Institute of Mental Health, Chevy Chase, Md., Nov. 1970.

BLACKSTONE, W. T., 'The Concept of Political Freedom', *Social Theory and Practice* 42 (1973).

BOHSTEDT, J., *Riots and Community Politics in England and Wales 1790–1810*, Harvard University Press, Cambridge, Mass., 1983.

BOND, J. E., *The Rules of Riot: Internal Conflict and the Law of War*, Princeton

University Press, Princeton, NJ, 1974.

BONNER, D., *Emergency Powers in Peacetime*, Sweet & Maxwell, London, 1987.

—— and STONE, R., 'The Public Order Act 1986: Steps in the Wrong Direction?', *Public Law* 1987.

BOWDEN, T., *The Breakdown of Public Security: The Case of Ireland 1916–1921 and Palestine 1936–1939*, Sage, London, 1977.

—— *Beyond the Limits of the Law: A Comparative Study of the Police in Crisis Politics*, Penguin Books, Harmondsworth, 1978.

BOWMAN, H. M., 'Martial Law and the English Constitution', *Michigan Law Review* 15: 2 (1916).

BOUTMY, É., *The English People: A Study of their Political Psychology*, Putnam, London, 1904.

BOYCE, D. G., '"Normal Policing": Public Order in Northern Ireland Since Partition', *Eire–Ireland* 14 (1979).

BRADLEY, A. W., 'Parliamentary Privilege, Zircon and National Security', *Public Law* 1987.

BRADY, C., *Guardians of the Peace*, Gill & Macmillan, Dublin, 1974.

BRAILSFORD, H. N., *Property or Peace*, Gollancz, London, 1934.

BREWER, J., *The Sinews of Power: War, Money and the English State, 1688–1783*, Century Hutchinson, London, 1988.

—— and STYLES, J. (eds.), *An Ungovernable People: The English and their Law in the Seventeenth and Eighteenth Centuries*, Hutchinson, London, 1980.

BREWER, J. D., GUELKE, A., HUME, I., MOXON-BROWNE, E., and WILFORD, R., *The Police, Public Order and the State: Policing in Great Britain, Northern Ireland, the Irish Republic, the USA, Israel, South Africa, and China*, Macmillan, London, 1988.

BROGAN, D. W., *The English People: Impressions and Observations*, Hamish Hamilton, London, 1943.

BROGDEN, M., 'A Police Authority–the Denial of Conflict', *Sociological Review* 25 (1977).

—— *The Police: Autonomy and Consent*, Academic Press, London, 1982.

—— *On the Mersey Beat: Policing Liverpool Between the Wars*, Oxford University Press, Oxford, 1991.

BROWN, J. and HOWES, G. (eds.), *The Police and the Community*, Saxon House, London, 1975.

BROWNE-WILKINSON, N., 'The Independence of the Judiciary in the 1980s', *Public Law* 1988.

BUNYAN, T., *The History and Practice of the Political Police in Britain*, Julian Friedmann, London, 1976.

BURKE, E., *Thoughts and Details on Scarcity*, originally presented to the Right Honorable William Pitt in the month of November, 1795, F. & C. Rivington, London, 1800.

BURN, W. L., *The Age of Equipoise*, Allen & Unwin, London, 1964.

BURROW, J. W., *A Liberal Descent: Victorian Historians and the English Past*, Cambridge University Press, Cambridge, 1981.

—— *Whigs and Liberals: Continuity and Change in English Political Thought*, Oxford University Press, Oxford, 1988.

BUTLER, J., *Government by Police*, Dyer Brothers, London, 1879.

BUTTERFIELD, H., *The Englishman and His History*, Cambridge University Press, Cambridge, 1944.

BUZAN, B., *People, States and Fear: An Agenda for International Security Studies in the Post-Cold War Era*, Routledge & Kegan Paul, London, 1973.

CAIN, M., *Society and the Policeman's Role*, Routledge, London, 1973.

—— 'Towards a Political Sociology of the British Police: A Review of 1979 and 1980', in R. Donelan (ed.), *The Maintenance of Order in Society*, Canadian Police College, Ottawa, 1982.

CALVERT, H., *Constitutional Law in Northern Ireland: A Study in Regional Government*, Stevens, London, 1968.

CAMPBELL, C., 'Emergency Law in Ireland, 1918–25', Ph.D. thesis, Queen's University of Belfast 1989.

CAMPBELL, J., 'Stubbs and the English State', The Stenton Lecture, University of Reading, 1989.

CARD, R., *Public Order: The New Law*, Butterworths, London, 1987.

CHAMBERLIN, R., *The Idea of England*, Thames & Hudson, New York, 1986.

CHANCELLOR, V. E., *History for Their Masters: Opinion in the English History Textbook 1800–1914*, Adams & Dart, Bath, 1970.

CHECKLAND, S., *British Public Policy 1776–1939: An Economic, Social and Political Perspective*, Cambridge University Press, Cambridge, 1983.

CHESSHYRE, R., 'This is no riot', *Sunday Times Magazine*, 15 Oct. 1989.

—— *The Force: Inside the Police*, Sidgwick & Jackson, London, 1989.

CHIBNALL, S., *Law and Order News: An Analysis of Crime Reporting in the British Press*, Tavistock Publications, London, 1977.

CHOWDHURY, S. R., *Rule of Law in a State of Emergency: The Paris Minimum Standards of Human Rights Norms in a State of Emergency*, St Martin's Press, New York, 1989.

CLARK, J. C. D., *Revolution and Rebellion: State and Society in England in the Seventeenth and Eighteenth Centuries*, Cambridge University Press, Cambridge, 1986.

—— (ed.), *Ideas and Politics in Modern Britain*, Macmillan, London, 1990.

CLARKE, S. W., 'The Rule of DORA', *Journal of Comparative Legislation and International Law* 3rd ser. 1 (1919).

CLUTTERBUCK, R. L., 'A Third Force?', *Army Quarterly* 104 (1973).

—— 'The Police and Urban Terrorism', *Police Journal* 68: 3 (1975).

—— *Britain in Agony: The Growth of Political Violence*, Faber, London, 1978.

COAKLEY, R. W., *The Role of Federal Military Forces in Domestic Disorders 1789–1878*, US Army Center of Military History, Washington DC, 1988.

COCKBURN, J. S., 'Patterns of Violence in English Society: Homicide in Kent 1560–1985', *Past and Present* 130 (1991).

COHEN, P., 'The Police, the Home Office, and Surveillance of the British Union of Fascists', *Intelligence and National Security* 1 (1986).

COHEN, S. and SCULL, A. (eds.), *Social Control and the State*, Martin Robertson, Oxford, 1983.

COLLEY, L., *Britons: Forging the Nation 1707–1837*, Yale University Press, New Haven, Conn., 1992.

COLLINI, S., 'Hobhouse, Bosanquet and the State: Philosophical Idealism and Political Argument in England 1880–1918', *Past and Present* 72 (1976).

COLLS, R. and DODD, P. (eds.), *Englishness: Politics and Culture 1880–1920*, Croom Helm, London, 1986.

COLSON, E., *Tradition and Contract: The Problem of Order*, Aldine, Chicago, 1974.

Conservative Research Department, 'Law and Order', *Politics Today* 22 (Dec. 1983).

COOK, C. (ed.), *Defence of the Realm Manual*, 7th edn., HMSO, London, 1919.

CORRIGAN, P. and SAYER, D., *The Great Arch: English State Formation as a Cultural Revolution*, Blackwell, Oxford, 1985.

COSER, L., *The Functions of Social Conflict*, Routledge, London, 1956.

—— 'Some Social Functions of Violence', *The Annals of the American Academy of Political and Social Science*, May 1966.

COTTER, C. P., 'Emergency Detention in Wartime: The British Experience', *Stanford Law Review* 6 (Mar. 1954).

COWELL, D., JONES, T., and YOUNG, J. (eds.), *Policing the Riots*, Junction Books, London, 1982.

CRESSY, D., 'Describing the Social Order in Elizabethan and Stuart England', *Literature and History* 3 (1976).

CRICK, B. and ROBSON, W. A. (eds.), *Protest and Discontent*, Penguin Books, Harmondsworth, 1970.

CRITCHLEY, T. A., *The Conquest of Violence: Order and Liberty in Britain*, Constable, London, 1970.

—— *A History of Police in England and Wales*, Constable, London, 1978.

CROSSICK, G., *The Lower Middle Class in Britain 1870–1914*, Croom Helm, London, 1977.

CRUICKSHANKS, E. and ERSKINE-HILL, H., 'The Waltham Black Act and Jacobitism', *Journal of British Studies* 24: 3 (1985).

DARVALL, F. O., *Popular Disturbances and Public Order in Regency England*, 2nd edn., Oxford University Press, Oxford, 1969.

DAVEY, B. J., *Lawless and Immoral: Policing a Country Town, 1838–1857*, Leicester University Press, Leicester, 1983.

DE SMITH, S. A., *Constitutional and Administrative Law*, 5th edn. by H. Street and R. Brazier, Penguin Books, Harmondsworth, 1985.

DESMARAIS, R. H., 'The Supply and Transport Committee, 1919–26: A Study of the British Government's Method of Handling Emergencies Stemming from Industrial Disputes', Ph.D. thesis, University of Wisconsin 1970.

—— 'The British Government's Strikebreaking Organization and Black Friday', *Journal of Contemporary History* 6: 2 (1971).

DICEY, A. V., 'The Prevalence of Lawlessness in England', *The Nation*, 2 Aug. 1883.

—— *Introduction to the Study of the Law of the Constitution*, Macmillan, London, 1885.

DODD, C., 'The Case of Marais', *Law Quarterly Review* 18 (1902).

DONAJGRODSKI, A. P. (ed.), *Social Control of Nineteenth Century Britain*, Croom Helm, London, 1977.

DONELAN, R. (ed.), *The Maintenance of Order in Society*, Canadian Police College, Ottawa, 1982.

DUNBABIN, J. P. D., *Rural Discontent in Nineteenth-Century Britain*, Faber, London, 1974.

DYSON, K. F., *The State Tradition in Western Europe: A Study of an Idea and an Institution*, Martin Robertson, Oxford, 1980.

ECKSTEIN, H., 'The Sources of Leadership and Democracy in Britain', in S. H. Beer and A. B. Ulam (eds.), *Patterns of Government: The Major Political Systems of Europe*, 2nd edn., Random House, New York, 1962.

EGAN, B. and McCORMACK, V., *Burntollet*, LRS Publishers, 1969.

EICHENBERG, R. E., *Public Opinion and National Security in Western Europe*, Macmillan, London, 1989.

EMSLEY, C., 'The Bedfordshire Police 1840–1856: A Case Study in the Working of the Rural Constabulary Act', *Midland History* 7 (1982).

—— 'The Military and Popular Disorder in England 1790–1801', *Journal of the Society for Army Historical Research* 61 (1983).

ENGLANDER, D., 'Military Intelligence and the Defence of the Realm: The Surveillance of Soldiers and Civilians in Britain During the First World War', *Bulletin of the Society for the Study of Labour History* 52: 1 (1987).

—— 'Police and Public Order in Britain, 1914–1918', in Emsley, C. and Weinberger, B. (eds.), *Policing Western Europe: Politics, Professionalization and Public Order*, Greenwood, London, 1991.

ESCOTT, T. H. S., *England: Its People, Polity and Pursuits*, Cassell, Peter, Galpin, & Co., London, 1879.

EWING, K. D. and GEARTY, C., *Freedom under Thatcher: Civil Liberties in Modern Britain*, Oxford University Press, Oxford, 1990.

Farrell, M., *Arming the Protestants: The Formation of the Ulster Special Constabulary and Royal Ulster Constabulary, 1920–7*, Pluto, London, 1983.

FEATHERSTONE, S., 'The Nation as Pastoral in British Literature of the Second World War', *Journal of European Studies* 16 (1986).

FINLASON, W. F., *A Review of the Authorities as to the Repression of Riot or*

Rebellion, with Special Reference to the Criminal or Civil Liability, Stevens & Sons, London, 1868.

FLETCHER, A. and STEVENSON, J. (eds.), *Order and Disorder in Early Modern England*, Cambridge University Press, Cambridge, 1985.

FORSTER, H., 'Shooting the Elephant: Historians and the Problem of Frontier Lawlessness', in R. Beales and D. Sullivan (eds.), *The Political Context of Law: Proceedings of the 7th British Legal History Conference, Canterbury 1985*, Hambledon Press, London, 1987.

FOX, K. O., 'The Tonypandy Riots', *Army Quarterly* 104: 1 (1973).

—— 'Public Order: The Law, and the Military', *Army Quarterly* 104: 3 (1974).

FRASER, D., *Power and Authority in the Victorian City*, St Martin's Press, New York, 1979.

FYSON, R., 'The Crisis of 1842: Chartism, the Colliers' Strike and the Outbreak in the Potteries', in J. Epstein and D. Thompson (eds.), *The Chartist Experience: Studies in Working-Class Radicalism and Culture, 1830–60*, Macmillan, London, 1982.

GATRELL, V. A. C. and HADDEN, T. B., 'Criminal Statistics and Their Interpretation', in E. A. Wrigley (ed.), *The Study of Nineteenth Century Society*, Cambridge University Press, Cambridge, 1970.

—— LENMAN, B. and PARKER, G. (eds.), *Crime and Law: The Social History of Crime in Western Europe since 1500*, Europa, London, 1980.

GEARY, R., *Policing Industrial Disputes: 1893 to 1985*, Cambridge University Press, Cambridge, 1985.

GORER, G., *Exploring English Character*, Cresset, London, 1955.

GRACE, E. and LEYS, C., 'The Concept of Subversion and its Implications', in C. E. S. Franks (ed.), *Dissent and the State*, Oxford University Press, Toronto, 1989.

GRAINGER, J. H., *Character and Style in English Politics*, Cambridge University Press, Cambridge, 1969.

—— *Patriotisms: Britain, 1900–1939*, Routledge, London, 1986.

GREENLEAF, W. H., *Order, Empiricism, and Politics: Two Traditions of English Political Thought 1500–1700*, Oxford University Press, London, 1964.

GREER, S. C. and WHITE, A., *Abolishing the Diplock Courts: The Case for Restoring Jury Trial to Scheduled Offences in Northern Ireland*, Cobden Trust, London, 1986.

—— *The Police, Public Order and Western Society*, Wheatsheaf, Brighton, 1987.

GRIFFITH, J. A. G., 'The Crichel Down Affair', *Modern Law Review* 18 (1955).

—— *The Politics of the Judiciary*, 2nd edn., Fontana, London, 1981.

GROSSMAN, B. A., 'The Discretionary Enforcement of Law', in S. F. Sylvester and E. Sargarin (eds.), *Politics and Crime*, Praeger, New York, 1972.

HABERMAS, J., 'What Does Crisis Mean Today? Legitimation Problems in Late Capitalism', *Social Research* 40: 4 (1973).

HADDEN, T., 'The Law in their Hands', *Times Literary Supplement*, 4–10 Mar. 1988.

HALL, S., *Drifting Into a Law and Order Society*, Cobden Trust, London, 1980.

—— 'The Lessons of Lord Scarman', *Critical Social Policy* 2: 2 (1982).

—— and JEFFERSON, T., *Resistance Through Rituals: Youth Subculture in Post-War Britain*, Hutchinson, London, 1976.

—— CRICHTER, C., JEFFERSON, T., CLARKE, J., and ROBERTS, B., *Policing the Crisis: Mugging, the State, and Law and Order*, Macmillan, London, 1978.

HAMILL, D., *Pig in the Middle: The Army in Northern Ireland 1969–1984*, Methuen, London, 1985.

HAMILTON, H., *England, a History of the Homeland*, Norton, New York, 1948.

HAND, G. J. (ed.), *Report of the Irish Boundary Commission*, Irish Universities Press, Shannon, 1969.

HARRIS, R. and SEWILL, B., *British Economic Policy, 1970–74: Two Views*, Institute of Economic Affairs, London, 1975.

HARRISON, B., *Peaceable Kingdom: Stability and Change in Modern Britain*, Clarendon Press, Oxford, 1982.

HARRISON, F., *Martial Law: Six Letters to the 'Daily News'*, The Jamaica Committee, London, 1867.

—— 'The Religion of Inhumanity', *Fortnightly Review*, June 1873.

HARRISON, M., *Crowds and History: Mass Phenomena in English Towns, 1790–1835*, Cambridge University Press, Cambridge, 1988.

HARVEY, J. and HOOD, K., *The British State*, Lawrence & Wishart, London, 1958.

HAY, D. and SNYDER, F. (eds.), *Policing and Prosecution in Britain 1750–1850*, Oxford University Press, Oxford, 1989.

HAYTER, A. J., *The Army and the Crowd in Mid-Georgian England*, Macmillan, London, 1978.

HEATH, E., 'A State of Secrecy', *New Statesman and Society*, 10 Mar. 1989.

HERRUP, C., 'Crime, Law and Society', *Comparative Studies in Society and History* 27: 1 (1985).

—— *The Common Peace: Participation and the Criminal Law in Seventeenth-century England*, Cambridge University Press, Cambridge, 1987.

HEUSTON, R. F. V., '*Liversidge* v. *Anderson* in Retrospect', *Law Quarterly Review* 86 (1970).

HEZLET, A., *The B Specials: A History of the Ulster Special Constabulary*, Stacey, London, 1972.

HILEY, N., 'British Internal Security in Wartime: The Rise and Fall of P.M.S. 2, 1915–1917', *Intelligence and National Security* 1: 3 (1986).

HILLYARD, P. and PERCY-SMITH, J., *The Coercive State*, Fontana, London, 1988.

HOBSBAWM, E. J., *Primitive Rebels: Studies in Archaic Forms of Social Movement in the 19th and 20th Centuries*, Manchester University Press, Manchester, 1959.

—— and RUDÉ, G., *Captain Swing*, Penguin Books, Harmondsworth, 1973.

HOLDAWAY, S. (ed.), *The British Police*, Arnold, London, 1979.

—— 'Police Accountability: A Current Issue', *Public Administration* 60 (1982).

—— *Inside the British Police: A Force at Work*, Blackwell, Oxford, 1983.

HOLMES, R., *The Little Field Marshal: Sir John French*, Cape, London, 1981.

HOPKIN, D. R., 'The Llanelli Riots, 1911', *Welsh Historical Review* 11: 4 (1983).

HUEFFER, F. M., *The Heart of the Country: A Survey of a Modern Land*, Alston Rivers, London, 1906.

—— *The Spirit of the People: An Analysis of the English Mind*, Alston Rivers, London, 1907.

HUMPHRIES, S., *Hooligans or Rebels? An Oral History of Working-Class Youth 1889–1937*, Blackwell, Oxford, 1981.

HYNES, S., *A War Imagined: The First World War and English Culture*, Macmillan, London, 1990.

IGNATIEFF, M., 'It's a Riot', *London Review of Books*, 20 Aug. 1981.

INGRAHAM, B. L., *Political Crime in Europe: A Comparative Study of France, Germany, and England*, California University Press, Berkeley, Calif., 1979.

INNES, J., 'Jonathan Clark, Social History and England's "Ancien Régime"', *Past and Present* 115 (May 1987).

INNES, J. and STYLES, J., 'The Crime Wave: Recent Writing on Crime and Criminal Justice in Eighteenth-century England', *Journal of British Studies* 25 (1986).

JACOB, J., 'Some Reflections on Governmental Secrecy', *Public Law* 1974.

JAMES, M. E., 'The Concept of Order and the Northern Rising 1569', *Past and Present* 60 (1973).

JEFFERSON, T. and GRIMSHAW, R., *Controlling the Constable: Police Accountability in England and Wales*, Cobden Trust, London, 1984.

JEFFERY, K., 'The British Army and Internal Security 1919–1939', *Historical Journal* 24: 2 (1981).

—— *The British Army and the Crisis of Empire 1918–22*, Manchester University Press, Manchester, 1984.

—— 'Military Aid to the Civil Power in the United Kingdom: An Historical Perspective', in P. J. Rowe and C. J. Whelan (eds.), *Military Intervention in Democratic Societies*, Croom Helm, London, 1985.

—— and HENNESSY, P., *States of Emergency: British Government and Strike-breaking since 1919*, Routledge, London, 1983.

JENNINGS, A. (ed.), *Justice Under Fire*, Pluto Press, London, 1988.

JENNINGS, I., *The Sedition Bill Explained*, New Statesman and Nation, London, 1934.

JESSOP, R., *Traditionalism, Conservatism and British Political Culture*, Allen & Unwin, London, 1974.

JEVONS, W. S., *The State in Relation to Labour*, Macmillan, London, 1882.

JOHNSON, N., *In Search of the Constitution*, Pergamon Press, Oxford, 1977.

JONES, D. J. V., *Crime, Protest, Community and Police in Nineteenth-century Britain*, Routledge, London, 1982.

—— 'The New Police, Crime, and People in England and Wales 1829–1888', *Transactions of the Royal Historical Society* 33 (1983), 151–68.

JONES, T., *Whitehall Diary*, ed. K. Middlemas, ii, London, 1969; iii, Oxford University Press, London, 1971.

KAEUPER, R. W., 'Law and Order in 14th Century England: The Evidence of

Special Commissions of Oyer and Terminer', *Speculum* 54 (1979).

—— *War, Justice and Public Order: England and France in the Later Middle Ages*, Oxford University Press, Oxford, 1988.

KAMM, R. M., 'The Home Office, Public Order, and Civil Liberties, 1880–1914', Ph.D. thesis, Cambridge University 1981.

KAVANAGH, D., 'The Deferential English: A Comparative Critique', *Government and Opposition* 6: 3 (1971).

—— *British Politics: Continuities and Change*, Oxford University Press, Oxford, 1990.

KEETON, G. W., 'Liversidge v. Anderson', *Modern Law Review* 5 (1941).

KEIR, D. L. and LAWSON, F. H., *Cases in Constitutional Law*, 5th edn., Oxford University Press, London, 1967.

KEITH, A. B., *The Constitution Under Strain*, Stevens & Sons, London, 1942.

KELLER, L., 'Public Order in Victorian London: The Interaction Between the Metropolitan Police, the Government, the Urban Crowd, and the Law', Ph.D. thesis, Cambridge University 1976.

KENDALL, W., *The Revolutionary Movement in Britain, 1900–1921: The Origins of British Communism*, Weidenfeld, London, 1969.

KETTLE, M., 'The Politics of Policing and the Policing of Politics', in P. Hain (ed.), *Policing the Police*, ii, John Calder, London, 1980.

—— *Uprising! The Police, the People, and the Riots in Britain's Cities*, Pan Books, London, 1982.

KIDD, R., *British Liberty in Danger*, Lawrence & Wishart, London, 1940.

KITSON, F., *Low Intensity Operations*, Faber, London, 1971.

KNORR, K. (ed.), *Historical Dimensions of National Security Problems*, National Security Education Program, University Press of Kansas, Lawrence, Kan., 1976.

KOHN, G. C., *Dictionary of Wars*, Facts on File, New York and Oxford, 1986.

LAMARQUE, J., 'La Théorie de la necessité et l'Article 16 de la Constitution de 1958', *Revue de la droit public et de la science politique en France et à l'étranger* 77 (1961).

LAMBERT, J. L., *Police Powers and Accountability*, Croom Helm, London, 1985.

LANGBEIN, J. H., 'Albion's Fatal Flaws', *Past and Present* 98 (1983).

LASKI, H., 'Civil Liberties in Great Britain in Wartime', *Bill of Rights Review* 2 (1942).

LASLETT, P., *The World We Have Lost*, 3rd edn., Methuen, London, 1983.

LASSWELL, H. D., 'The Garrison State and the Specialists on Violence', *American Journal of Sociology* 46 (1941).

Law Commission, *Codification of the Criminal Law: Treason, Sedition and Allied Offences*, Working Paper No. 72, London, 1977.

LeMAY, G. H. L., *The Victorian Constitution: Conventions, Usages, and Contingencies*, Duckworth, London, 1979.

LEWIS, G. C., *On Local Disturbances in Ireland*, B. Fellowes, London, 1836.

LEYS, C., *Politics in Britain*, Heinemann, London, 1983.

LINEBAUGH, D. H. P. and THOMPSON, E. P. (eds.), *Albion's Fatal Tree*, Allen Lane, London, 1975.

LIPSKY, M. and OLSON, D. J., *Commission Politics: The Processing of Racial Crisis in America*, Transaction Books, New Brunswick, NJ, 1977.

LOMAS, O. G., 'The Executive and the Anti-Terrorist Legislation of 1939', *Public Law* 1980.

LOW, S., *The Governance of England*, T. F. Unwin, London, 1914.

LOWRY, D. R., 'Internment: Detention Without Trial in Northern Ireland', *Human Rights* 5 (1976).

—— 'Terrorism and Human Rights: Counter-insurgency and Necessity at Common Law', *Notre Dame Lawyer* 53: 49 (1977).

LUSTGARTEN, L., *The Governance of Police*, Sweet & Maxwell, London, 1986.

McAUSLAN, P. and MacELDOWNEY, J. F. (eds.), *Law, Legitimacy, and the Constitution: Essays Marking the Centenary of Dicey's 'Law of the Constitution'*, Sweet & Maxwell, London, 1986.

McCABE, S., WALLINGTON, P., ALDERSON, J., GOSTIN, L., and MASON, C., *The Police, Public Order, and Civil Liberties: Legacies of the Miners' Strike*, Routledge, London, 1988.

MACFARLANE, A., 'History, Anthropology and the Study of Communities', *Social History* 5 (1977).

—— *The Culture of Capitalism*, Blackwell, Oxford, 1987.

—— with HARRISON, S., *The Justice and the Mare's Ale: Law and Disorder in Seventeenth-century England*, Blackwell, Oxford, 1981.

MAINWARING, G., *Observations on the Present State of the Police of the Metropolis*, J. Murray, London, 1821.

MAINWARING-WHITE, S., *The Policing Revolution: Police Technology, Democracy and Liberty in Britain*, Harvester, Brighton, 1983.

MANSERGH, N., *The Unresolved Question: The Anglo-Irish Settlement and its Undoing 1912–72*, Yale University Press, New Haven, Conn., 1991.

MARK, R., *A History of Police in England and Wales*, Foreword by T. A. Critchley, Constable, London, 1978.

—— *In the Office of Constable*, Collins, London, 1978.

MARKESINIS, B. S., 'The Right to be Let Alone versus Freedom of Speech', *Public Law* 1986.

MARSHALL, G., *Police and Government: The Status and Accountability of the English Constable*, Methuen, London, 1965.

—— 'The Armed Forces and Industrial Disputes in the United Kingdom', *Armed Forces and Society* 5 (1979).

MARTIN, F. X. and BYRNE, F. J. (eds.), *The Scholar Revolutionary: Eoin MacNeill 1867–1945 and the Making of a New Ireland*, Irish Universities Press, Shannon, 1973.

MARTIN, K., *The British Public and the General Strike*, Leonard and Virginia Woolf, London, 1926.

MARWICK, A. J. B., 'Middle Opinion in the 1930s', *English Historical Review* 79 (1964).

—— *The Deluge: British Society and the First World War*, 2nd edn., Macmillan, London, 1973.

MARX, G. T., 'Civil Disorder and the Agents of Social Control', *Journal of Social Issues* 26 (1970).

MASON, A., 'The Government and the General Strike', *International Review of Social History* 14: 1 (1969).

MASSINGHAM, H. J., *Genius of England*, Chapman & Hall, London, 1937.

MASTERMAN, C. F. G., 'Where Ignorant Armies Clash by Night', *Commonwealth*, Aug. 1901.

—— *The Condition of England*, Methuen, London, 1909.

—— *England After War: A Study*, Harcourt Brace, New York, 1923.

MATHER, F. C., *Public Order in the Age of the Chartists*, Manchester University Press, Manchester, 1959.

—— 'The General Strike of 1842', in J. Stevenson and R. Quinault (eds.), *Popular Protest and Public Order: Six Studies in British History, 1790–1920*, Allen & Unwin, London, 1974.

MAY, R. and COHEN, R., 'The Interaction Between Race and Colonialism: A Case Study of the Liverpool Race Riots of 1919', *Race and Class* 16: 2 (1974).

Metropolitan Police Force, *Public Order Review: Civil Disturbances 1981–1985*, London, 1986.

MIDDLEMAS, K., *Politics in Industrial Society: The Experience of the British System since 1911*, Deutsch, London, 1979.

MIDWINTER, E., *Law and Order in Early Victorian Lancashire*, University of York, 1968.

MILLER, W. R., *Cops and Bobbies: Police Authority in New York and London 1830–1870*, Chicago University Press, Chicago, 1977.

MINGAY, G. E. (ed.), *The Rural Idyll*, Routledge, London, 1989.

MOORE, D. C., 'Political Morality in Mid-Nineteenth Century England: Concepts, Norms, Violations', *Victorian Studies* 13: 1 (Sept. 1969).

—— *The Politics of Deference: A Study of the Middle Nineteenth-Century English Political System*, Harvester, Hassocks, 1976.

MORGAN, J., *Conflict and Order: The Police and Labour Disputes in England and Wales 1900–1939*, Clarendon Press, Oxford, 1987.

MORRIS, G. S., 'The Emergency Powers Act 1920', *Public Law* 1979.

MORRIS, T., 'The Case for a Riot Squad', *New Society*, 29 Nov. 1985.

MORTON, G. J., *Just the Job: Some Experiences of a Colonial Policeman*, Hodder & Stoughton, London, 1957.

MUENGER, E., *The British Military Dilemma in Ireland: Occupation Politics, 1886–1914*, Kansas University Press, Lawrence, Kan., 1991.

NAIRN, T., *The Break-up of Britain*, 2nd edn., Verso, London, 1981.

National Council of Civil Liberties, *Report of a Commission of Inquiry appointed to examine the Purpose and Effect of the Civil Authorities (Special Powers) Acts (Northern Ireland) 1922 and 1933*, London, 1936.

NEAL, F., *Sectarian Violence: The Liverpool Experience 1819–1914*, Manchester University Press, Manchester, 1988.

NEUMANN, F. L., *The Rule of Law: Political Theory and the Legal System in Modern Society*, Berg, Leamington Spa, 1985.

NEVILLE, R. G., 'The Yorkshire Miners and the 1893 Lockout: The Featherstone "Massacre"', *International Review of Social History* 21 (1976).

NIEBURG, H. L., 'Violence, Law and the Informed Polity', *Journal of Conflict Resolution* 13 (1969).

NIPPEL, W. E., '"Reading the Riot Act": The Discourse of Law Enforcement in 18th Century England', *History and Anthropology* 1: 2 (1985).

NORTON, P. (ed.), *Law and Order and British Politics*, Gower, Aldershot, 1984.

NORTHAM, G., *Shooting in the Dark: Riot Police in Britain*, Faber, London, 1988.

O'BOYLE, M. P., 'Emergency Situations and the Protection of Human Rights', *Northern Ireland Law Quarterly* 28 (1977).

O'DOWD, L., ROLSTON, B., and TOMLINSON, M., *Northern Ireland: Between Civil Rights and Civil War*, CSE Books, London, 1980.

O'HALLORAN, C., *Partition and the Limits of Irish Nationalism*, Gill & Macmillan, Dublin, 1987.

O'HIGGINS, P., 'The Lawless Case', *Cambridge Law Journal* 16 (1962).

—— 'English Law and the Irish Question', *Irish Jurist* 1 (1966).

OLIVER, I., *Police, Government and Accountability*, Macmillan, London, 1987.

PALLEY, C., 'The Evolution, Disintegration and Possible Reconstruction of the Northern Ireland Constitution', *Anglo-American Law Review* 1: 3 (1972).

PALMER, S. H., *Police and Protest in England and Ireland 1780–1850*, Cambridge University Press, Cambridge, 1988.

—— 'Major General Sir Charles James Napier: Irishman, Chartist, and Commander of the Northern District in England, 1839–41', *Irish Sword* 16 (1982).

PATTERSON, H., *Class Conflict and Sectarianism: The Protestant Working Class and the Belfast Labour Movement 1868–1920*, Blackstaff, Belfast, 1980.

PEARSON, G., *Hooligan: A History of Respectable Fears*, Macmillan, London, 1983.

PELLEW, J., *The Home Office: From Clerks to Bureaucrats, 1848–1914*, Heinemann, London, 1982.

PERKINS, K., 'Soldiers or Policemen?', *British Army Review* 45 (1973).

PHILIPS, D., 'Riots and Public Order in the Black Country, 1835–1860', in R. Quinault and J. Stevenson (eds.), *Popular Protest and Public Order: Six Studies in British History 1790–1920*, Allen & Unwin, London, 1974.

—— *Crime and Authority in Victorian England: The Black Country 1835–1860*, Croom Helm, London, 1977.

—— '"A New Engine of Power and Authority": The Institutionalization of Law Enforcement in England, 1780–1830', in V. A. C. Gatrell, B. Lenman, and

G. Parker (eds.), *Crime and the Law: The Social History of Crime in Western Europe since 1500*, Europa, London, 1980.

—— '"A Just Measure of Crime, Authority, Hunters and Blue Locusts": The "Revisionist" Social History of Crime and the Law in Britain, 1780–1850', in S. Cohen and A. Scull (eds.), *Social Control and the State*, Martin Robertson, Oxford, 1983.

PICKERING, P. A., 'Class Without Words: Symbolic Communication in the Chartist Movement', *Past and Present* 112 (1986).

PLEHWE, R., 'Police and Government: The Commissioner of Police for the Metropolis', *Public Law* 1974.

POCOCK, J. G. A., *The Ancient Constitution and the Feudal Law*, Cambridge University Press, Cambridge, 1957.

—— 'The Limits and Divisions of British History', *American Historical Review*, 1982.

'The Police of London', *Quarterly Review* 129 (1870).

POLLOCK, F., 'What is Martial Law?', *Law Quarterly Review* 18 (1902).

PONTING, C., 'R. v. *Ponting*', *Journal of Law and Society* 14: 366 (1987).

PORTER, B., 'The Origins of Britain's Political Police', Warwick Working Papers in Social History No. 3 (1985).

—— 'The Historiography of the Early Special Branch', *Intelligence and National Security* 1 (1986).

—— *Origins of the Vigilant State*, Weidenfeld, London, 1987.

POWELL, E. and MAUDE, A., *Biography of a Nation*, J. Baker, London, 1955.

PRICE, R. N., 'Society, Status and Jingoism: The Social Roots of Lower Middle Class Patriotism 1870–1900', in G. Crossick (ed.), *The Lower Middle Class in Britain 1870–1914*, Croom Helm, London, 1977.

PRIESTLEY, J. B., *English Journey*, Harper and Brothers, London, 1934.

—— *The English*, Heinemann, London, 1973.

PROTHERO, M., *The History of the Criminal Investigation Department at Scotland Yard from Earliest Times Until Today*, Herbert Jenkins, London, 1931.

PULLING, A. (ed.), *Manual of Emergency Legislation*, Darling, London, 1914.

QUINAULT, R. and STEVENSON, J. (eds.), *Popular Protest and Public Order: Six Studies in British History 1790–1920*, Allen & Unwin, London, 1974.

RADZINOWICZ, L., *Sir James Fitzjames Stephen 1829–1894 and His Contribution to the Development of Criminal Law*, Selden Society, London, 1957.

—— 'New Departures in Maintaining Public Order in the Face of the Chartist Disturbances', *Cambridge Law Journal*, Apr. 1960.

—— *A History of the English Criminal Law*, iv, Stevens, London, 1968.

—— and HOOD, R., *A History of the English Criminal Law and its Administration from 1750*, v, *The Emergence of Penal Policy*, Stevens, London, 1986.

REBER, K., *Das Notrecht des Staates*, Polygrafischer Verlag, Zurich, 1938.

REINACH, T., *De l'état de siège*, F. Pichon, Paris, 1885.

REINER, R., *The Politics of the Police*, Wheatsheaf, Brighton, 1985.

REINER, R., *Chief Constables*, Oxford University Press, Oxford, 1991.

REITH, C., *The Police Idea*, Oxford University Press, London, 1938.

—— *Police Principles and the Problem of War*, Oxford University Press, London, 1940.

—— *The British Police and the Democratic Ideal*, Oxford University Press, London, 1942.

—— *A New Study of Police History*, Oliver & Boyd, Edinburgh, 1956.

REYNOLDS, G. W. and JUDGE, A., *The Night the Police Went on Strike*, Weidenfeld, London, 1968.

RICHMOND, C. F., 'Ruling Classes and Agents of the State: Formal and Informal Networks of Power', unpublished colloquium paper, St Peter's College, Oxford, 1991.

RICHTER, D. C., 'Public Order and Popular Disturbances in Great Britain, 1865–1914', Ph.D. thesis, University of Maryland 1964.

—— 'The Role of Mob Riot in Victorian Elections, 1865–1885', *Victorian Studies* 15 (1971–2).

—— *Riotous Victorians*, Ohio University Press, Athens, Oh., 1981.

ROACH, J. and THOMANEK, J. (eds.), *The Police and Public Order in Europe*, Croom Helm, London, 1985.

ROBERTS, A., 'The Police at Midnight', *New Statesman*, 22 Sept. 1961.

ROBERTSON, K. G., *Public Secrets: A Study in the Development of Government Secrecy*, Macmillan, London, 1982.

ROGERS, L., 'The War and the English Constitution', *The Forum*, July 1915.

—— *Crisis Government*, Allen & Unwin, London, 1934.

ROGERS, N., 'Jacobite Riots in Early Hanoverian England', in E. Cruickshanks (ed.), *Ideology and Conspiracy: Aspects of Jacobitism, 1689–1759*, J. Donald, Edinburgh, 1982.

ROGERS, P., 'The Waltham Blacks and the Black Act', *Historical Journal* 17 (1974).

ROLLO, J., 'The Special Patrol Group', in P. Hain (ed.), *Policing the Police*, ii, John Calder, London, 1980.

ROLPH, C. H., *The Police and the Public: An Enquiry Presented by C. H. Rolph*, Heinemann, London, 1962.

ROMAIN, P., *L'État de siège politique*, Imprimerie des Orphelins-apprentis, Albi, 1918.

ROSSITER, C. L., *Constitutional Dictatorship: Crisis Government in the Modern Democracies*, Princeton University Press, Princeton, NJ, 1948.

ROWE, P. J. and WHELAN, C. J. (eds.), *Military Intervention in Democratic Societies*, Croom Helm, London, 1985.

RUBIN, G. R., 'The Royal Prerogative or a Statutory Code? The War Office and Contingency Legal Planning, 1885–1914', in R. Eales and D. Sullivan (eds.), *The Political Context of Law*, Hambledon Press, London, 1987.

—— and SUGARMAN, D. (eds.), *Law, Economy and Society 1750–1914: Essays in the History of English Law*, Professional Books, Abingdon, 1984.

RUBINSTEIN, W. D., 'Education and the Social Origins of British Elites 1880–1970', *Past and Present* 112 (1986).

RULE, J. B., *Theories of Civil Violence*, University of California Press, Berkeley, Calif., 1988.

SAMUEL, R. (ed.), *Patriotism: The Making and Unmaking of British National Identity*, Routledge, London, 1989.

—— and THOMPSON, P. J. (eds.), *The Myths We Live By*, Routledge, London, 1990.

SAVILLE, J., *1848; The British State and the Chartist Movement*, Cambridge University Press, Cambridge, 1987.

SAYER, D., 'British Reactions to the Amritsar Massacre 1919–1920', *Past and Present* 131 (1991).

SCARMAN, LORD, 'A Code of English Law?', Lecture, University of Hull, 25 Feb. 1966, Hull University Press, Hull, 1966.

—— *English Law: The New Dimension*, Stevens, London, 1974.

—— 'Human Rights in an Unwritten Constitution', *Denning Law Journal* 129 (1987).

SCOTT, J. C., *Weapons of the Weak: Everyday Forms of Peasant Resistance*, Yale University Press, New Haven, Conn., 1985.

SCRATON, P. (ed.), *Law, Order and the Authoritarian State*, Open University Press, Milton Keynes, 1987.

SEARLE, G. R., *The Quest for National Efficiency: A Study in British Politics and Political Thought, 1899–1914*, Blackwell, Oxford, 1971.

SEELEY, J. R., *The Expansion of England*, Macmillan, London, 1883.

SEMMEL, B., *The Governor Eyre Controversy*, MacGibbon & Kee, London, 1962.

SILVER, A., 'The Demand for Order in Civil Society: A Review of Some Themes in the History of Urban Crime, Police and Riot', in D. J. Bordua (ed.), *The Police: Six Sociological Essays*, Wiley, New York, 1967.

—— 'Social and Ideological Bases of British Elite Reactions to Domestic Crisis in 1829–1832', *Politics and Society* 2 (Feb. 1971).

SIMON, J., *Speeches on the General Strike*, Macmillan, London, 1926.

SIMPSON, A. W. B., *In the Highest Degree Odious: Detention without Trial in Wartime Britain*, Clarendon Press, Oxford, 1992.

SIMPSON, H. B., 'The Office of Constable', *English Historical Review* 10 (1895).

SIMSON, H. J., *British Rule, and Rebellion*, Blackwood, London, 1938.

SKINNER, Q., *The Foundations of Modern Political Thought*, i, Cambridge University Press, Cambridge, 1978.

—— 'The Idea of Negative Liberty: Philosophical and Historical Perspectives', in R. Rorty, J. B. Schneewind, and Q. Skinner, *Philosophy in History*, Cambridge University Press, Cambridge, 1984.

SMITH, P. T., *Policing Victorian London: Political Policing, Public Order, and the London Metropolitan Police*, Greenwood, London, 1985.

SMITH, R. J., *The Gothic Bequest: Medieval Institutions in British Thought, 1688–1863*, Cambridge University Press, Cambridge, 1987.

SNYDER, F. and HAY, D. (eds.), *Labour, Law and Crime in Historical Perspective*, Tavistock Publications, London, 1987.

Society of Conservative Lawyers, *Public Order*, Conservative Political Centre, London, 1970.

The Special Constable: His Duties and Privileges, Arthur Pearson, London, 1914.

SPJUT, R. J., 'Defining Subversion', *British Journal of Law and Society* 6 (1979).

—— 'The "Official" Use of Deadly Force by the Security Forces Against Suspected Terrorists: Some Lessons from Northern Ireland', *Public Law*, Spring, 1986.

—— 'Deadly Force and Riot Control in Northern Ireland', *Public Law*, Spring, 1987.

SPRING, D., 'Walter Bagehot and Deference', *American Historical Review* 81 (1976).

STALKER, J., *Stalker*, Harrap, London, 1988.

STAMMERS, N., *Civil Liberties in Britain During the Second World War: A Political Study*, Croom Helm, London, 1983.

STEEDMAN, C., *Policing the Victorian Community: The Formation of English Provincial Police Forces, 1856–80*, Routledge, London, 1984.

STEPHEN, J. F., *General View of the Criminal Law*, Macmillan, London, 1863.

—— *A History of the Criminal Law of England*, Macmillan, London, 1883.

—— 'Foundations of the Government of India', *The Nineteenth Century* 80 (Oct. 1883).

—— *Liberty, Equality, Fraternity*, ed. R. J. White, Cambridge University Press, Cambridge, 1967.

STEVENS, I. N. and YARDLEY, D. C. M., *The Protection of Liberty*, Blackwell, Oxford, 1982.

STEVENSON, J., *Popular Disturbances in England 1700–1870*, Longmans, London, 1979.

—— 'Social Control and the Prevention of Riots in England, 1789–1829', in A. P. Donajgrodski (ed.), *Social Control in Nineteenth-century Britain*, Croom Helm, London, 1977.

STOCKDALE, E., *Law and Order in Georgian Bedfordshire*, Bedfordshire Historical Record Society, Bedford, 1982.

STONE, L., 'Interpersonal Violence in English Society 1300–1980', *Past and Present* 101 (Nov. 1983), 22–33.

STORCH, R. D., 'The Plague of the Blue Locusts: Police Reform and Popular Resistance in Northern England 1840–57', *International Review of Social History* 20: 1 (1975), 61–90.

—— 'The Policeman as Domestic Missionary: Urban Discipline and Popular Culture in Northern England 1850–1880', *Journal of Social History* 9: 4 (1976).

—— '"Please to Remember the Fifth of November": Conflict, Solidarity and Public Order in Southern England, 1815–1900', in R. D. Storch (ed.), *Popular Culture and Custom in Nineteenth-century England*, Croom Helm, London, 1982.

—— 'Policing Rural Southern England Before the Police: Opinion and Practice, 1830–1856', in D. Hay and F. Snyder (eds.), *Policing and Prosecution in Britain 1750–1850*, Oxford University Press, Oxford, 1989.

STREET, H., *Freedom, the Individual and the Law*, 2nd edn., MacGibbon & Kee, London, 1967.

—— 'The Prevention of Terrorism (Emergency Provisions) Act 1974', *Criminal Law Review* 1975.

SUGARMAN, D. (ed.), *Legality, Ideology and the State*, Academic Press, London, 1983.

SUPPERSTONE, M., *Brownlie's Law of Public Order and National Security*, 2nd edn., Butterworth, London, 1981.

SWIFT, R., 'Anti-Catholicism and Irish Disturbances: Public Order in Mid-Victorian Wolverhampton', *Midland History* 9 (1984).

TAYLOR, P., *Stalker: The Search for the Truth*, Faber, London, 1987.

THOMIS, M. and HOLT, P., *Threats of Revolution in Britain 1789–1848*, Macmillan, London, 1977.

THOMPSON, D. and EPSTEIN, J. (eds.), *The Chartist Experience: Studies in Working Class Radicalism and Culture, 1830–1860*, Macmillan, London, 1982.

THOMPSON, E. P., *Whigs and Hunters: The Origin of the Black Act*, Allen Lane, London, 1975.

—— 'The Peculiarities of the English', in *The Poverty of Theory*, Merlin, London, 1978.

THOMPSON, F. M. L., 'Social Control in Victorian Britain', *Economic History Review*, 2nd ser., 34: 2 (1981).

—— *The Rise of Respectable Society: A Social History of Victorian Britain*, Fontana, London, 1988.

THORNTON, A. P., *The Habit of Authority: Paternalism in British History*, Allen & Unwin, London, 1964.

THURLOW, R., 'British Fascism and State Surveillance, 1934–45', *Intelligence and National Security* 3 (1988).

TILLY, C. (ed.), *The Formation of National States in Western Europe*, Princeton University Press, Princeton, NJ, 1975.

—— 'The Web of Contention in Eighteenth-century Cities', in L. A. Tilly and C. Tilly (eds.), *Class Conflict and Collective Action*, Sage, London, 1981.

TOMLINSON, M., *et al.* (eds.), *Whose Law and Order? Aspects of Crime and Social Control in Irish Society*, Sociological Association of Ireland, Belfast, 1988.

TOWNSHEND, C., 'Martial Law: Legal and Administrative Problems of Civil Emergency in Britain and the Empire 1800–1940', *Historical Journal* 25 (1982).

—— *Political Violence in Ireland: Government and Resistance since 1848*, Clarendon Press, Oxford, 1983.

TOWNSHEND, C., 'Northern Ireland', in R. J. Vincent (ed.), *Foreign Policy and Human Rights*, Cambridge University Press, Cambridge, 1985.

—— *Britain's Civil Wars: Counterinsurgency in the Twentieth Century*, Faber, London, 1986.

—— 'Military Force and Civil Authority in the United Kingdom, 1914–1921', *Journal of British Studies* 28 (1989).

—— '"One man whom you can hang if necessary": The Discreet Charm of Nevil Macready', in J. Hattendorf and M. Murfitt (eds.), *The Limits of Military Power*, Macmillan, London, 1990.

TROUP, SIR E., 'Police Administration, Local and National', *Police Journal* 1 (1928).

TUCK, M., *Drinking and Disorder: A Study of Non-Metropolitan Violence*, Home Office Research and Planning Unit Study 108, HMSO, London, 1989.

TWINING, W. L., 'Emergency Powers and Criminal Process: The Diplock Report', *Criminal Law Review* 1973.

VICK, C., 'An Introduction to Aspects of Public Order and Policing', in J. R. Thackrah (ed.), *Contemporary Policing: An Examination of Society in the 1980s*, Sphere, London, 1985.

VINCENT, D., 'Communication, Community and the State', in C. Emsley and J. Walvin (eds.), *Artisans, Peasants and Proletarians 1760–1860*, Croom Helm, London, 1985.

—— 'The Origins of Public Secrecy in Britain', *Transactions of the Royal Historical Society* 6th ser. 1 (1991).

WADDINGTON, P. A. J., 'Are Our Politicians Chasing an Illusion?', *Police*, 15: 3 (Nov. 1982).

—— *The Strong Arm of the Law: Armed and Public Order Policing*, Clarendon Press, Oxford, 1991.

WALDEN, K., *Visions of Order*, Butterworths, Toronto, 1982.

WALKER, C., *The Prevention of Terrorism in British Law*, Manchester University Press, Manchester, 1986.

—— 'Shooting to Kill: Some of the Issues in *Farrell* v. *Secretary of State for Defence*', *Modern Law Review* 43 (1980).

WALLACE, S., *War and the Image of Germany: British Academics 1914–1918*, J. Donald, Edinburgh, 1988.

WALSH, D. P. J., *The Use and Abuse of Emergency Legislation in Northern Ireland*, Cobden Trust, London, 1983.

WARREN, A., 'Forster, the Liberals and New Directions in Irish Policy 1880–1882', *Parliamentary History* 6: 1 (1987).

WARREN, C., 'The Police of the Metropolis', *Murray's Magazine* 4 (1888).

WEBER, J. K., 'The King's Peace: A Comparative Study', *Journal of Legal History* 10 (1989).

WEINBERGER, B., 'Police Perceptions of Labour in the Inter-War Period: The Case of the Unemployed and of Miners on Strike', in F. Snyder and D. Hay (eds.),

Law, Labour and Crime in Historical Perspective, Tavistock Publications, London, 1987.

—— *Keeping the Peace? Policing Strikes in Britain, 1906–1926* (Berg, Oxford, 1990).

WEISSER, H., 'Chartism in 1848: Reflections on a Non-Revolution', *Albion* 13 (Spring 1981).

WELLS, R., *Insurrection: The British Experience 1795–1803*, Alan Sutton, Gloucester, 1983.

WESTERN, J. R., *The English Militia in the Eighteenth Century*, Routledge, London, 1965.

WESTLEY, W. A., *Violence and the Police: A Sociological Study of Law, Custom, and Morality*, MIT Press, Cambridge, Mass., 1970.

WHELAN, C. J., 'Military Intervention in Industrial Disputes', *Industrial Law Journal* 18 (1979).

WIENER, M. J., *English Culture and the Decline of the Industrial Spirit, 1850–1980*, Cambridge University Press, Cambridge, 1981.

WIENER, P. P. and FISHER, J. (eds.), *Violence and Aggression in the History of Ideas*, Rutgers University Press, New Brunswick, NJ, 1974.

WILCOX, A. F., 'Military Aid to the Civil Power', *New Law Journal*, 1976.

WILKINSON, R., *Gentlemanly Power: British Leadership and the Public School Tradition*, Oxford University Press, Oxford, 1964.

WILLIAMS, D. G. T., *Not in the Public Interest: The Problem of Security in Democracy*, Hutchinson, London, 1965.

—— *Keeping the Peace: The Police and Public Order*, Hutchinson, London, 1967.

—— 'Protest and Public Order', *Cambridge Law Journal* 28: 1 (Apr. 1970).

—— *The Accountability of the Police* (Tilberg Law Lectures 1978), Cambridge University Press, Cambridge, 1979.

—— 'The Donoughmore Report in Retrospect', *Public Administration* 60: 2 (1982).

WILSON, H. H. and GLICKMAN, H., *The Problem of Internal Security in Great Britain 1948–1953*, Doubleday, Garden City, NY, 1954.

YOUNG, T., assisted by Kettle, M., *Incitement to Disaffection*, Cobden Trust, London, 1976.

Index